THE BOOK OF THEATRE QUOTES

Notes, Quotes and Anecdotes of the Stage

I hope that this will provide some amusement. with best wishes for a Happy Christmas '83

love.

Rebecca x.

THE BOOK OF THEATRE QUOTES

Notes, Quotes and Anecdotes of the Stage

Compiled by Gordon Snell

Angus & Robertson Publishers

Previous books by the same author:

FOR CHILDREN
The King of Quizzical Island
Amy Johnson — Queen of the Air

Angus & Robertson Publishers
London . Sydney . Melbourne . Singapore . Manila

*This book is copyright. Apart from any fair dealing for
the purposes of private study, research, criticism or review,
as permitted under the Copyright Act, no part may be reproduced
by any process without written permission. Inquiries should
be addressed to the publisher.*

First published in the United Kingdom by Angus & Robertson
(UK) Ltd, 1982
First published in Australia by Angus & Robertson Publishers
Australia, 1982

Copyright © this collection Gordon Snell, 1982

ISBN 0 207 14576 8

Typeset in 10pt Garamond & 8pt Helios Bold by Setrite Typesetters, Hong Kong
Printed in Hong Kong

For Maeve with all my love

Acknowledgements

I should like to thank the following people who helped me with anecdotes and personal experiences:

David Allthorpe
Nigel Anthony
Moira Armstrong
Richard Baker
Jeremy Beckett
Christopher Bell
Jacqui Bianchi
Kate Binchy
Joy Boatman
Peggy Branford
Gordon Clyde
James Dale
Dominic Dromgoole
Patrick Dromgoole
Ernest Dudley

Mabel Evelyn
Polly Gray
Eddie Harris
Alan Haydock
Andrew Hewson
Anne Howells
Kay Kirby
Dorothy Lane
Bruce Laughland
T. P. McKenna
Elizabeth McNamara
Gerry McCrudden
Adrian Mitchell
Mysie Monté
Conrad Nicholson

Edgar Norfolk
Patrick Oliver
Peter O'Toole
Nick Parsons
Jim Pope
Joan Ryan
The Editors of 'The Stage'
Reginald Salberg
Michael Smee
R. D. Smith
Philip Stone
Robin Twite
Grace Webb
Tudor Williams
Alistair Wilson

I should also like to acknowledge with thanks the help and co-operation of the BBC, from whose programmes a number of these quotations are taken.

Contents

1. The Abbey Theatre, Dublin

Abbey Theatre

Dr J. F. Larchet witnessed the early days of the Abbey Theatre from the vantage point of the orchestra pit, and said that you could see an amazing variety of people in the audience:

Indeed I have seen sitting in the front row of the pit, during the troubled times, Michael Collins and one or two other leaders. And every time Michael Collins laughed, he breathed on the head of Sir Neville Macready, who was sitting in the back row of the stalls—and at that time, Sir Neville had offered a thousand pounds for Michael Collins, dead or alive.

The rowdy first performances of J. M. Synge's 'The Playboy of the Western World' were recorded by Joseph Holloway in his journal:

Saturday 26 January 1907
The Abbey was thronged in the evening to witness the first performance of Synge's three-act comedy 'The Playboy of the Western World', which ended in fiasco owing to the coarseness of the dialogue. The audience bore with it for two and a half acts and even laughed with the dramatist at times, but an unusually brutally coarse remark put into the mouth of 'Christopher Mahon', the playboy of the title, set the house off into hooting and hissing amid counter applause, and the din was kept up till the curtain closed in.... Despite the fact that Synge in a note on the programme says, 'I have used one or two words only

that I have not heard among the country people of Ireland, or spoken in my own nursery before I could read the newspapers', I maintain that his play of 'The Playboy' is not a truthful or just picture of the Irish peasants, but simply the outpouring of a morbid, unhealthy mind ever seeking on the dunghill of life for the nastiness that lies concealed there.... Synge is the evil genius of the Abbey and Yeats his able lieutenant. Both dabble in the unhealthy....

Monday 28 January 1907
...we arrived at the Abbey. Two stalwart police at the vestibule suggested trouble, and we found plenty and to spare when we went in. The performance was just concluding amid a terrific uproar (the piece had not been listened to, we were told). The curtains were drawn aside, and W. G. Fay stood forward amid the din. After some minutes, in a lull, he said, 'You who have hissed tonight will go away saying you have heard the play, but you haven't.'

'We heard it on Saturday!' came from the back of the pit, and the hissing and hooting renewed.

The scene which followed was indescribable. Those in the pit howled for the author, and he with Lady Gregory and others held animated conversation in the stalls.... Small knots of people argued the situation out anything but calmly, and after

2. A scene from the 1975 production of 'The Playboy of the Western World' by J.M. Synge

about a quarter of an hour's clamour, the audience dispersed hoarse.

Tuesday 29 January 1907
Arrived at the Abbey when 'Riders to the Sea' was half through.... I noticed that the youths in the stalls were mostly under the influence of drink (and learned that the management had allowed them in for nothing to back up the play that the crowded pit had come there to howl down). This precious gang of noisy boys hailed from Trinity, and soon after 'The Playboy' commenced one of their number (Mr Moorhead) made himself objectionable and was forcibly removed by Synge and others, after a free fight amongst the instruments of the orchestra....

This set the noise in motion, and W. B. Yeats again came on the scene and with raised hand secured silence. He referred to the removal of one drunken man and hoped all that were sober would listen to the play. The noise continued, and shortly after a body of police led on by W.B. marched out of the side door from the scene dock and ranged along the walls of the pit.... Yeats also was busy just now as a spy aiding the police in picking out persons disapproving of the glorification of murder on the stage....

At the end chaos seemed to have entered the Abbey, and the college youths clambered on to the seats and began the English national anthem, while those in the body of the hall sang something else of home growth. I felt very sad while the scene continued. The college boys had ultimately to be forcibly ejected by the police, and they marched off in a body singing, police-protected, to the college. One of them was arrested for beating the police and fined five pounds. Two of those who were ejected from the pit were fined forty shillings each, W. B. Yeats prosecuting.

Despite all, 'The Playboy' was not heard!

As a result of the rowdy reception of 'The Playboy', the Abbey Theatre box office enclosed a printed note with the voucher they sent to people who applied for seats:

'Should it be impossible to hear the play the night you select we will send you another voucher on receiving your application.'

According to Oliver St John Gogarty, the Abbey Theatre in the early days 'sent out an SOS for geniuses' and everybody applied, including James Joyce. He went in to see Lady Gregory, but was ushered out of the presence after only a minute. There and then, Joyce made up a limerick for the occasion:

There was a kind lady called Gregory,
Said: 'Come to me, poets in beggary,'
But found her imprudence
When thousands of students
Cried: 'Oh, we are in that category!'

St John Ervine paid this tribute to Miss Horniman, principal benefactress of the Abbey Theatre:

I liked her—I found her a kind and helpful woman. She was very kind to me. She had her faults, she was a human being. She was possibly vain, though I never saw any sign of it. She spent her money lavishly in the cause of the theatre, and the whole of what may be called 'Modern Theatre' is I think if not entirely, very largely, due to what that woman did. She was far more important in the theatre than Lady Gregory or Miss Lilian Baylis, two women whom I regard as over-rated—and she never got any thanks from anybody.

She was a curious woman.... I once amused her by telling her that she looked like the original District Visitor—and that is true, but you know there was a certain kind of elegance about the way she dressed. The style suited her. She was a spinster, she looked like a spinster, and she behaved like a spinster—but she was a rebellious woman, and a courageous woman, and she didn't care two hoots what anybody thought of her. If she wanted to support a thing, she supported it. It was she who started Shaw; it was she who started Yeats; it was she who started the Abbey Theatre; it was she who started the Gaiety Theatre in Manchester, and theatres in America derive from her. If she hadn't done the work she did, the theatre in this country would be in a very grave plight.

The company's style in those first days was refreshingly original to the eyes of an English critic, A. B. Walkley, who wrote in 'The Times Literary Supplement' in May 1903:

As a rule, the players stand stock still. The listeners do not distract one's attention by fussy stage business; they just stay where they are and listen. When they do move it is without premeditation, at haphazard, even with a little natural clumsiness, as of people who are not conscious of being stared at in public. Hence a delightful effect of spontaneity. Add that the scenery is of Elizabethan simplicity—performance is a sight good for sore eyes—eyes made sore by the perpetual movement and glitter of the ordinary stage.

There were some original rehearsal methods too—the Fay brothers, who led the company, used to take the cast for a trip out to the Dublin Hills on a Saturday afternoon so that they could try out their voices, speaking against the sound of the river.

Nowadays, the fame of the Abbey is such that actors are proud to claim a connection with it—even, as playwright Denis Johnston says, a totally spurious connection:

Oddly enough, all over the world, there are people whom one has never heard of in Dublin, who are continuously described in playbills as 'late of the Abbey Theatre Company'. Indeed, if all the so-called members of the Abbey Company were gathered together for one show, according to my calculations they could put on Cecil B. de Mille's 'Quo Vadis', with the possible omission of the sixty lions....

Abuse of Actors

An Elizabethan law declared:

All Bearwards, Common Players of Interludes, Counterfeit Egyptians etc. shall be taken, adjudged and deem'd Rogues, Vagabonds, and beggars, and shall sustain all pain and punishment, as by this Act is in that behalf appointed.

After the Communist revolution in China, theatrical performers were recruited from some novel sources. Acrobatic thieves, who were trained to leap and clamber in order to get into inaccessible places and steal, found themselves drafted into state theatre groups. And Esther Cheo Ying, who was in the revolutionary army, recalled in her book 'Black Country Girl in Red China':

Street performers on the fringes of the semi-criminal classes were put into theatres left vacant by the strip-tease artists and their ilk. I saw them putting on their show in market places collecting a few cents one week, and then the next in theatres performing to enthusiastic crowds and given grand titles such as 'Honoured State Artiste'. Later they travelled abroad delighting sophisticated audiences with their feats.

In the seventeenth century, Samuel Butler, in his book 'Characters', penned this scathing portrait of the acting profession:

A player is a representatif by his calling, a person of all qualities; and though his profession be to counterfeit, and he never means what he says, yet he endeavours to make his words and actions always agree.

His labour is to play, and his bus'nes to turn passion into action—The more he dissembles, the more he is in earnest, and the less he appears himself, the truer he is to his profession—The more he deceives men, the greater right he does them; and the plainer his dealing is, the less credit he deserves. He assumes a body like an apparition, and can turn himself into as many shapes as a witch. His business is to be somebody else, and he is never himself, but when he has nothing to do. He gets all he speaks by heart, and yet never means what he says. He is said to enter when he comes out, and to go out when he goes in. When he is off the stage he acts a gentleman, and in that only makes his own part himself—When he plays love and honour in effigie, the Ladies take him at his word, and fall in love with him in earnest; and, indeed, they may be truly said to fall in love, considering how much he is below them. This blows him up with so much vanity, that he forgets what he is, and as he deluded them, so they do him. He is like a Motion made by clockwork, the Poet winds him up, and he walks and moves till his part is run down, and then he is quiet. He is but a puppet in great, which the poet squeaks to, and puts into what posture he pleases; and though his calling be but ministerial to his author, yet he assumes a magistery over him, because he sets him on work, and he becomes subordinate accordingly. He represents many excellent virtues, as they light in his part, but knows no more of them than a picture does who it was drawn for. His profession is a kind of metamorphosis, to transform himself out of one shape into another, like a taylors sheet of paper, which he folds into figures.

His prime qualifications are the same with those of a lyar, confidence and a good memory; as for wit he has it at second hand, like his cloaths. The ladies take his counterfeit passions in earnest, and accompany him with their devotions, as holy sisters do a gifted hypocrite at his holding-forth, and when he gives the false alarm of a fight they are as much concern'd, as if he were in real danger, or the worst were not past already. They are more taken with his mock love and honour, than if it were real, and, like ignorant dealers, part with right love and honour for it. His applause and commendation is but a kind of manufacture form'd by clapping of hands; and though it be no more than men set dogs together by the ears with, yet he takes it as a testimony of his merit, and sets a value on himself accordingly.

The seventeenth-century satirist Tom Brown wrote:

It is as hard a matter for a pretty woman to keep herself honest in a theatre, as 'tis for an apothecary to keep his treacle from the flies in hot weather, for every libertine in the audience will be buzzing about her honey-pot.

Doctor Samuel Johnson said of the actress Mrs Pritchard as Lady Macbeth:

She was a vulgar idiot. She never read any part of the play, except her own part, and she said gownd.

James Boaden described how an early nineteenth-century actor was put down by the wits of the time:

Daly, the Irish manager, was tempted to try his fortune here, as a successor to Barry, in perhaps his master-work, 'Othello'. The punsters despatched him in their usual manner: 'A poor Player, That struts and frets his hour upon the stage And then is heard—no Moor.'

John Keats wrote in a letter to his sister in 1819:

The Covent Garden Company is execrable. Young is the best among them and he is a ranting coxcombical tasteless Actor—a Disgust, a Nausea—and yet the very best after Kean. What a set of barren asses are actors!

Of course, actors and actresses have been known to insult other members of their own profession...and they have even used modern technology to do so: the telephone answering machine was put to imaginative use by one actress—let us call her Mary X—who had been infuriated by the behaviour of another—let us call her Jane Y. So infuriated, that she went out one day, leaving this recorded message to greet callers on the phone:

'This is Mary X's number. I'm going out for a walk round the park to try and get over my rage at the appalling behaviour of that stinking bloody bitch, Jane Y....'

And she went on in even more colourful tones, which amazed and delighted the first of her callers, who told a friend: 'You must ring Mary's number—it's hilarious!' A whole string of people rang to hear the recorded message, and it wasn't very long before a stern reply was being recorded on Mary's tape. It was a warning from Jane Y's solicitor....

Dorothy Parker describes an actress's tombstone:

Her name, cut clear upon this marble cross,
Shines as it shone when she was still on
    earth;
While tenderly the mild, agreeable moss
Obscures the figures of her date of birth.

Abuse of Critics

David Garrick:

> ...thus actors try their art,
> To melt that Rock of Rocks—the critic's
> heart.

T. P. McKenna:

Actors feel a sense of comradeship, rather like soldiers in an army—because of the dangers of the profession. And you'd rather have an accolade from another actor, whom you respect, than from a critic, any day. Such compliments are more exhilarating than any notice.

In August 1966 John Osborne wrote in 'The Sunday Telegraph':

Theatre critics should be regularly exposed, like corrupt constabularies or faulty sewage systems. Indeed, as the structure of institutional theatre grows, I would employ gentle, subsidised chuckers-out so that most daily critics might be barred from openings altogether, along with actors' agents and boxes of chocolates. If they would only heed my advice, the National Theatre would engage someone to write a regular consumer's guide to critics. It could be an amusing addition to an already attractive and handsome programme....

My own attitude to critics is clear and entirely reasonable. It is one of distrust and dislike based on predictability and historical fact. I regard them as something like kinky policemen on the cultural protectionist make, rent collectors, screws, insurance men, customs officers and Fairy Snowmen. One should simply not open one's door to them.

Oscar Wilde expressed similar sentiments to John Osborne's, more succinctly, in 'The Critic as Artist' with this description of critics and the work they review:

Mediocrity weighing mediocrity in the balance, and incompetence applauding its own brother....

And Mícheál MacLiammóir said:

Literature is the only art whose critics use the same medium as that used by the artist who supplies them with their material. How astonishing it would be if the actor's performance were to be criticised through the medium of acting: how many of the existing dramatic critics would remain in their job? For how long, oh Lord, how long?

In 'A Resounding Tinkle' N. F. Simpson lets the author—as well as the critics—have their say about the play that is in progress. Interrupting the action, the Author addresses the audience thus:

It seemed the only way. I think we have all been trying as hard as can reasonably be expected not to show our exasperation—I certainly have—because we do all like, naturally, to feel we've been provided with a meaning; something we can carry round with us like an umbrella for a few days. We all feel rather lost without a meaning to seize hold of; rather like a snake charmer in front of a boa constrictor and no flute. Or whatever they use. And in this search for a meaning we have some very good allies in the critics. They know a great deal about these things. They are trained to find meanings, and even if there are no meanings to be found they rarely come unprovided with spare meanings which with a little wire and string can often be fastened quite securely. So it is to the critics that for all our sakes I have decided to turn. We've got to turn somewhere.

And the Critics duly appear and have their say—and an intense and meaning-packed say it is:

MISS SALT. I'd rather like to take up this idea of the skit again, or the parody of it, because—and this is surely the whole point which none of us has made yet—here is a play in which the writer is imitating himself repeatedly all through the play. He is in fact actually burlesquing his own self-mimicry and in quite the most devastating way from first to last. That I think is inherent in the whole thing.

PEPPER. He's satirizing farce, of course, too. That comes across quite unmistakably. As one of the characters says somewhere in the play—this is the custard-pie farce of the intellect.

MUSTARD. Comedy. Custard-pie comedy. Of the abstract. But to get back to this point about burlesque. It is, basically, a parody of a skit on satire that he's burlesquing, and the farce is so to speak a by-product of that. I don't think he's aiming at farce at all. The farce is in a sense what we, the audience, *contribute*.

CHAIRMAN. The audience. Did anyone else, I wonder, feel—as I certainly did—that the barrier between audience and actors was being quite deliberately dismantled? Mrs Vinegar?

MRS VINEGAR. It's been done before. And done better.

MUSTARD. You mean the Verfremdungseffekt. The alienation effect.

MISS SALT. It's Brecht, of course—though with a very different aim from that of Brecht.

PEPPER. No. I don't see Brecht here at all.

MISS SALT. It's the Brechtian technique carried on *beyond* Brecht. Isn't that it?

MUSTARD. Beyond, and in a sense of course at a tangent to Brecht. It's as though he'd gone off on a branch line some way back which is carrying him further than Brecht was able to go but in a quite different direction.

MISS SALT. And, of course, *facing* Brecht as he moves away from him. The farther he goes *beyond* Brecht, therefore, the farther he is retreating *from* him.

PEPPER. I can accept Brecht as a starting-point. But a starting-point is something you move away from, and in my view the author of this play has been doing just that. He has been putting more and more ground between himself and his model—if that's what Brecht is, though I doubt it—and they have been getting farther and farther apart, these two, until both of them are specks on the horizon. Which is why I think we're quite wrong to be discussing this play or whatever it is as if it were 'The Comedy of Errors' rewritten by Lewis Carroll to provide a part for Godot or somebody.

CHAIRMAN. Yes. Well, now our time is running out and I think we ought to say something about the ending—which we've none of us yet seen of course. Is it possible that some of the shortcomings of the play so far could be redeemed by the ending? Mrs Vinegar?

MRS VINEGAR. I doubt whether I could sit through any more of it. I have never begrudged danger money to steeplejacks and people of that kind, and I do think it's high time someone suggested boredom money for critics. The ending? No. I think the piece is beyond redemption. The best that can be hoped for from the ending is that sooner or later it will arrive.

Frank Sullivan, the American columnist and humourist, wrote an interview with a theatre

critic, expert in the art of the cliché. The following is part of it:

Q. Now, then, when great ladies of the stage are in a cast—

A. They are never in a cast. They grace a cast.

Q. I beg your pardon. When they grace a cast, how do they act?

A. With emotional intensity, consummate artistry, and true awareness. They are superb as. They are magnificent in the role of. It is good to have them back.

Q. And how are their performances etched?

A. Finely. They have the ring.

Q. What ring?

A. The ring of authority. They bring new understanding to the role of Shakespeare's immortal heroine. They make the part come alive.

Q. I see. Now, Mr Arbuthnot, when Thornton Sherwood writes a play—

A. Sir, the mot juste continues to elude you. Playwrights do not write plays. They fashion them.

Q. How?

A. With due respect for the eternal verities.

Q. How else?

A. With deft strokes, scalpel wit, loving care, penetrating insight, and masterly craftsmanship.

Q. Why?

A. So that Joshua Logan may direct the plays with authority and imagination.

Q. What kinds of plays are there?

A. Oh, their number is legion. There are dramas of frustration and dramas of extramarital love, or the eternal triangle. There are plays that are penetrating studies and plays that are valuable human documents. There are pageants, which ought to be glittering, if possible.

Tragedies should, of course, be stark, and melodramas lurid, and spectacles, to be de rigueur, should be lavish, colourful, or handsome. But lampoons must be merry, farces must be rollicking, and comedies must be either of ancient vintage or sophisticated.

Q. What does the playwright do in a sophisticated comedy?

A. He pokes fun at our foibles. He dissects our tribal mores.

Q. Using what kind of vein?

A. A rich vein of satire.

Q. The task of the playwright sounds onerous enough, Mr Arbuthnot.

A. Oh, you have no idea of the angles he must consider. He must, for instance, make sure that his play has compelling moments. He must take care that it is well knit and fast-moving, and that it is brilliant in conception, builds up to an exciting climax, and ends on a happy note. Then, there is the character insight.

Q. What about that?

A. Well, he must provide plenty of it, along with a scope.

Q. Must have a scope, too, eh?

A. Yes, preferably wide.

Q. Why?

A. So that his play may provide a rich or rewarding experience. So that it may be first-rate entertainment, a major event of the theatrical season, and the most important contribution to the drama in years. In short, so that it may be a Must.

John Kemble, a nineteenth-century actor, once said of critics:

Damn these fellows, they will have their way; in fact, I would sooner they cut me up all to pieces than not notice me at all.

Act Natural

In 'Dames of the Theatre', Eric Johns wrote:

Mrs Kendal had a high opinion of her husband's talent as an actor and would often recall the scene in 'The Queen's Shilling' in which he displayed his remarkable gift of turning pale whenever he wished, just as Duse had been able to blush at will on stage. Mr Kendal played a wounded soldier and at one point in the action the colonel gripped his arm where he had been wounded and the soldier visibly blanched with pain, often causing women in the audience to faint.

Mrs Kendal's brother, T. W. Robertson, pioneered the 'naturalistic' movement in the nineteenth-century theatre and was anxious that the stock exaggerations should be shunned by the actors—so in his lists of characters he added comments like this:

The author requests this part may be played with a slight French accent. He is not to pronounce the words absurdly or duck his head towards his stomach like the conventional stage Frenchman.

The naturalistic settings which later began to seem stifling to many theatre people, were originally quite a revolutionary idea. The actor-manager Sir Squire Bancroft gets the real credit—or blame—for the innovation. From the 1860s onwards he used such settings especially for the plays of T. W. Robertson, the author of 'Caste'. As Frances Donaldson wrote in 'The Actor-Managers':

Twenty years earlier Madame Vestris had used scenic cloths, carpets and elaborate furnishings, but it was left to the Bancrofts to employ these so successfully that they became an accepted part of theatrical productions. They put real rugs on the floor, real furniture on the sets, the rooms in which their performances took place had real ceilings and, which caused at the time the greatest sensation of all, real knobs on the door-handles. Their style became known as the 'cup-and-saucer' comedy because of the realistic effects in the kitchen scene in 'Caste'. Before this time it was customary in a conversation scene merely to bring down two or three chairs to the middle of the stage for the actors to sit on while talking and afterwards to take them away.

And Joseph Addison said:

A little skill in criticism would inform us that shadows and realities ought not to be mixed together in the same piece; and that scenes which are designed as the representations of nature, should be filled with resemblances, and not with the things themselves. If one would represent a wide, open country filled with herds and flocks, it would be ridiculous to draw the country only upon the scenes, and to crowd several parts of the stage with sheep and oxen. This is joining together inconsistencies, and making the decoration partly real and partly imaginary.

Victorian dramatists and theatre managers did not shrink from showing the more sordid side of city life—in fact they showed it with such enthusiastic realism that some audiences and critics felt they went too far. George R. Sims, who wrote that much under-rated poem of social protest beginning 'It is Christmas Day in the Workhouse', also wrote a number of plays. One of them, 'The Lights o' London', staged in 1881, quite overwhelmed a contemporary critic:

If anything, it is all too real, too painful, too smeared with the dirt and degradation of London life, where drunkenness, debauchery, and depravity are shown in all their naked hideousness. Amidst buying and selling, the hoarse roars of costermongers, the jingle of the piano-organ, the screams of the dissolute, fathers teach their children to cheat and lie, drabs swarm in and out of the public-house, and the hunted Harold, with his devoted wife, await the inevitable capture in an upper garret of a house which is surrounded by the police.

Actor-Managers

Mr Whitely, a manager of a touring troupe of a century ago, was far from modest about his acting skills, according to Pierce Egan in 'The Life of an Actor':

Mr Whitely was remarkably fond of the old method of acting, viz, a great halt or twitch in the gait, a very grave face on all occasions, and an inflexible regard in tragedy for the interests of ti-ti-tum, ti-tum, ti-tum, ti-tum-ti. He had a great opinion of his own powers, and was certain that, however mean the character or part might be considered in the drama, he had the ability to make it appear conspicuous; and to prove this imaginary power, frequently threw himself into such situations, which always created merriment and sarcastic humour in his company, and laughter in the audience. . . .

He was fond of declaring that the inattention of managers in the cast of parts was shameful; that he knew a good actor could make the most trifling characters appear glorious; 'and,' said he, 'to evince the truth of my assertion, you shall see me undertake one of the worst parts in ''Richard the Third'' '. The next day's playbill pompously announced, in large letters, the part of the

LIEUTENANT OF THE TOWER

for that night only,

by MR WHITELY

(being his first appearance in that character)

When John Holloway joined Edmund Tearle's theatre company, he was expected to learn five sizeable parts in five days before making his debut with them. There was one part in a melodrama that he simply had not had time to master before the performance, noted by David Holloway in 'Playing the Empire':

When he was due to play this part for the first time, John, almost in tears, went to Tearle's dressing-room and said he did not know the words, and therefore could not go on.

'That's all right, my boy,' Tearle replied. 'Just go on and make a noise.'

This proved to be Tearle's own method. If he had failed to master his words he would quite literally go on and make a noise, stunning the audience with a series of bull-like roars and gentle bleats from which not one single word was intelligible, but with the whole performance projected with such assurance that the audience was fooled. It was, as John discovered, up to the other actors to build into their own lines enough of Tearle's ('As the Lord Richard said . . .') to keep the audience informed as to the progress of the play.

Edmund Tearle had some most novel excuses when he failed to learn his lines. When he still did not know the role of Mephistopheles in a version of 'Faust' by the time the dress rehearsal came round, he said:

'I could not learn the words because there was a thunderstorm. If I had read the words of the devil during a storm I should have been struck by lightning.'

The performance that night was ragged, to say the least....

The rest of the cast did what they could as Tearle wandered round the stage booming and bleating. In the third act John had an inspiration: he ran all his lines together into one long speech, reaching a climax and exiting leaving Tearle silent and alone in the centre of the stage. Wisely the stage manager rang down the curtain. John sat waiting in his dressing-room for Tearle's wrath to explode, but the star only looked puzzled when he came in.

'What happened in that scene?' he asked.

John replied, 'I don't know, guv'nor, but I don't think you said much.'

This seemed to satisfy Tearle, for he went out shaking his head and muttering, 'I suppose I was a bit fluffy.'

In his essay 'The Last of the Actor-Managers' Richard Huggett recounts a story which is a favourite of actors remembering Robert Atkins:

They will tell of the time when he was invited by the Flower family to direct at Stratford-on-Avon during the war. The Flowers, who virtually owned Stratford, were respectable churchgoing worthies and owners of the famous brewery. It was inevitable that Robert should be at loggerheads with them and thus it turned out. Their chief objection to Robert was his language which was no less uninhibited in Stratford than it had been in London. Their disapproval found an unexpected outlet: they did not invite him to read the lesson during the memorial service held on Shakespeare's birthday which was the traditional privilege of the resident director. Robert was deeply upset by this and stormed angrily into the vestry after the service had finished.

'Can you give me,' he boomed at the rector, 'one single cogent reason why I shouldn't read the fucking lesson?'

The Irish actor-manager Anew McMaster had a cunning way of helping his memory when he played some of the long Shakespearean roles. In soliloquies he would deliver one part of the speech leaning against a pillar on the right of the stage, then cross the stage to another pillar for the next part, and so on. Each pillar had part of the speech written on the back of it. One night, when the stage-hands had set the stage in haste, Anew McMaster began one of his big speeches in the middle, paused, and was heard to mutter in rage: 'Wrong bloody pillar!'

3. An actor-manager, from an 1834 print

Ad Lib

The phrase 'ad lib' comes from the Latin ad libitum, meaning 'to choice' or 'at pleasure'. But there is usually little pleasure for actors who find themselves having to ad lib because of circumstances beyond their control. Some of the most excruciating tales of the theatre involve such enforced improvisation. . . .

Reginald Salberg:

A young and inexperienced actress was on stage with a star player, when the phone rang, for no reason at all. The stage management had simply made a mistake. The actress was flustered, but was immensely reassured that all would be well, when the star calmly picked up the receiver. His experience would cope with the situation. The star listened to the phone for a few seconds, then handed it to her, saying: 'It's for you, darling!'

A similar situation where experience triumphed over innocence involved a young actor who was on stage playing a scene with an actor who was older. . .and a lot more wily.

The leading lady did not come on to join them when she was supposed to. Desperately the young actor filled in the pause by saying to his companion, 'I really think we must thrash this matter out!'

The older actor folded his arms with a smile and said: 'What an excellent idea! You begin!'

Guns can be awkward on stage, especially when they fail to go off at the right dramatic moment. It is a situation that requires quick thinking, as in the case where one actor levelled a gun at another and pulled the trigger with a shout of murderous triumph. There was no sound.

The victim obligingly, however, fell to the ground. The killer looked at the gun admiringly and said: 'These silencers are really amazing!'

Another somewhat cautious actor, who had a scene where he shot himself, used to carry a little bottle so that if the gun did not go off, he could be seen to poison himself instead. Unfortunately the actor playing the doctor who was supposed to rush on and examine the body wasn't paying much attention on the night when the gun failed and the suicide had taken poison. The doctor duly rushed on, made his examination and announced: 'Dead! Shot, straight through the heart!'

You can sometimes hear one actor say jokingly to another, 'The boot was poisoned,' whereupon both of them fall about laughing. It is an allusion to one of the classic stories that circulate in the profession, illustrating the resourcefulness of actors in dire situations. The story is that there was a scene where one actor had to shoot another. He pulled the trigger once: not a sound. He tried again, with the same result. And again. Furiously he threw the gun away. He produced a dagger and raised it to strike; the blade fell off. While the potential victim cowered in helpful desperation, the killer, equally desperate, picked up a large vase standing on a table and lifted it above his head. It slipped from his grasp, crashed to the floor and broke.

Both actors by now felt that inanimate objects were plotting against them, and the audience was beginning to mutter and even chuckle. The killer swung his foot and pretended to give the victim a vicious kick, whereupon the victim slumped thankfully to the floor. There he gave one agonised convulsion, and fell dead, crying out: 'The boot was poisoned!'

Disaster was avoided once at Perth Rep by some desperate ad libbing in the play 'Seagulls over Sorrento', about four volunteers arriving at a remote naval station in northern Scotland, where a secret torpedo is undergoing trials. In an early scene the captain, accompanied by a lieutenant and a petty officer, explains to the four new arrivals that there will be no leave while the trials are on and that they are sworn to secrecy about the whole project. Unfortunately, the captain one night launched into a speech from near the end of the play instead, described here by Alistair Wilson:

Tony Groser, playing the Cockney seaman, saw the prompter's agonised face, came to attention, took one pace forward and yelled: 'Sir!'

The captain, realising that something was wrong, but with no idea what, mumbled and dithered for a moment, failed to accept the prompt, looked helplessly round and, in true service style, bawled out: 'Carry on, sub-lieutenant!' and marched off.

The young actor playing the lieutenant gulped, panicked, shouted: 'Carry on, petty officer!' and ran off.

The petty officer turned pale under his make-up, gobbled for a second, then shouted: 'Atten-shun! Dis-miss!' and fled.

In a deadly silence, the four of us left on stage stared at each other. The young assistant stage manager playing the raw recruit, eased surreptitiously towards the prompter. Lofty, played by Brian Mosley, later a stalwart in 'Coronation Street', let his jaw hang open as his contribution. Tony Groser, an experienced actor, looked at me and moved downstage. I moved to him, in my character as the dour and uncommunicative Scot.

'I expect what the cap'n was going to say,' said Tony, taking me by the arm, 'was that we're 'ere on a top secret mission, I fink!'

'Aye,' I said, 'something tae dae wi' torpedoes, I fancy. Did ye see yon submarine outside?'

'That's right, that's right!' Tony said, delighted. 'Yuss, and I expect we won't get no leave till the trials are over, what do you fink, 'aggis, eh?'

'Right,' I said, 'and we'll be sworn to secrecy, forbye, I'm thinking.'

'Sure to be!' said Tony. He stood and considered for a moment. 'Yuss, well, I fink that'll be everything,' he said, and turned upstage to carry on with his correct lines. As he did so he muttered to me: 'So much for the plot!'

Athene Seyler remembered a time when a fellow actress had to do some desperate improvising in order to get on to the stage at all:

There was one occasion, playing in a little provincial theatre where the scenery was really rather too big for the size of the stage, and the second act, I think it was, was in a bedroom with a very large, old-fashioned wardrobe in it. During the scene, my mother had to come on. There was only one door on to the scene, and I realised when I heard a rattling and saw the knob of the door going round and round and round that the door had thoroughly stuck and she couldn't get on.

After a second of walking about and doing my hair and looking in the glass and thinking, 'What in the name of fortune are we going to do?' the door of the wardrobe opened and my mother made a dignified entrance, stepping down over the drawer underneath it as if it was quite usual to enter the scene through the wardrobe.

So we played the scene and then she went back to the door to get off. The carpenter hadn't been found, it was still shut: so with great aplomb she walked to the wardrobe, and got into it and went through it and made her exit that way!

When Harry Secombe was playing the part of d'Artagnan in the comedy musical 'The Four Musketeers' at Drury Lane, he was stricken by laryngitis. But the show went on, thanks to the fact that he had made a tape-recording of his numbers in advance, just in case. He was able to mime to the songs—especially important in the two romantic ballads he had to sing. The laryngitis lasted well over a week, and at first Harry mimed accurately and credibly. But after a couple of performances, his sense of fun took over. One audience was

4. Harry Secombe as D'Artagnan in 'The Four Musketeers' at Drury Lane Theatre

startled, then delighted, to see him suddenly clench a rose between his teeth—while the song continued pouring forth—and do an impersonation of Carmen. At another show he drank a glass of water during the song. And finally, as the song came to its poignant end, he opened his cloak to reveal a notice on his chest reading: 'Normal service will be resumed as soon as possible'.

Charles Lamb, in 'The Essays of Elia', remembered an off-stage ad lib from an actor called Dodd, one of the best players of the part of Sir Andrew Aguecheek in 'Twelfth Night'.

I know one instance of an impromptu which no length of study could have bettered. My merry friend, Jem White, had seen him one evening in Aguecheek, and recognising Dodd the next day in Fleet Street, was irresistibly impelled to take off his hat and salute him as the identical knight of the preceding evening, with a 'Save you, Sir Andrew'.

Dodd, not at all disconcerted at this unusual address from a stranger, with a courteous half-rebuking wave of the hand, put him off with an 'Away, Fool'.

Perhaps the most skilled ad libbers in the history of the theatre were the actors of the Italian Commedia dell'Arte. This is how one of them, Evariste Gherardi, described their style:

The Italian actors learn nothing by heart; all they need, when they perform a comedy, is to know what the subject is, just before they go on.... A man who is called a 'good Italian comedian' is a man with understanding, who relies for his acting more on imagination than on memory. He matches his actions to his words, and makes both fit in with the performance of his fellow actors, doing all that's needed to respond to them—and he does it all so well, that you'd think everything had been carefully worked out beforehand.

Agents

Here are some of the printable comments that have been made about agents:

Why bother to go to a different agent? Changing agents is like changing deck chairs on the 'Titanic'.

He only heard from his agent twice: once to say he was sorry but he'd lost all the actor's photographs, and six months later to say he was going out of business....

The most wanted criminal in Britain and the USA knew exactly how to elude his pursuers: he didn't bother about plastic surgery or false passports—he just joined X's agency and was never heard of again.

An author was sitting beside his agent at the first night of his new play. As the curtain was about to go up, the author turned and whispered: 'Are you as nervous as I am—or only ten per cent as nervous?'

In defence of agents, Kenneth More wrote in 'More or Less':

I have frequently heard actors criticise agents. Sometimes I have done so myself. I suppose we all basically resent paying them ten per cent. Some actors even say they will have a clause in their will so that when they die ten per cent of their ashes are sprinkled over their agent. But without an agent most actors and actresses would never survive.

The agent has to sell his clients to people who, very often, have never heard of them and are not particularly interested in remedying that situation. The agent has also to cheer up his client until he lands a part. And sometimes, ironically, he may have to cut him down to size because he is becoming unreasonable or big-headed. He helps with advice of all kinds, from tax

5. Kenneth More

questions to matrimonial problems, and is a father confessor, when nobody else wants to listen. And remember, the agent makes nothing for himself until he has found work for his client. As the agent likes to tell it, the client then takes ninety per cent of what he has earned for him!

Reginald Salberg recalls:

An agent once recommended an actor to me and I said I would interview him. Before the day fixed for that interview, I discovered he was playing at Richmond, and as I was in London I went to see him—and didn't like his performance. I kept the appointment to see him but warned the agent that I wouldn't be able to offer him work as I'd seen him act and was unimpressed. The agent, one of the old school, looked aghast, and said reproachfully: 'You went to see him act. How unfair!'

Amateur Dramatics

Amateur theatricals and the fractious feelings they cause were observed and recorded with her customary perception by Jane Austen in 'Mansfield Park':

Everything was now in a regular train—theatre, actors, actresses, and dresses, were all getting forward; but though no other great impediments arose, Fanny found, before many days were past, that it was not all uninterrupted enjoyment to the party themselves, and that she had not to witness the continuance of such unanimity and delight as had been almost too much for her at first. Everybody began to have their vexation. Edmund had many. Entirely against his judgment, a scene-painter arrived from town, and was at work, much to the increase of the expenses, and what was worse, of the éclat, of their proceedings; and his brother, instead of being really guided by him as to the privacy of the representation, was giving an invitation to every family who came in his way. Tom himself began to fret over the scene-painter's slow progress, and to feel the miseries of waiting. He had learned his part—all his parts—for he took every trifling one that could be united with the butler, and began to be impatient to be acting; and every day thus unemployed was tending to increase his sense of the insignificance of all his parts together, and make him more ready to regret that some other play had not been chosen.

Fanny, being always a very courteous listener, and often the only listener at hand, came in for the complaints and distresses of most of them. She knew that Mr Yates was in general thought to rant dreadfully; that Mr Yates was disappointed in Henry Crawford; that Tom Bertram spoke so quick he would be unintelligible; that Mrs Grant spoilt everything by laughing; that Edmund was behindhand with his part; and that it was misery to have anything to do with Mr Rushworth, who was wanting a prompter through every speech. She knew, also, that poor Mr Rushworth could seldom get anybody to rehearse with him: his complaint came before her as well as the rest; and so decided to her eye was her cousin Maria's avoidance of him, and so needlessly often the rehearsal of the first scene between her and Mr Crawford, that she had soon all the terror of other complaints from him. So far from being all satisfied and all enjoying, she found everybody requiring something they had not, and giving occasion of discontent to the others. Everybody had a part either too long or too short—nobody would attend as they ought—nobody would remember on which side they were to come in—nobody but the complainer would observe any directions.

A northern English drama group entered an amateur festival with a medieval costume drama. The play opened to show the leading actor, a handsome six-foot man in impressive lordly outfit, reading from a huge leather-bound volume. In the script, the page enters and says to him: 'My Lord—the King is here.'

Nervous on the night, the young page entered and instead said his only other line, which should come at the end of the play: 'My Lord—the King is dead!'

The leading actor slammed his book shut, stalked across the stage and, towering above the cringing youth, said: 'That's reet, lad—tha's buggered t' play!'

An amateur drama group staged a full-length Shakespeare production which was acclaimed by all their friends and families and praised by the local press too. Not long afterwards they arranged a coach trip to Stratford-on-Avon to see the same play. When they got back, someone asked the leading man if the production had been anything like their own.

'It wasn't bad,' he replied. 'Laurence Olivier played my part.'

At a one-act play festival in Glasgow, a local drama group decided to be adventurous, and do an act from 'Macbeth'. They were awful. The adjudicator did not want to be too hard on them, but he could hardly avoid saying that their performance was really not up to much.

A kindly man, he was afraid they might be feeling very depressed at his criticism, so he went round backstage when they were clearing up later, found the actors and explained what a difficult play they had chosen. He looked at the petite Glasgow girl who had played Lady Macbeth and said:

'Of course, Lady Macbeth is a particularly hard role. It's a part that taxes the talents of even our foremost professional West End actresses.'

'Is that a fact?' said the girl. 'I found it nae bother at a'.'

Professionals can sometimes be pretty scathing about the activities of amateurs, as this example from Wilfred Brambell's 'All Above Board' shows:

We struggled valiantly but in vain to establish theatre in that town. Little by little, over a period of eighteen months, our public drifted away from us and returned to the YMCA where they paid to see their friends cavorting in lamp shades. I think it was a pity.

6. Ellen Terry as Lady Macbeth

Animals

Joseph Addison claimed in 'The Spectator' that Christopher Rich, proprietor of Drury Lane around the beginning of the eighteenth century, refrained for many years from staging a production of 'Dick Whittington and his Cat'. He was anxious to have real mice in the show and was afraid that the cat would be unable to kill them all, leaving the theatre infested. . . .

The nineteenth-century melodramas featured some extremely skilful animal performers as well as some exotic ones, according to James L. Smith in 'Victorian Melodramas':

In 'The Caravan' by Frederick Reynolds (1803), the hero's dog leaps from a rock into the sea to save a child from drowning. 'The Dog of Montargis' (1814), which Thomas Dibdin cribbed from Pixerécourt, is even cleverer. He digs up the body of his murdered master, raises the alarm, pursues the killer and at the showdown springs at the villain's throat; the actor wore protective bandages which hid small sachets of convincing 'blood'. Monkeys, jackals, lions, elephants and giant cobras came soon after, and in Fitzball's 'Thalaba the Destroyer' (1836) ostriches made their debut on the melodramatic stage.

When Kenneth More was in Charlie Denville's company at the Grand Theatre at Byker in Newcastle, one of the plays was 'Son of the Sheikh'. He described it in his book 'More or Less':

Charlie Denville explained the background of the play to us.

'This is an eastern play, of course,' he said. 'Tons of atmosphere. It's an oasis, so we've got to have animals and sawdust. Animals for colour and effect.'

'What sort of animals have you in mind, Charlie?' I asked him.

'A camel, for one. The ship of the desert.'

'But where are you going to find a camel in Byker?'

'It's all been taken care of, dear boy. I've been to the local zoo, and they'll let me have one.'

'Do you know what to feed a camel on?'

'No, but it's going to eat anything I give it. We'll also have a few chickens and ducks.'

'But you don't have chickens and ducks in the middle of the Sahara.'

'I do,' Charlie replied with finality. 'Anything that moves and flies is good value. The whole stage is going to be covered in sawdust, and the scene will be set for three nights, so the animals can stay on the stage when the theatre's closed'.

This play proved a terrible experience for us all. By the third night, the stage was covered with animal droppings. We had chickens, ducks, two goats and two donkeys, all contributing. The birds fluttered into the orchestra pit and had to be driven out by musicians wielding flutes and cornets like clubs. The whole theatre stank to high heaven. Stagehands, who were playing the bandits, would trip me up and roll my face in the mess, having the time of their lives. And to cap it all, there was no room for the camel to get on the stage properly.

It was essential that he was seen, to prove that a camel was actually in the cast, and ideally the brute should have come loping across the desert with the hero on his back to rescue my wife and me from the villains. But so much other livestock was crowding the stage that there simply wasn't room for him.

So the camel came in, just as far as the base of his neck, with the rest of his body outside in the wings. This semi-entrance at least proved he existed.

A pantomime dame cleaning a dolphin's

teeth with a giant toothbrush was one of the more curious scenes in what was altogether a curious event: a pantomime called 'Robinson Crusoe on Dolphin Island' at the London Dolphinarium in 1971. The principal stars were dolphins, penguins and sea-lions, and they gave eight performances daily, seven days a week.

An animal trainer who had many creatures in his 'stable' was about to be interviewed for a television programme about two of them, a falcon and a mouse, which he said lived happily together in the same cage. And indeed, he had the falcon on his wrist and the mouse was sitting on the table. During the rehearsal he explained how friendly they were, and just as the interviewer was registering his surprise and delight, the falcon suddenly leaned forward and gobbled up the mouse. The owner frowned, looked puzzled, and said: 'Oh dear! He's never done that before!'

When the live broadcast went on the air shortly afterwards, the trainer explained how the falcon lived happily with a mouse, adding, 'Unfortunately he can't be here at the moment. . . .'

A dedicated Method actor was playing the part of Long John Silver and went in search of the perfect parrot to suit the role. After hunting through many pet shops he still wasn't satisfied, but at the last shop he described the exact kind of bird he had in mind—size, colouring, timbre of squawk and all. The pet shop owner said: 'I have one exactly like that, due to come in this week. Can you come back on Friday?'

'I can't come on Friday,' said the actor. 'That's the day I'm having my leg amputated.'

7. 'Dick Whittington and his Cat', Sadler's Wells, 1852

Applause

It was once the custom in the London theatre for the audience to applaud frequently during the performance if they liked a particular speech, or even a particular reaction. Colley Cibber wrote in the seventeenth century:

You have seen a Hamlet perhaps, who, on the first Appearance of his Father's Spirit, has thrown himself into all the straining Vociferation requisite to express Rage and Fury, and the House has thunder'd with Applause.

And Sarah Siddons was at first surprised and put out when she found that this constant applause was not the custom in Edinburgh:

On the first night of my appearance I was surprised and not a little mortified at that profound silence which was indeed an awful contrast to the bursts of applause I had been used to hear in London. No, not a hand moved till the end of the scene, but then indeed I was most amply remunerated. Yet, while I admire the fine taste and the judgement of this measure, I am free to confess it renders the task of an actor almost too laborious, because customary interruptions are not only gratifying and cheering, but they are also really necessary in order to gain breath and voice to carry one on through some violent exertions; though after all it must be confessed that silence is the most flattering applause an actor can receive.

When Richard Flanagan staged 'Romeo and Juliet' at the Queen's Theatre, Manchester, he engaged Harcourt Williams to play Romeo. On the first night, the actor had just left the stage after the balcony scene when he heard a great burst of applause from the audience. He turned and saw that Flanagan was on stage, bowler hat in his hand, taking a bow for the scenery....

8. Charles Laughton and Athene Seyler

Charles Laughton was adept at getting the audience to applaud even his ailments. During the run of 'The Party' in London, he was sometimes afflicted by a fit of coughing. He would sign apologetically for the curtain to be brought down, then after a pause he would come out in front of it, still coughing and wheezing, and get a round of sympathetic applause. When the coughing fit had subsided, he made humble apologies to the audience and then announced that he would continue with the play. More applause. When the curtain rose again, there was further clapping—and the show went on....

Audiences

In 1582 Stephen Gosson wrote, in 'Plays confuted in five actions':

In the playhouses at London, it is the fashion of youths to go first into the yard, and to carry their eye through every gallery, then like unto ravens where they spy carrion, thither they fly, and press as near to the fairest as they can.

Elizabethans themselves did not always have a very high opinion of theatre audiences— quite the contrary. Henry Crosse said in 1603:

Now the common haunters are for the most part, the lewdest persons in the land, apt for pilfery, perjury, forgery, or any rogueries; the very scum, rascality, and baggage of the people, thieves, cut-purses, shifters . . . briefly, an unclean generation, and spawn of vipers. Must not here be good rule, where is such a brood of Hell-bred creatures? For a Play is like a sink in a town, whereunto all the filth doth run; or a boil in the body, that draweth all the ill humours unto it.

Eighteenth-century theatregoing had its hazards: for a time, there was a fashion among the more boisterous and boorish young men for nose-tweaking. If any member of the audience loudly applauded a speech or an exit, he might find one of these funsters leaning over suddenly and pinching him on the nose.

At a performance of 'Macbeth' Joseph Addison was much put out by the behaviour of a woman of quality, sitting not far from him:

A little before the rising of the Curtain, she broke out into a loud Soliloquy, 'When will the dear Witches enter'; and immediately upon their first Appearance, asked a Lady that sat three Boxes from her, on her Right Hand, if those Witches were not charming Creatures. A little after, as Betterton was in one of the finest Speeches of the Play, she shook her Fan at another Lady, who sat as far on the left Hand, and told her with a Whisper, that might be heard all over the Pit, 'We must not expect to see Balloon to Night'. Not long after, calling out to a young Baronet by his Name, who sat three Seats before me, she asked him whether Macbeth's Wife was still alive; and (before he could give an Answer) fell a talking of the Ghost of Banquo. She had by this time formed a little Audience to her self, and fixed the Attention of all about her. But as I had a mind to hear the Play, I got out of the Sphere of her Impertinence, and planted my self in one of the remotest Corners of the Pit.

In Australia there was an attempt to start up commercial theatre only seven years after the very first theatrical performance by convicts in 1789. Allan Aldous wrote in 'Theatre in Australia':

Commercialism began in Australia in 1796 when an ex-convict, Robert Sidway, who had established himself as a storekeeper, built the Botany Bay Theatre, mainly of saplings. Admission prices ranged from one shilling in the gallery to five shillings for boxes, payable in meat, flour, or the inevitable liquor if the theatregoer was deficient in ready cash. Audiences were composed of soldiery, free settlers and ticket-of-leave convicts. The players, too, were mostly of convict origin. Although a commercial success—criticism was then an undeveloped craft and so there is no record of artistic standards—the theatre lasted but two years. Many of the ex-convicts still retained the old itch and it was their wont to go to the playhouse, observe who was in the audience, and then depart to rob their homes at leisure. Things came to such a pass that Phillip had it razed. Another theatre opened two years later met a similar fate.

For thirty years occasional amateur performances in large rooms in private homes provided the only theatrical fare.

THEATRICAL PLEASURES. PL.3.

London Pub. by Thos. McLean. 26. Haymarket.

Snug in the Gallery.

9. 'Snug in the Gallery', a caricature of a boisterous eighteenth-century th

The proprietor and barman of the Eagle Inn in Melbourne built the city's first theatre in 1841, a wooden structure called the Pavilion. Paul McGuire described it in his book 'The Australian Theatre':

The entrance was by half a dozen creaking steps from Bourke Street, and the dress circle was achieved by a doubtful sort of ladder. The whole construction was inclined to sway in the wind. Lit by candles and swing lamps, its fire hazard was high. Those who had umbrellas, usually took them to the play, for the roof and walls were leaky.

Blanchard Jerrold, in 'London: A Pilgrimage', looked at the young audiences in the 'penny gaffs' of nineteenth-century London:

The true penny gaff is the place where juvenile Poverty meets juvenile Crime. We elbowed our way into one, that was the foulest, dingiest place of public entertainment I can conceive: and I have seen, I think, the worst, in many places. The narrow passages were blocked by sharp-eyed young thieves, who could tell the policeman at a glance, through the thin disguise of private clothes. More than one young gentleman speculated as to whether he was wanted; and was relieved when the sergeant passed him. A platform, with bedaubed proscenium, was the stage; and the boxes were as dirty as the stalls of a common stable.

'This does more harm than anything I know of,' said the sergeant, as he pointed to the pack of boys and girls who were

10. 'The Penny Gaff' by Gustave Doré, 1872

laughing, talking, gesticulating, hanging over the boxes—and joining in the chorus of a song, a trio were singing.

An overwhelming cocked hat, a prodigious shirt collar, straps reaching half way to the knees, grotesque imitations of that general enemy known to the Whitechapel loafer as a 'swell', caricatures of the police, outrageous exaggerations of ladies' finery, are conspicuous in the wardrobe of the penny gaff. What can that wardrobe be? An egg chest, an old bedstead, a kitchen drawer? In vain do I strive to convey to the reader the details of the picture, of which my fellow pilgrim has caught some of the salient points. The odour—the atmosphere—to begin with, is indescribable. The rows of brazen young faces are terrible to look upon. It is impossible to be angry with their sauciness, or to resent the leers and grimaces that are directed upon us as unwelcome intruders. Some have the aspect of wild cats. The lynx at bay, has not a crueller glance than some I caught from almost baby faces.

The trio sing a song, with a jerk at the beginning of each line, in true street style; accompanying the searing words with mimes and gestures, and hinted indecencies, that are immensely relished. The boys and girls nod to each other, and laugh aloud: they have understood. Not a wink has been lost upon them: and the comic ruffian in the tall hat has nothing to teach them. At his worst they meet him more than half way. For this evening these youngsters will commit crimes —the gaff being the prime delight of the pickpocket.

Although nowadays children are often the most honest and invigorating audiences to perform for, Sybil Thorndike found them less than enchanting when they were allowed to eat during school matinees, according to Sheridan Morley's 'Sybil Thorndike: A Life in the Theatre':

Some kind friend would occasionally provide the little darlings with bags of buns and sweets at the beginning of the performance . . . a chocolate—a little innocent chocolate —can make such a noise with its wrappings and its clothings, and after the crinkling is done one can almost detect whether it's a nut, or a foul ginger, or the noiseless cream;

and teas—teas—teas—and the paying for teas—could any sounds be more ruinous to the performance of a play? Why is this ever allowed? I'd have all bars and teas and foods whipped from the sacred confines.

Jacqui Bianchi attended a performance of 'The Comedy of Errors' at Stratford-upon-Avon in 1966:

I was in the gallery, in front of an elderly American couple who seemed to be enjoying themselves hugely, lapping up the complications caused by two sets of identical twins with evident delight. In the interval, they told each other how much they were enjoying the play, and were thoroughly happy until the curtain-calls. Then, when the Dromios (excellent performances by Michael Williams and Robert Lloyd) ran on from opposite sides of the stage, the lady clutched her husband with a cry of: 'Gee, there are two of them!' What she thought had been happening on the stage, I could only surmise.

David Allthorpe recalls:

There was some confusion among patrons of the Theatre Royal, Norwich, when the Royal Shakespeare Company visited the theatre in 1972 with productions of 'The Merchant of Venice' and Gorki's 'The Lower Depths'. There was disappointment for a few members of the audience who found they were watching Gorki's sombre play instead of the expected 'Merchant', so the management instructed the box office to check with people booking for the scheduled Gorki nights during the run that they knew which play was on. One customer, asked if he wanted tickets for 'The Lower Depths', replied: 'I don't care where they are, as long as I can see.'

A. E. Wilson wrote in 'Theatre Guyed':

Between the acts there is a general rush from the stalls into the foyer, and those in the gallery, ceasing to drape themselves over the railing and uncurling themselves from the unnatural and torturing positions into which they have been compelled to place themselves, retreat from their dizzy perches in order to breathe once again and to ease for a little their cramps and pains.

The fashionable throng in the foyer submits itself to be trodden upon and crushed with the utmost good humour and enjoyment. The foyers of most theatres are ingeniously constructed to give the minimum amount of room to the maximum number of people. The result is a delightfully free and uneasy atmosphere of intimacy. You are not only able to rub shoulders with society, the celebrated and the notorious, but to tread on their toes and to dig your elbows viciously into their ribs into the bargain.

Indeed those who mingle in the scrum are offered an unparalleled opportunity of getting their own back on those against whom they may have some private grudge. I bear in this way the scars of injuries inflicted by many of my enemies.

Peter Brook describes the effect of the audience on directors and performers in his book 'The Empty Space':

The director tries to preserve a vision of the whole, but he rehearses in fragments and even when he sees a run-through it is unavoidably with foreknowledge of all the play's intentions. When an audience is present, compelling him to react as an audience, this foreknowledge is filtered away and for the first time he finds himself receiving the impressions given by the play in their proper time-sequence, one after another. Not surprisingly he finds that everything appears different.

For this reason any experimenter is concerned with all aspects of his relationships with an audience. He tries by placing the audience in different positions to bring about new possibilities. An apron stage, an arena, a fully lit house, a cramped barn or room—already these condition different events. But the difference may be superficial: a more profound difference can arise when the actor can play on a changing inner relationship with the spectator. If the actor can catch the spectator's interest, thus lower his defences and then coax the spectator to an unexpected position or an awareness of a clash of opposing beliefs, of absolute contradictions, then the audience becomes more active. This activity does not demand manifestations—the audience that answers back may seem active, but this may be quite superficial—true activity can be invisible, but also indivisible.

And Brook staged one experimental production which must have been really bewildering for the audience:

Our own purpose was uniquely selfish—we wanted to see some of our experiments in performance conditions. We did not give the audience a programme, list of authors, of names, of items, nor any commentary or explanation of our own intentions.

The programme began with Artaud's three-minute play, 'The Spurt of Blood', made more Artaud than Artaud because his dialogue was entirely replaced by screams. Part of the audience was immediately fascinated, part giggled. We meant it seriously, but next we played a little interlude that we ourselves considered a joke. Now the audience was lost: the laughers did not know whether to laugh any more, the serious-minded who had disapproved of their neighbours' laughter no longer knew what attitude to take. As the performance continued, the tension grew: when Glenda Jackson, because a situation demanded it, took off all her clothes a new tension came into the evening because the unexpected now might have no bounds. We could observe how an audience is in no way prepared to make its own instant judgements second for second.

In a particularly intense moment of 'The River Line' with one of the principal characters speaking his dying words, an American voice was heard clearly from the stalls, saying: 'I think, Charlie, I shall take brother John those Balmoral short-cakes....'

A theatre management which 'papers the house' is not going in for a bout of redecoration but simply giving away a lot of complimentary tickets to swell the audience. You can sometimes hear an actor comment gloomily about a full house: 'Yes—but it's mostly paper....'

Audience Participation

'The Spectator' in December 1711 reported the strutting of a member of the audience, so flamboyant that it took attention from the play and even got mixed up with it—in spite of the law referred to in many plays' advertisements that 'By her Majesty's Command, no Persons are to be admitted behind the Scenes':

This was a very lusty Fellow, but withal a sort of Beau, who getting into one of the Side-Boxes on the Stage before the Curtain drew, was disposed to shew the whole Audience his Activity by leaping over the Spikes; he pass'd from thence to one of the ent'ring Doors, where he took Snuff with a tolerable good Grace, display'd his fine Cloaths, made two or three feint Passes at the Curtain with his Cane, then faced about and appear'd at t'other Door: Here he affected to survey the whole House, bow'd and smil'd at Random, and then shew'd his Teeth (which were some of them indeed very white): After this he retir'd behind the Curtain, and obliged us with several Views of his Person from every Opening.

During the Time of acting he appear'd frequently in the Prince's Apartment, made one at the Hunting-Match, and was very forward in the Rebellion. If there were no Injunctions to the contrary, yet this Practice must be confess'd to diminish the Pleasure of the Audience, and for that Reason presumptuous and unwarrantable: But since her Majesty's late Command has made it criminal, you have Authority to take Notice of it.

Audiences became so used to spectators wandering on to the stage that when David Garrick played King Lear in Dublin, a contemporary biographer, Thomas Davies, recorded in 'Memoirs of the Life of David Garrick' in 1780:

When the old King was recovering from his delirium, and sleeping with his head on Cordelia's lap, a gentleman stepped at that instant from behind the scenes, and threw his arms around Mrs Woffington who acted in that character; nor did I hear that the audience resented, as they ought, so gross an affront offered to them, and to common decency.

But it was in Dublin that the movement to get spectators banned from the stage itself was really launched, by Thomas Sheridan, who managed the Smock Alley theatre for twenty-three years in the mid-eighteenth century. After the 'Kelly riot' in 1746 Sheridan successfully sued his assailant for assault, thereby helping to get acting accepted as a gentlemanly profession.

At the trial Kelly's lawyer said: 'I have often seen a gentleman soldier, and a gentleman taylor; but I have never seen a gentleman player.'

Thomas Sheridan replied, with a bow: 'Sir, I hope you see one now.'

And Garrick was later to achieve the same success in London; as a triumphant historian recorded of Sheridan's Dublin success:

From that hour, not even the first Man of Quality in the Kingdom ever asked, or attempted to get behind the Scenes; and before that happy era, every person who was Master of a Sword, was sure to draw it on the Stage-door-keeper, if he denied him entrance.

There was no-one more willing than Henry Fielding's Mr Partridge to react to the stage characters as though they were real:

The grave-digging scene next engaged the attention of Partridge, who expressed much surprize at the number of skulls thrown upon the stage. To which Jones answered, 'That it was one of the most famous burial-places about town.'—'No wonder then,' cries Partridge, 'that the place is haunted. But I never saw in my life a worse grave-digger. I had a sexton, when I was a clerk, that should have dug three graves while he is digging one. The fellow handles a spade as if it was the first time he had ever had one in his hand. Ay, ay, you may sing. You had rather sing than work, I believe.' Upon Hamlet's taking up the skull, he cried out, 'Well! it is strange to see how fearless some men are: I never could bring myself to touch anything belonging to a dead man, on any account.'—He seemed frightened enough too at the ghost, I thought.

One of the nineteenth-century touring companies was travelling through the western United States. During a performance of 'Othello', Iago had reached with relish a particularly fiendish part of his plot against the Moor. Someone at the back of the audience stood up, levelled his gun at the stage and shot Iago dead. Then he turned the gun on himself and blew out his own brains.

Drink can sometimes lead to audience comments that just have to be brazened out. There's a story about Robert Newton on tour as Richard III. He and a fellow actor went on an all-day spree and got to the theatre only just in time to dress, make up and go on stage.
When the curtain rose and Robert Newton somewhat slurringly began his first speech, a voice from the audience shouted accusingly: 'You're drunk!'
Newton stopped, came downstage and spoke across the footlights:
'You think I'm drunk? Wait till you see the Archbishop of Canterbury!'

T. P. McKenna remembers an embarrassing scene when he was with the Abbey

Theatre company during their period at the Queen's Theatre in Dublin. A group of his contemporaries from his home village in County Cavan decided to come and see him perform. With football crowd style loyalty they called out whenever he came on or said a line: 'Good old T.P.! Come on there! Good man yourself!'
He didn't get any of the laughs that were in the play's lines, but he got lots of others—in fact the rest of the audience was so entertained by the roars of the claque that they started to join in.

Samuel Beckett's 'Waiting for Godot' caused some violent audience reactions when it was first staged in London— sometimes the comments even had a Beckett-like quality of their own.
At one performance, when the two tramps were in the midst of their philosophising, a man in the audience stood up and shouted furiously: 'Why don't they get some work?' Instantly another member of the audience on the other side of the theatre stood up and shouted back: 'They haven't got the time!'

When Peter O'Toole was playing Jimmy Porter in John Osborne's 'Look Back in Anger' he found matinee audiences a bit of a trial. He nevertheless tried to give of his best; but at one matinee, just as the two of them were playing the intense and touching scene recalling their baby-talk, and murmuring sadly 'Poor Squirrels', 'Poor Bears', a rasping matronly voice from the stalls rang out with the question: 'Why isn't he wearing a tie?'

In his 'Notes from the Underground' Charles Marowitz described how he launched his Open Space Theatre with a play called 'Fortune and Men's Eyes', which involved the audience environmentally as soon as they came in:

The author John Herbert was a young inmate at the Canadian reformatory he writes about, and the shock of that experience conditions what could easily have become a bogus play. The object of the environmental entrance was to give members of the audience a palpable sensation of what it is like to be trundled into a cold, forbidding, state institution. We forced the audience to come down the fire-escape; a narrow, chilling flight of iron stairs above which towered a hundred fire-escapes. On one of them, a prison guard holding a machine gun, coolly surveyed their passage. As they walked downstairs, they passed a barred window through which two desolate convict faces stared out at them. Once inside the building, they were submitted to the indignity of fingerprinting and then ushered through a door which led them into a prison cell. There they stood, sometimes for as long as ten minutes, while an impassive guard stood watch outside. On the loud-speaker system, they heard the bored voice of a prison official bleating pointless institutional information. Eventually, the cell door clanked open and they were guided through the set (four prison bunks) and into their seats.

There were some who giggled through the ceremony and others who took it in dead earnest. One lady grew hysterical and demanded her money back. One man adamantly refused to be fingerprinted and began berating the actors as if they were guards and he a victim of the state. Once seated, many people humbly asked permission to use the toilets, and others, speaking in hushed tones, asked if it was all right to smoke.

Of course, an environmental entry is a 'gimmick', but a gimmick which emotionally conditions an audience to the play it is going to see, in my view, justifies itself. The great lesson of 'Fortune and Men's Eyes' (a lesson learned even more forcibly after the West End transfer) was that The Open Space was not a 'theatre' but a place, the character of which could and should change with each play. The

rostra on which the seats stood were mobile and for each production they were rearranged so that the actor-audience relationship was never predictable. Each play required, not so much a 'setting' as an ambiance and every part of the theatre—including where the audience sat (or did not sit), the stairs leading to the theatre, the foyer, and loos—was subject to aesthetic considerations. It became clear that the thrill of a small theatre was not only the close proximity with actors, but the possibility of recreating the environment anew with every play. There was a possibility to pitch the audience into the play spatially thereby rigging their perspective; thereby also altering the feel and amplitude of the theatrical experience.

This was American playwright Sam Shepard's comment on the theory and practice of what's called 'environmental theatre' and its attempts to involve the audience in the action:

There's a whole myth about environmental theatre as it's being practised now in New York. The myth is that in order for the audience to be actively participating in the event that they're watching they have to be physically sloshed into something, which isn't true at all. An audience can sit in chairs and be watching something in front of them, and can be actively participating in the thing that's confronting them, you know. And it doesn't necessarily mean that if an audience walks into the building and people are swinging from the rafters and spaghetti's thrown all over them, or whatever the environment might be, that their participation in the play is going to be any closer. In fact it might very well be less so, because of the defences that are put up as soon as that happens.

Auditions

This is how Thomas Snagge described his audition for David Garrick in his book, 'Recollections of Occurrences':

I rushed to the encounter with all the ardour and consequence of success that a volunteer would shew for a glorious national conflict. But scarce had I spoken three speeches e'er the little man bit his lips, and perhaps his tongue too, to prevent a smile of discouragement to my tragedy declaiming? Nor had I proceeded three more, than he turned smartly round upon his heel. 'Very well! Sir, indeed! Enough! I have not time to hear more.' Then with his usual quickness: 'Oh! ay! Saunders. I want to speak with you,' and then, as if he had seen somebody unexpectedly at a distance, he shot off like an arrow from a bow.

During this, my grand rehearsal, the actors and actresses were hiding their faces, tittering and peeping at the side-wings while the prompter with a sly and half-encouraging sneer: 'Well spoke, Sir! With good emphasis and good discretion.' Shortly Mr Garrick returned.

'Sir, you have some little cadences I must teach you to avoid and some exuberances to retrench. You may, in time, do. I'll see you again soon. Call. Call here, or in Southampton Street.' Then on the light fantastic toe he capered off, bawling loudly, 'Here, Johnson! Johnson! let me see the Box Book.'

This was like a sudden paralytic stroke! My genius was wounded, benumbed! The high blaze of fame was clouded and I set out on my retreat with a palsied despondency. Yet I buoyed my spirits up with the satisfying anchor of reflection that I had not committed any egregious palpable blunder in repeating the words, tho' I might be a little extravagant in the action. Nor could I suppose there were any very unpromising appearance in my person, voice or pronunciation, and that some hopes might be placed on the attention I had received and the flattering symptoms of so cordial a 'very well' from the little man and the friendly desire to call again (without once considering this to be the mode of dismissal, as I often afterwards found).

At sixteen Jane Carr auditioned for one of the schoolgirl parts in 'The Prime of Miss Jean Brodie':

When I auditioned for Peter Wood for this show, I didn't just have to read. He told me to go across the stage, turn and say something amazing about myself. So I walked across, turned and screamed: 'I hate rice.' And eventually I got the part.

At seventeen, Liv Ullmann came to Oslo, planning to go to a theatre school. In her book, 'Changing', she wrote:

After my audition—Juliet and Ophelia—I stood in a corridor and waited for the list to be posted of those who had been accepted. And when it happened, a tall, awkward boy placed himself next to me and read aloud the names of the chosen ones. While something was dying within me, because I was not included, I understood, when he suddenly stopped at the next-to-the-last name, that he was. He barely smiled, and walked quietly out of the room as if nothing had happened to him.

For years I followed his career. I hoped to find some justice in my defeat by seeing his success.

Now he is a fish dealer in Sweden and, I hear, very satisfied with things.

Backstage

Joseph Addison wrote in 'The Spectator' on eighteenth-century theatrical improvements in stage effects:

Their Lightnings are made to flash more briskly than heretofore; their Clouds are also better furbeloved, and more voluminous.... They are also provided with above a dozen Showers of Snow, which, as I am informed, are the plays of many unsuccessful Poets artificially cut and shredded for that use.

One piece of backstage equipment gave a new phrase to the language which is still very much in use: 'to steal someone's thunder'. Nearly three centuries ago John Dennis invented a new machine for making the sound of thunder in the theatre. After it was used in one of his plays, a rival copied it for another theatre, causing Dennis to exclaim angrily: 'He's stolen my thunder!'

Thomas Snagge wrote, in 'Recollections of Occurrences':

Working in the trade is very different from seeing the finished performance before the curtain, where all is dressed and polished for show. In the morning all is gloom, negligence and hurry...actors in their great coats and dishevelled hair, yawning out their parts and hasting it over to get out of the house, to walk, talk and be admired... actresses muffled, and drawling out their words with simpers and affectation. The general bustle is to get over the confinement of the drill.

The technical staff at the Old Vic were waiting one morning for Tyrone Guthrie to arrive for a lighting rehearsal. It was a bright day outside, and it happened that a beam of sunlight was coming through a small window high up in the theatre and slanting down on to the stage, creating a splendidly picturesque effect.

The stage manager called out to his assistant, 'Make sure you put a curtain over that window—if he sees that, he'll want it in the show!'

A voice boomed out from the back of the stalls: 'Too late, John. Saw it. Like it. Want it!'

Perhaps the oddest theatre curtain was one that Louella Houston came across in her American travels:

We played in a town called Bozeman, Montana, and it's the only place in the world I have seen a curtain go down instead of being pulled up in the air. We had a lot of strings and various things on the stage, and we had to be very careful nobody walked on the stage; and the stage manager said to us: 'Oh, I gotta stay on the stage because I got to let the curtain down for you.'

My husband said, 'What do you mean?'

So he said, 'The curtain goes down in there—down in that, where the footlights are.' And, I might add, the footlights were kerosene lamps—they didn't have electric light in the theatre at that time—and we were quite worried about it.

Anyway, we saw how the curtain was worked, and we got one of our attendants to work the curtain and roll it down into the stage. And then, at the finish of the act he had to roll it up!

Bardlerising

A bardleriser is my name for anyone who has adapted, re-vamped, or re-interpreted the Bard. Many do it for fun, but some writers have gone at it with totally serious intent to make what they were sure were 'improvements' on Shakespeare's original text. . . .

Nahum Tate, who became Poet Laureate in 1692, was one of the most prolific and popular of the bardlerisers. His version of 'King Lear', produced in 1681, was enthusiastically received and for many years was the version most commonly used. It had a love interest between Cordelia and Edgar and a happy ending, and left out the Fool altogether. Garrick appeared in this version, though he later performed in one which was billed as having 'restorations from Shakespeare'. But the Fool was not one of the restorations—Garrick did consider putting him back, but finally agreed with others that 'the feelings of Lear would derive no advantage from the buffooneries of the parti-coloured jester'.

The result is that in the big storm scene Lear enters with Kent instead of with the Fool and nevertheless proceeds to call him 'my boy' and 'my poor knave'. As for the lines, Tate sometimes seems to like change for the sake of change; otherwise it's hard to see why he would take the original:

Blow winds, and crack your cheeks! Rage,
　　　blow.
You cataracts, and Hurricanoes spout,
Till you have drenched our steeples,
　　　drowned the Cocks. . .

and alter it to:

Blow winds, and burst your cheeks, rage
　　　louder yet,
Fantastic lightning singe, singe my white
　　　head;

Spout Cataracts, and Hurricanoes fall,
Till you have drowned the towns and
　　　palaces
Of proud ingrateful Man.

This is the final scene in Nahum Tate's happy-ever-after version:

　　　(Re-enter Edgar with Gloster.)
ALBANY. Look, Sir, where pious Edgar
　　comes,
Leading his Eye-less Father. O my Liege!
His wond'rous Story will deserve your
　　Leisure;
What he has done and suffer'd for your
　　Sake,
What for the fair Cordelia's.
GLOSTER. Where's my Liege? Conduct me to
　　his Knees, to hail
His second Birth of Empire; my dear Edgar
Has, with himself, reveal'd the King's blest
　　Restauration.
LEAR. My poor dark Gloster.
GLOSTER. O let me kiss that once more
　　sceptred Hand!
LEAR. Hold, thou mistak'st the Majesty,
　　kneel here;
Cordelia has our Pow'r, Cordelia's Queen.
Speak, is not that the noble Suff'ring Edgar?
GLOSTER. My pious Son, more dear than my
　　lost Eyes.
LEAR. I wrong'd him too, but here's the fair
　　Amends.
EDGAR. Your Leave, my Liege, for an
　　unwelcome Message.
Edmund (but that's a Trifle) is expir'd;
What more will touch you, your imperious
　　Daughters,
Goneril and haughty Regan, both are dead,
Each by the other poison'd at a Banquet;
This, Dying, they confest.
CORDELIA. O fatal Period of ill govern'd Life!
LEAR. Ingratefull as they were, my Heart
　　feels yet
A Pang of Nature for their wretched
　　Fall;—

But, Edgar, I defer thy Joys too long:
Thou serv'dst distrest Cordelia; take her
   Crown'd;
Th' imperial Grace fresh blooming on her
   Brow;
Nay, Gloster, thou hast here a Father's
   Right,
Thy helping Hand t'heap Blessings on their
   Heads.
KENT. Old Kent throws in his hearty Wishes
   too.
EDGAR. The Gods and you too largely
   Recompence
What I have done; the Gift strikes Merit
   dumb.
CORDELIA. Nor do I blush to own my Self
   o'er-paid
For all my Suff'rings past.
GLOSTER. Now, gentle Gods, give Gloster his
   Discharge.
LEAR. No, Gloster, thou hast Business yet
   for Life;
Thou, Kent, and I, retir'd to some cool Cell
Will gently pass our short Reserves of Time
In calm Reflections on our Fortunes past,
Cheer'd with Relation of the prosperous
   Reign
Of this celestial Pair; thus our Remains
Shall in an even Course of Thoughts be
   past,
Enjoy the present Hour, nor fear the last.
EDGAR. Our drooping Country now erects
   her Head,
Peace spreads her balmy Wings, and Plenty
   blooms.
Divine Cordelia, all the Gods can witness
How much thy Love to Empire I prefer!
Thy bright Example shall convince the
   World
(Whatever Storms of Fortune are decreed)
That Truth and Vertue shall at last succeed.
                    (*Exeunt Omnes*.)

*'Coriolanus' was something of a favourite
with the bardlerisers. It appeared in several
eighteenth-century versions: at Drury Lane
in 1719 as 'The Invader of his Country;
or, The Fatal Resentment' and at Covent
Garden in 1754 as 'Coriolanus, or The
Roman Matron'. Another version in 1749
succeeded in preserving the Unity of Place,
adapting the play so that the entire action*

*took place in the Volscian camp. Earlier,
Nahum Tate blithely rewrote the entire
fifth act for his version, 'The Ingratitude
of a Commonwealth'.*

**Dryden and Davenant's version of 'The
Tempest' showed a passion for symmetry
and pairing: they introduced Sycorax, a sister
to Caliban; Dorinda, a sister for Miranda; and
Hippolito, 'one that never saw woman'—not
to mention Milcha, a mate for Ariel, who pops
up at the end, and is described as:**

. . .a gentle Spirit for my Love, who twice
seven years has waited for my freedom.

**The final pairing-off of Ferdinand with
Miranda, and Hippolito with Dorinda gives
plenty of scope for coy humour, beginning
with some arch remarks from Prospero to his
daughters:**

PROSPERO. My Ariel told me, when last night
   you quarreled,
You said you would for ever part your
   beds;
But what you threatened in your anger,
   Heaven
Has turned to Prophecy:
For you, Miranda, must with Ferdinand
And you, Dorinda, with Hippolito
Lie in one Bed hereafter.
ALONZO. And Heaven make
Those Beds still fruitful in producing
   children,
To bless their Parents' youth, and
   Grandsires' age.
MIRANDA (to DORINDA). If Children come
   by lying in a Bed,
I wonder you and I had none between us.
DORINDA. Sister, it was our fault, we meant
   like fools
To look 'em in the fields, and they it
   seems
Are only found in Beds.
HIPPOLITO. I am o'erjoyed
That I shall have Dorinda in a bed;
We'll lie all night and day together there,
And never rise again.
FERDINAND (aside to him). Hippolito! you yet
   are ignorant
Of your great Happiness, but there is
   somewhat
Which for your own and fair Dorinda's sake
I must instruct you in.
HIPPOLITO. Pray teach me quickly
How Men and Women in your World
   make love,
I shall soon learn I warrant you.

Sir William Davenant, who adapted 'The Tempest' with Dryden, also managed a spectacular piece of compression on two of Shakespeare's plays. He amalgamated 'Much Ado About Nothing' and 'Measure for Measure' into one play, calling the result 'The Law Against Lovers'.

Davenant, incidentally, was always impressed by Ben Jonson's simple epitaph: 'O rare Ben Jonson'. But somehow his own epitaph, copied from it, didn't have the same ring about it; it read: 'O rare Sir William Davenant'.

It is perhaps just as well for Garrick's reputation that one of his literary efforts has not survived: his version of 'Hamlet'. Garrick pruned what he called the 'tedious interruptions' and 'absurd digressions' so that 'this brilliant Creation of the Poet's Fancy is purged from the Vapours and Clouds which obscured it; and like his own Firmament, it appears to be finely fretted with Golden Stars'. Among the things he cut out were Hamlet's and Laertes' voyages, and the Grave-diggers; he also wrote in some extra speeches for himself. His version, however, did not please his audiences—and it certainly did not please the Shakespearean scholar George Steevens, who wrote suggesting that Garrick should make use of the bits he had cut:

You had better throw what remains of the piece into a farce, to appear immediately afterwards. No foreigner would ever believe it was formed out of the loppings and excrescences of the tragedy itself. You may entitle it 'The Grave-diggers; with the pleasant humours of Osrick, the Danish Macaroni'.

What were things like during the preparations for the first-ever productions of Shakespeare's plays? Maurice Baring, in an extract from 'Diminutive Dramas', suggested what might have happened at a rehearsal in the Globe Theatre in 1595.

LADY MACBETH. Get out, damned spot! Get out, I say! One, two, three, four: why, there's plenty of time to do't. Oh! Hell! Fie, fie, my Lord! a soldier and a beard! What have we got to fear when none can call our murky power to swift account withal? You'd never have thought the old man had so much blood in him!

THE AUTHOR. I don't think you've got those lines quite right yet, Mr Hughes.

LADY MACBETH. What's wrong?

THE STAGE MANAGER. There's no 'get'. It's 'one, two': and not 'one, two, three, four'. Then it's 'Hell is murky'. And there's no 'plenty'. And it's 'a soldier is afeared', and not 'a soldier and a beard'.

THE AUTHOR. And after that you made two lines into rhymed verse.

MR HUGHES. Yes, I know I did. I thought it wanted it.

THE PRODUCER. Please try to speak your lines as they are written, Mr Hughes.

(Enter Mr Burbage, who plays Macbeth.)

MR BURBAGE. The scene doesn't go. Now don't you think Macbeth had better walk in his sleep instead of Lady Macbeth?

THE STAGE MANAGER. That's an idea.

THE PRODUCER. I think the whole scene might be cut. It's quite unnecessary.

LADY MACBETH. Then I shan't come on in the whole of the fifth act. If that scene's cut I shan't play at all.

THE STAGE MANAGER. We're thinking of transferring the scene to Macbeth. (To the Author.) It wouldn't need much altering. Would you mind rewriting that scene, Mr Shakespeare? It wouldn't want much alteration. You'd have to change that line about Arabia. Instead of this 'little hand', you might say: 'All the perfumes of Arabia will not sweeten this horny hand.' I'm not sure it isn't more effective.

THE AUTHOR. I'm afraid it might get a laugh.

MR BURBAGE. Not if I play it.

THE AUTHOR. I think it's more likely that Lady Macbeth would walk in her sleep, but—

MR BURBAGE. That doesn't signify. I can make a great hit in that scene.

LADY MACBETH. If you take that scene from me, I shan't play Juliet to-night.

THE STAGE MANAGER (aside to Producer). We can't possibly get another Juliet.

THE PRODUCER. On the whole, I think we must leave the scene as it is.

MR BURBAGE. I've got nothing to do in the last act. What's the use of my coming to rehearsal when there's nothing for me to rehearse?

THE PRODUCER. Very well, Mr Burbage. We'll go on to the Third Scene at once.

We'll go through your scene again later, Mr Hughes.

MR BURBAGE. Before we do this scene there's a point I wish to settle. In Scene V, when Seyton tells me the Queen's dead, I say: 'She should have died hereafter; there would have been a time for such a word'; and then the messenger enters. I should like a soliloquy here, about twenty or thirty lines, if possible in rhyme, in any case ending with a tag. I should like it to be about Lady Macbeth. Macbeth might have something touching to say about their happy domestic life, and the early days of their marriage. He might refer to their courtship. I must have something to make Macbeth sympathetic, otherwise the public won't stand it. He might say his better-half had left him, and then he might refer to her beauty. The speech might begin:

O dearest chuck, it is unkind indeed
To leave me in the midst of my sore need.

Or something of the kind. In any case it ought to rhyme. Could I have that written at once, and then we could rehearse it?

THE PRODUCER. Certainly, certainly, Mr Burbage. Will you write it yourself, Mr Shakespeare, or shall we get someone else to do it?

THE AUTHOR. I'll do it myself if someone will read my part.

THE PRODUCER. Let me see; I forget what is your part.

THE STAGE MANAGER. Mr Shakespeare is playing Seyton. (Aside.) We cast him for Duncan, but he wasn't up to it.

THE PRODUCER. Mr Kydd, will you read Mr Shakespeare's part?

BANQUO. Certainly.

THE PRODUCER. Please let us have that speech, Mr Shakespeare, as quickly as possible. (Aside.) Don't make it too long. Ten lines at the most.

THE AUTHOR (aside). Is it absolutely necessary that it should rhyme?

THE PRODUCER (aside). No, of course not; that's Burbage's fad.

(Exit the Author into the wings.)

Macbeth and Macduff then go through a fractious rehearsal of the fight scene, and

the Author returns with his new speech written. Asked to read it, he recites Macbeth's great speech: 'Tomorrow, and tomorrow, and tomorrow...' But the reaction is not too favourable:

MR BURBAGE. Well, you don't expect me to say that, I suppose. It's a third too short. There's not a single rhyme in it. It's got nothing to do with the situation, and it's an insult to the stage. 'Struts and frets' indeed! I see there's nothing left for me but to throw up the part. You can get anyone you please to play Macbeth. One thing is quite certain, I won't.

(Exit Mr Burbage, in a passion.)

The critic and satirist A. E. Wilson suggested giving 'Hamlet' a new lease of life by adapting it into some other style:

It is so full of gloom and superstition, for instance, as to be almost Celtic. It is, in fact, like one of those jolly dismal plays with which the Irish Players used to entertain us.

What an Irish play it would make. Hamlet, naturally, would have to be a sort of playboy of Elsinore as the plot involves the killing of his 'da' just according to the pleasant fancy of J. M. Synge in 'The Playboy of the Western World'. We should call him 'Mike O'Hamlet' and Ophelia, I fear, would have to be Pegeen O'Feely.

We will take the scene wherein Ophelia first imparts to her father Polony (Polonius) her account of Hamlet's strange behaviour and her fears that he is not quite all there:

PEGEEN. 'Tis sewing I was in me little bit of a room, God save us all, when Mike O'Hamlet did be coming in and all and be all wild like. There was no hat upon the head of him and the breeches and stockings of him all twisty and the face of him like the whiteness of the shirts the holy saints in heaven do be wearing.

POLONY. Whisht, now, 'tis the polis be lepping after him may be and he like to be destroyed so it is, before the rising of the blessed dawn.

PEGEEN. Whisht yourself, father, 'tis telling you I am. The knees of me was knocking like two skellingtons do be clapping together in the winds of heaven. There was himself with the face of a fellow did be after knocking the eye from a peeler

34

or a little queer man did be chased by all the scarlet devils in hell and himself after telling me the horrors and screechings in the dark places.

POLONY. 'Tis after being destroyed for the love of you he is, I am thinking, and you a fine, tidy girl all the sons of the kings of the Western world do be after seeking.

PEGEEN. The divil do I know but it's afeard of him so I am now.

POLONY. Well, glory be to God and what did himself be after saying?

PEGEEN. The young gossoon took me by the wrist, so he did, and he held me the way he would be crushing the very bones of me till it's like I was to be crying out in great anguish.

POLONY. Be the holy saints hark at that now!

PEGEEN. And then he goes to the length of his arm and gives me a queer look in the face I'm thinking, the way he would be after making a fine bit of a drawing of it. Then he did be after giving my arm a queesy weesy shake and wag his head like the boughs of the great trees do be shivering in the breezes of the golden dawn.

POLONY. Do you say that now, Pegeen O'Feely?

PEGEEN. I do surely and him making a great sighing would put you thinking would crack the great bulk of him and put him out of the wide world. Then it's letting me go it is and himself turning his head over his shoulder the way he would be seeing without the eyes of him and he going out into the brightness of the day and the light of them shining on me the way you would be thinking they was the holy lamps of the blessed saints.

Wilson also felt that 'Hamlet' would go well if translated into what he called 'Americanese' so that the 'rogue and peasant slave' speech would begin: 'Gee! what a bonehead and poor sap am I...' and the 'To be or not to be' soliloquy would go like this:

To quit or not to quit; that's what I'm up
    against
Ought I to stick the darn thing out
And let old man Fortune make a monkey of
    me
Or take a crack against this brand of
    bellyaches

And swipe the lot of them. To pass out; to
    sleep
No more; and by a sleep to say we end
The katzenjammer and all the other things
    that give us the willies.
I'll tell the world it would be better. To
    pass out; to hit the hay
To hit the hay; perhaps to dream: Gee! that
    would be tough;
For while we're sleeping in the boneyard
    what dreams may come when we
    have handed in our cheques,
That makes you think: There's the respect
That makes your life just one long tough
    break
For who would stand for a kick in the pants
    or a sock on the jaw
The panning of some ritzy guy
The pain in the neck when some frail has
    given you the icy mitt
When he might stage a fade out with a bare
    rib tickler . . . .

One of Wilson's suggestions for restoring Shakespeare to popularity in the 1930s was to get Noel Coward to rewrite 'Romeo and Juliet'. The scene of the lovers' parting might go something like this:

JULIA (sweetly). O, Ro, must you be going? It isn't four o'clock yet. Another cocktail, darling?

ROMEO. Thanks.

JULIA. And anyway, don't be stupid, darling. That wasn't the lark, silly. It was the thingummyjig, believe me.

ROMEO. Rot; it was the lark. The beastly thing's always singing at this devastating hour of the morning. And it's getting light and I'd rather leave and live than be caught by your beastly husband and kicked out.

JULIA (yawning). Oh, very well, then. Have it your own way, darling.

ROMEO. Beastly fag getting up. I'll stay. Give me another cocktail.

JULIA. Sweetest.

ROMEO (drinking cocktail). Angel face. (A pause.) But it wasn't a nightingale.

JULIA. It was.

ROMEO. Oh, do shut up talking about it. You make me sick.

JULIA (sweetly insistent). But dearest, it was the nightingale.

ROMEO. Oh, what does it matter, you ass.
Let's get back to bed and forget it.
(They go.)

Bardlerising can have more serious intentions. This is how Edward Bond described his version of the 'Lear' story, according to Malcolm Hay and Philip Roberts' book, 'Edward Bond: A Companion to the Plays':

...Shakespeare took this character and I wished to correct it so that it would become a viable model for me and, I would like to think, for our society. Shakespeare does arrive at an answer to the problems of his particular society, and that was the idea of total resignation, accepting what comes, and discovering that a human being can accept an enormous lot and survive it. He can come through the storm. What I want to say is that this model is inadequate now, that it just does not work. Acceptance is not enough. Anybody can accept. You can go quietly into your gas chamber...you can sit quietly at home and have an H-bomb dropped on you. Shakespeare had time. He must have thought that in time certain changes would be made. But time has speeded up enormously, and for us, time is running out....

In 'The Macbeth Murder Mystery', James Thurber described his meeting at an English country hotel with an American woman who had bought a paperback 'Macbeth', having mistaken it for a detective story. She had read it and unravelled the mystery, proclaiming to Thurber that it was really Macduff who murdered Duncan. Thurber was intrigued:

I read the play over carefully that night, and the next morning, after breakfast, I sought out the American woman. She was on the putting green, and I came up behind her silently and took her arm. She gave an exclamation. 'Could I see you alone?' I asked, in a low voice. She nodded cautiously and followed me to a secluded spot. 'You've found out something?' she breathed. 'I've found out,' I said, triumphantly, 'the name of the murderer!' 'You mean it wasn't Macduff?' she said. 'Macduff is as innocent of those murders,' I said, 'as Macbeth and the Macbeth woman.' I opened the copy of the play, which I had with me, and turned to Act II, Scene 2. 'Here,' I said, 'you will see where Lady Macbeth says, "I laid their daggers ready. He could not miss 'em. Had he not resembled my father as he slept, I had done it." Do you see?' 'No,' said the American woman, bluntly, 'I don't.' 'But it's simple!' I exclaimed. 'I wonder I didn't see it years ago. The reason Duncan resembled Lady Macbeth's father as he slept is that it actually was her father!' 'Good God!' breathed my companion, softly. 'Lady Macbeth's father killed the King,' I said, 'and, hearing someone coming, thrust the body under the bed and crawled into the bed himself.' 'But,' said the lady, 'you can't have a murderer who only appears in the story once. You can't have that.' 'I know that,' I said, and I turned to Act II, Scene 4. 'It says here, "Enter Ross with an old man." Now, that old man is never identified and it is my contention he was old Mr Macbeth, whose ambition it was to make his daughter Queen. There you have your motive.' 'But even then,' cried the American lady, 'he's still a minor character!' 'Not,' I said, gleefully, 'when you realize that he was also one of the weird sisters in disguise!' 'You mean one of the three witches?' 'Precisely,' I said. 'Listen to this speech of the old man's. "On Tuesday last, a falcon towering in her pride of place, was by a mousing owl hawk'd at and kill'd." Who does that sound like?' 'It sounds like the way the three witches talk,' said my companion, reluctantly. 'Precisely!' I said again. 'Well,' said the American woman, 'maybe you're right, but—' 'I'm sure I am,' I said. 'And do you know what I'm going to do now?' 'No,' she said. 'What?' 'Buy a copy of "Hamlet",' I said, 'and solve that!' My companion's eye brightened. 'Then,' she said, 'you don't think Hamlet did it?' 'I am,' I said, 'absolutely positive he didn't.' 'But who,' she demanded, 'do you suspect?' I looked at her cryptically. 'Everybody,' I said, and disappeared into a small grove of trees as silently as I had come.

Samuel Beckett

The Irish author and critic Vivian Mercier described Samuel Beckett's 'Waiting for Godot' as 'a play in which nothing happens, twice'. Mercier, the author of a book about Beckett's work entitled 'Beckett/Beckett', went to the same school as Samuel Beckett —Portora Royal School, Enniskillen—in 1928, five years after Beckett left. But he didn't know of him until 1934, when in July that year the headmaster issued his regular letter which went to Old Portora pupils as well as present ones. In it, Beckett was singled out (if misspelled):

. . .Old Portorans seem to be going strong in the literary world. S. B. Becket has now brought out a volume entitled 'More Pricks than Kicks'. It is described as 'a piece of literature memorable, exceptional, the utterance of a very modern voice'. The Spectator devoted a column of criticism, mostly favourable, to this book. We must heartily congratulate its author on such a reception to his first work of fiction. His 'Proust' was published a couple of years earlier.

Vivian Mercier comments:

Although Enniskillen is in Northern Ireland, so that the subsequent banning of 'More Pricks than Kicks' in the Irish Free State had no legal effect there, I noticed that the book did not turn up in the school library: Portora in those years was just beginning to admit that it had been the alma mater of Oscar Wilde and wanted no fresh notoriety.

11. A scene from Beckett's 'Waiting for Godot' at the Arts Theatre, 1955

Brendan Behan

In the BBC Television programme, 'Monitor', Brendan Behan talked to Colin MacInnes, who asked him about his work:

BRENDAN BEHAN. About my work...
somebody said 'What's your message?'
on an American broadcast. I said, 'I'm
not a postman...I don't deliver
messages.' The only message that I know
that I've got is that there should be no
war, in particular, for anybody—and that
we've all got to get by. About the
hereafter—well, I don't know, sometimes
I...I'm a daylight atheist. If I'm in
daylight and the sun is shining, I
couldn't...care less; I'm like the Swedes.
But somebody said that the Swedes have
the highest suicide rate in the world. It's
a lot of rubbish. The reason the Swedes
have a high suicide rate is that they give
the returns—whereas in England or
Ireland or Scotland or Wales if somebody
croaks themselves, they say: 'Oh, he
didn't know the gun was loaded,' or 'He
didn't know that seven million aspirins
could knock you off!' (Laughs.) I could
think of more pleasant ways of croaking
yourself, incidentally. But about my own
work, as I think you know, I very seldom
speak about it.

COLIN MACINNES: I'd like you to, though.
Will you just today, please speak about
it? We'd like to hear....

12. Brendan Behan

BRENDAN BEHAN. Well, it's kind of you to ask
me, but the only thing I can say is this:
Camus said, when he got the Nobel
Prize, he said: 'The duty of a writer is
not to those that are in power, but to
those that are subject to them....'

Sarah Bernhardt

At the Comédie Française, according to her book, 'Memoirs', Sarah Bernhardt caused violent tussles at rehearsal, all because of a bit of moonlight:

I was crossing the bridge, my pale face wild with grief, and the ball-wrap, which was intended to cover my shoulders, dragging along, just held by my limp fingers, while my arms were hanging down as though despair had deprived me of their use. I was bathed in the white light of the moon, and the effect, it seems, was deeply striking and impressive. Suddenly a nasal, aggressive voice cried out: 'One moon effect is enough. Turn it off for Mlle Bernhardt.'

I sprang forward to the front of the stage. 'Excuse me, M Perrin,' I exclaimed, 'you have no right to take my moon away. The manuscript reads, ''Berthe advances, pale, convulsed with emotion, the rays of the moon falling on her.'' I am pale and I am convulsed. I must have my moon.'

'It is impossible!' roared Perrin. 'Mlle Croizette's line, ''You love me, then,'' and her kiss must have this moonlight. She is playing the Sphinx, which is the chief part in the play, and we must leave her the principal effect.'

'Very well, then; give Croizette a brilliant moon and give me a less brilliant one. I don't mind that, but I must have my moon.'

All the artistes and all the employés of the theatre put their heads in at all the doorways and openings, both on the stage and in the house itself. The 'Croizettists' and the 'Bernhardtists' began to comment on the discussion.

Octave Feuillet was appealed to, and he got up in his turn.

'I grant that Mlle Croizette is very beautiful in her moon effect. Mlle Sarah Bernhardt is ideal, too, with her ray of moonlight. I want the moon, therefore, for them both.'

Perrin could not control his anger. There was a discussion between the author and the director, followed by others between the artistes, and between the doorkeeper and the journalists who were asking him questions. The rehearsal was interrupted; I declared that I would not play the part unless I had my moon. For the next two days I received no notice of another rehearsal, but through Croizette I heard that they were trying my rôle of Berthe privately. They had given it to a young woman whom we had nicknamed 'The Crocodile', because she followed all the rehearsals just as that animal follows boats—she was always hoping to snatch up some rôle that might happen to be thrown overboard. Octave Feuillet refused to accept the change of artistes, and he came himself to fetch me, accompanied by Delaunay, who had negotiated matters.

'It's all settled,' he said, kissing my hands. 'There will be moon for both of you.'

13. Sarah Bernhardt as Hamlet

The first night was a triumph both for Croizette and for me. The party strife between the two clans waxed hotter and hotter, and this added to our success and amused us both immensely, for Croizette was always a delightful friend and a loyal comrade. She worked for her own ends, but never against anyone else.

Brooks Atkinson wrote in 'Broadway':

In January of 1901, Sarah Bernhardt introduced a dash of cosmopolitanism to Broadway by arriving for her sixth American tour with fifty trunks, five servants, one secretary, the great Benôit Constant Coquelin, a troupe of supporting actors, and a formidable repertory consisting of 'L'Aiglon', 'Cyrano de Bergerac', 'La Tosca', 'La Dame aux Camélias', and 'Hamlet'. Since she played in French, few people knew what she or any of her actors were saying. Once she skipped a whole scene, though no-one in the audience realized it. But Broadway audiences were sufficiently familiar with 'Hamlet' to say some very harsh things about the imperious French lady who had the effrontery to emasculate 'Hamlet' at $5.00 a ticket at the Knickerbocker Theater.

In 'Hamlet', Coquelin was obliging enough to play the First Grave-digger, although Madame had brought him to Broadway to play his greatest part, Cyrano, when the Rostand play turned up in the repertory. He was as good a Grave-digger as the French language permitted. But Bernhardt failed as Hamlet. Everyone denounced her performance indignantly: 'a farce'; 'in every way she is unfitted to Hamlet'; 'the grandeur of the play is lost'. Norman Hapgood, the most flexible and civilized of the critics, was more precise. He described her Hamlet as 'a pert, ill-mannered, spoiled, bad-tempered boy with little sense and a theatrical temperament', which sounds suspiciously like a portrait of Bernhardt.

Blood

There are various techniques for producing the instant effect of blood. For a stabbing, for instance, a knife with a hollow blade can be used: it has a tube inside it, leading to a rubber bulb concealed in the handle of the knife. The bulb is filled with stage blood, and squeezed at the moment of stabbing....
   And prop-making expert Roger Oldhamstead says in Motley's 'Theatre Props':

A successful method of producing a limited amount, perhaps just to smear the face or hands, is to use a ring, in which the original setting has been replaced by a small cube of sponge soaked in stage blood. The ring is worn with the setting facing inwards, and gentle pressure on the sponge produces enough blood to show, as a little goes a long way. There are many proprietary brands of blood available from all theatrical make-up suppliers, and they will wash off. These can be used on dummies, with the addition of a small quantity of emulsion medium. It is also possible to mix paint the appropriate colour, but it should be tested under the lights as stage blood often looks too pink; there should be plenty of depth and body in the colour.

Nineteenth-century melodrama allowed for plenty of blood and violence, and plenty of audience reaction to it, as in stage versions of 'Oliver Twist', described in John Hollingshead's 'My Lifetime':

Nancy was always dragged round the stage by her hair, and after this effort Sikes always looked up defiantly at the gallery, as he was doubtless told to do in the marked prompt copy. He was always answered by one loud and fearful curse, yelled by the whole mass like a Handel Festival chorus. The curse was answered by Sikes dragging Nancy twice round the stage, and then, like Ajax, defying the lightning. The simultaneous yell then became louder and more blasphemous. Finally when Sikes, working up to a well-rehearsed climax, smeared Nancy with red-ochre, and taking her by the hair (a most powerful wig) seemed to dash her brains out on the stage, no explosion of dynamite invented by the modern anarchist, no language ever dreamt of in Bedlam could equal the outburst. A thousand enraged voices, which sounded like ten thousand, with the roar of a dozen escaped menageries, filled the theatre and deafened the audience, and when the smiling ruffian came forward and bowed, their voices, in thorough plain English, expressed a fierce determination to tear his sanguinary entrails from his sanguinary body.

The classic scene in Victorian melodrama of the heroine tied to the railway track was given a new twist in a play called 'Under the Gaslight' by Augustin Daly, first staged in New York in 1867 and later popular in London too. In this, the heroine does the saving. She finds herself locked inside a station and therefore prevented from helping Snorkey, a friendly messenger, when he is caught by Byke, who is simply, and aptly, described in the cast list as 'Byke, a villain':

SNORKEY. Byke, what are you going to do?
BYKE. Put you to bed. (Lays him across the railroad track.)
SNORKEY. Byke, you don't mean to—My God, you are a villain!
BYKE (fastening him to rails). I'm going to put you to bed. You won't toss much. In less than ten minutes you'll be sound asleep. There, how do you like it? You'll get down to the Branch before me, will you? You'll dog me and play the eaves-

41

dropper, eh! Now do it if you can. When you hear the thunder under your head and see the lights dancing in your eyes, and feel the iron wheels a foot from your neck, remember Byke. (Exit.)

LAURA. Oh, Heavens, he will be murdered before my eyes! How can I aid him?

SNORKEY. Who's that?

LAURA. It is I, do you not know my voice?

SNORKEY. That I do, but I almost thought I was dead and it was an angel's. Where are you?

LAURA. In the station.

SNORKEY. I can't see you, but I can hear you. Listen to me, miss, for I've got only a few minutes to live.

LAURA (shaking door). And I cannot aid you.

SNORKEY. Never mind me, miss, I might as well die now and here, as at any other time. I'm not afraid. I've seen death in almost every shape, and none of them scare me; but for the sake of those you love, I would live. Do you hear me?

LAURA. Yes! yes!

SNORKEY. They are on the way to your cottage—Byke and Judas—to rob and murder.

LAURA (in agony). Oh, I must get out! (Shakes window bars.) What shall I do?

SNORKEY. Can't you burst the door?

LAURA. It is locked fast.

SNORKEY. Is there nothing in there? no hammer? no crowbar?

LAURA. Nothing. (Faint steam whistle heard in the distance.) Oh, Heavens! The train! (Paralysed for an instant.) The axe!!!

SNORKEY. Cut the woodwork! Don't mind the lock, cut round it. How my neck tingles! (A blow at door is heard.) Courage! (Another.) Courage! (The steam whistle heard again—nearer, and rumble of train on track—another blow.) That's a true woman. Courage! (Noise of locomotive heard, with whistle. A last blow—the door swings open, mutilated, the lock hanging—and Laura appears, axe in hand.)

SNORKEY. Here—quick! (She runs and unfastens him. The locomotive lights glare on scene.) Victory! Saved! Hooray! (Laura leans exhausted against switch.) And these are the women who ain't to have a vote! (As Laura takes his head from the track, the train of cars rushes past with roar and whistle.)

Perhaps the most 'politely' gruesome line in drama is spoken by the heroine in a melodrama of 1845 called 'The Green Bushes'. She says:

Pray, pray let me drag you to the spot where my husband lies weltering in his gore....

In the Drury Lane version of 'Bluebeard' in 1798, grisly scenes follow when the young wife persuades Bluebeard's servant to let her into the forbidden Blue Chamber:

SHACABAC puts the key into the lock; the Door instantly sinks, with a tremendous crash, and the BLUE CHAMBER appears streaked with vivid streams of Blood. The figures in the picture over the door change their position, and ABOMELIQUE is represented in the action of beheading the Beauty he was, before, supplicating. The Pictures, and Devices of Love, change to subjects of Horror and Death. The INTERIOR APARTMENT (which the sinking of the door discovers) exhibits various Tombs, in a sepulchral building—in the midst of which ghastly and supernatural forms are seen— some in motion, some fixed—in the centre is a large Skeleton, seated on a tomb (with a Dart in his hand) and, over his head, in characters of Blood, is written 'THE PUNISHMENT OF CURIOSITY'.

Theatre of Boredom

In 1866 one of the longest first nights on record took place, at Her Majesty's Theatre in London. The play, 'Oonagh; or The Lovers of Lisnamona', was literally never-ending: it was still going on after two o'clock in the morning, and showed no sign of ever finishing. The stage-hands decided to take matters into their own hands. They tugged the carpet from under the feet of the performers, who fell to the floor. The curtain was then rung down.

William Shakespeare wrote in his epilogue to 'King Henry VIII':

'Tis ten to one, this play can never please
All that are here. Some come to take their
    ease,
And sleep an act or two; but those, we fear,
We have frighted with our trumpets; so, 'tis
    clear,
They'll say 'tis naught: others, to hear the
    city
Abused extremely, and to cry, 'That's
    witty!'—
Which we have not done neither; that, I
    fear,
All the expected good we're like to hear
For this play at this time, is only in
The merciful construction of good women,
For such a one we show'd 'em. If they
    smile,
And say 'twill do, I know within a while
All the best men are ours; for 'tis ill hap,
If they hold, when their ladies bid 'em clap.

And in 'ABC of the Theatre', Humbert Wolfe wrote:

O is O'Neill. The theatre was packed,
though a few may have died in the 49th act.

'I have to confess to a low threshold of boredom,' said John Mortimer, introducing a collection of five of his one-act plays ('Five Plays'). He went on:

I have some sympathy with Sir Charles Dilke, who never saw more than one act of any play. He loved the theatre deeply, but enough, he no doubt felt, was as good as a feast. I have even more sympathy with that anonymous and candid MP who fell asleep during his own maiden speech. There is something a little desperate about seeing a character, who has occupied a year of your life, coming through the door at the opening of the third act. 'What, you again?' you may be inclined to mutter, gripping the pen to provide him with another, scarcely deserved page of dialogue. In a one-act play, the enthusiasm has no time to die. The only rule I have found to have any meaning in writing is to try and not bore yourself.

Bertolt Brecht

Some comments from Bertolt Brecht on the art of the theatre:

Spectator and actor ought not to approach one another but to move apart. Each ought to move away from himself. Otherwise the element of terror necessary to all recognition is lacking.

The bourgeois theatre's performances always aim at smoothing over contradictions, at creating false harmony, at idealization. Conditions are reported as if they could not be otherwise; characters as individuals, incapable by definition of being divided, cast in one block, manifesting themselves in the most various situations, likewise for that matter existing without any situation at all. If there is any development it is always steady, never by jerks; the developments always take place within a definite framework which cannot be broken through. None of this is like reality, so a realistic theatre must give it up.

In order to produce alienation-effects the actor has to discard whatever means he has learnt of getting the audience to identify itself with the characters which he plays. Aiming not to put his audience into a trance, he must not go into a trance himself. . . . At no moment must he go so far as to be wholly transformed into the character played. The verdict: 'He didn't act Lear, he was Lear' would be an annihilating blow to him.

Jean-Paul Sartre in a conversation on Bertolt Brecht ('Sartre on Theatre'):

SARTRE: What Brecht wanted and what our classical dramatists tried for was to cause what Plato called 'the source of all philosophy'—surprise, making the familiar unfamiliar. Incidentally, Voltaire used this method in his tales. All you have to do is to present characters from another world. Then you can laugh at them, because you tell yourself as you leave the theater, 'Why, that world is my world!' The ideal in Brecht's drama would be for the audience to be like a team of ethnographers suddenly coming across a savage tribe and, after they had approached them, finding that they were in fact exactly like themselves. It is at such moments that an audience comes to collaborate with an author: when it recognizes itself, but in a strange guise as if it were someone else; it brings itself into being as an object before its own eyes, and it sees itself, though without playing itself as a role, and thus comes to understand itself.

INTERVIEWER: You were saying a moment ago that the mainspring of a play should be Plato's surprise. Do you think that is all that's needed? Are there no other links between spectator and stage? Wouldn't that be rather a frigid performance?

SARTRE: No doubt. But that was not what Brecht wanted. All he wanted was that the spectator's emotions should not be blinkered. After all, his wife, Helene Weigel, who was also one of his best interpreters, reduced audiences to tears in 'Mother Courage'.

To 'show' and simultaneously to 'move' would be ideal. I don't think Brecht would have considered that contradiction an insuperable absurdity.

It all depends on the perspective you take when you want to tell a story. Either you take the eye of eternity—things are so, they will always be so, woman will always be the Eternal Feminine, and so on. If so, you fall back on the drama of 'human nature', which I call bourgeois. Or you look at it as a sign of the beginning of a movement or the continuation of a liquidation. That is to say, from the historical point of view, or better, the point of view of the future. In 'The Doll's House', which dealt with the emancipation of women at a time when it was barely thinkable, Ibsen chose the perspective of the future; it was from the point of view of the future that he saw the collapse of the domineering and vacuous husband and Nora's liberation.

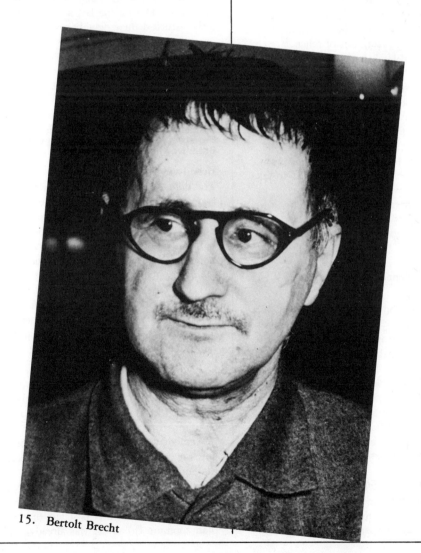

15. Bertolt Brecht

Broadway

The razzmatazz of publicity gimmicks was well in evidence in the Broadway of the early twentieth century and there was an easy method of casting, according to Brooks Atkinson in 'Broadway':

The section of Broadway between 37th Street and 42nd Street was known as the Rialto. Theatre people gathered there or promenaded there. Producers could sometimes cast a play by looking over the actors loitering on the Rialto; and out-of-town managers, gazing out of office windows, could book tours by seeing who was available.

Broadway was gay. It did foolish things with enthusiasm. The Hippodrome press department on Sixth Avenue organized a party of showgirls to be drawn up Broadway on sleds by elephants. An ostrich drew a light runabout through the streets. A baby elephant climbed five flights of stairs to take tea with Edna Wallace Hopper. The Hippodrome organized a sightseeing trip in a huge open bus for a tribe of Indians in full regalia. It was good for everybody, including the producers.

Broadway audiences in the 1900s were a voluble group:

In this era of good feelings, the relationship between audiences and actors was on the whole cordial and unsophisticated. Mrs Leslie Carter said that audiences invariably greeted the star with applause on her entrance. They applauded at the end of every act. If the performance pleased them they clapped, whistled, and stamped their feet at the final curtain. In melodramas, it was standard practice to hiss the villain and warn the hero or heroine of impending disaster.

Audiences were inclined to talk during performances. Richard Mansfield, Margaret Anglin, and Eleanor Robson on occasion stopped their performances and refused to continue until the audience was silent. They rebuked chatty audiences directly across the footlights. Matinee girls also had a reputation for bad manners. During the performance, they giggled and chatted with their friends and made audible comments about the actors: 'Isn't she just darling?' and 'I think he's the handsomest man I've ever seen.' During the last act, the matinee girls disturbed their neighbours by putting on their hats, veils, and jackets and rushing out of the theatre as soon as the curtain came down. They were in a hurry to get their ice-cream sodas before the calamity of having to go home.

Stanley Kauffmann gives these definitions of Broadway, Off-Broadway, and Off-Off-Broadway in 'Theatre Quarterly':

Broadway

The difference between Broadway and the two other types of New York theatre is easy to state. Broadway, by rule of Actors' Equity Association, is the area 'bounded by Fifth Avenue and Ninth Avenue from 34th Street to 56th Street and Fifth Avenue and the Hudson River from 56th Street to 72nd Street'. Within that area, or in any theatre anywhere seating more than 499 persons, any professional production must operate under full-scale Broadway contracts unless Equity consents otherwise in writing.

Off-Broadway

Off-Broadway is generally said to have begun under that name in 1952 with the Circle in the Square production of 'Summer and Smoke' in Sheridan Square. The movement was apparently the result of the post-war influx, into both theatre work and the audience, of more educated and artistically ambitious people. Off-Broadway was a mode of production that was fully or mostly professional, that cost less money than zooming Broadway was already

6. Broadway, New York, showing Astor House and the Post Office as they were in the 1890s

beginning to cost, and that would therefore permit productions of new plays and revivals too risky for full-scale budgets. For about ten years Off-Broadway flourished: then Broadway producers began to use it to produce shows that were on the Broadway border-line—'almost' commercial. The character of Off-Broadway began to change from a locus of some standing to a pocket-size Broadway or a place for Broadway tryouts. Partly in consequence of this change and partly because of general rises, Off-Broadway costs began to skyrocket. In December 1977 an Off-Broadway musical, 'The Misanthrope', closed soon after it opened at a reputed loss of 400,000 dollars. If this is only about half of what the loss would have been uptown, still it is very far from the limberness of 1952.

Off-Off-Broadway
Off-Off-Broadway inhabits the same geographical territory as Off-Broadway with the same excluded middle of Manhattan, but it is very much more free in organization and intent. It began recognizably around the end of the 1950s as a reaction against the increasing sleekness and expense of Off-Broadway, in order to safeguard experiment and reach and to go further with both. Off-Off-Broadway operates in many different kinds of places: a few relatively conventional theatres, but mostly in lofts, backs of bars, cafés, church basements, converted garages —sometimes the place is simply called a 'space'. (Henny Youngman has a joke on the subject, of course. Man, getting into taxi: 'Take me to one of those Off-Off-Broadway theatres.' Driver: 'You're in one.')

And this is how Stanley Kauffmann describes the current Broadway audience:

...most of it is the same middle class as fifty years ago, allowing for three important changes. First, there are now some middle-class blacks in the group. And of course there are now big Broadway shows with all-black casts that attract predominantly black audiences. (Is the title 'Bubbling Brown Sugar' much of a step upward from 'Blackbirds of 1927'? The show certainly wasn't.)

Second, that middle-class audience no longer lolls securely on convictions of its rightness. After at least thirty years of various anti-bourgeois attacks, from gentle spoofing to slashing hate, the middle class has not lowered its estimate of itself but is considerably more defensive than it used to be, less reflexively reliant on the approval of the world around.

Third, most of that audience now are college graduates, a much greater proportion than in its antecedent fifty years ago; and they are, or feel an obligation to be, more open-minded on matters that would have been restricted before. Authentic intellectual exploration and aesthetic innovation are not among those matters: but liberality of language, of sexual reference and behaviour are à la mode.

In the past fifty years that middle-class ritual, the theatre party, has blossomed. Such parties existed fifty years ago—my parents were sometimes in them; but they were not nearly as organized and influential as they are today. Now there are businesses set up to organize block sales of tickets to groups in the metropolitan area, which the group can then resell at a mark-up for philanthropic purposes. These theatre parties are now so profitable occasionally there is a 'Broadway Theatre Preview' to allow party organizers to see bits of upcoming shows so that they can advise their subscribers. One hears, and can readily believe, that some shows are designed with the party-public in mind. Pre-premiere subscriptions are money in the bank—sometimes a good deal of it.

Against all this good news about Broadway must be set some darker news. The expense of production is, as noted, higher, astronomically higher than it was. Fifty years ago a one-set, small-cast play could, with some scrimping. open on Broadway for an investment of 10,000 dollars. In 1977 'The Gin Game', a one-set, two-character play, cost 250,000 dollars. This means that hits are more necessary than ever. Fifty years ago there were occasional productions of plays that were not expected to be smash hits, were just expected to find 'their' audiences (as the phrase went) and to run for five or six weeks. No-one today would produce a new play with that intent. The play that comes to Broadway without long-run ambition is almost always either at the end of a long tour in which the investment has been recouped or else is a pre-tested British play with famous actors and with its possible deficit in the charge of some foundation.

Mrs Patrick Campbell

17. Mrs Patrick Campbell

Faced with a sparse audience Mrs Patrick Campbell would turn upstage and remark to a fellow performer: 'The Marquis and Marchioness of Empty are in front again!'

Performing the part of Mrs Alving in Ibsen's 'Ghosts', Mrs Campbell was described by James Agate as being like 'the Lord Mayor's coach with nothing inside it'.
　　But in that play she certainly showed how there is nothing like a bit of elaborate 'business' to wrench the audience's attention away from some other performer and on to yourself, according to Ronald Hayman's 'Gielgud':

Rehearsing 'Ghosts', she took a dislike to the actor who was playing Pastor Manders. She referred to him as 'that dreadful old man with sweat dropping down to his stomach' and in the long scene where Manders is liable to become the dominant character, she focused the audience's attention on herself by hanging a complete set of curtains.

Mrs Campbell was also able to cope magnificently with disastrous situations. Athene Seyler once said that she herself had a dread of finding that her underclothes had fallen down, on stage. That was why she had such an admiration for Mrs Campbell 'whose nether garments fell on the floor, and she picked them up with the greatest dignity and threw them at the back of the sofa....'

Carrying a Spear

In the time of the star actor-managers like Kean, the status of small-part actors was very lowly: they were known simply as 'walking gents', or 'general utilities'.

But some modern directors have given even the spear-carriers a sense of importance. Tyrone Guthrie was one of the most skilful and imaginative directors of crowd scenes, treating the elements of each scene like a composer orchestrating music. When he was producing 'Julius Caesar' he told the members of the crowd that they must each think out their own individual characters and their reactions to speeches like Antony's famous rabble-rousing one. It was no good relying on the old 'Rhubarb, rhubarb!'

The effect was splendid—until at one performance, by one of those odd flukes that happen in the theatre as in real life, there was a sudden pause and silence after a particular line, where normally there was immediate hubbub. This time, though, one crowd-member's line rang out loud and clear, and the dialogue went like this:

ANTONY. *Friends, Romans, countrymen, lend me your ears: I come to bury Caesar, not to praise him.*
VOICE FROM CROWD: *Morbid!*

18. A crowd scene in 'Julius Caesar', Drury Lane, 1881

50

Censored!

Even back in the fourth and fifth century AD, the Christian church was taking a sour view of the stage and its performers. Here is a selection from the decrees of various Church Councils of that time:

It shall not be lawful for any woman who is either in full Communion, or a probationer for Baptism, to marry or entertain any Comedians or Actors; whoever takes this liberty shall be excommunicated.

Concerning Players, we have thought fit to excommunicate them as long as they continue to Act.

The sons of Bishops, or other Clergymen, should not be permitted to furnish out Public Shows, or Plays, or be present at them.

The testimony of people of ill reputation, of Players, and others of such scandalous employments, shall not be admitted against any person.

A number of saints have ranged themselves firmly against all plays and players. St John Chrysostom in the fourth century, for instance:

What need I comment on the lewdness of those spectacles, and give a detailed description? For what is to be met with there but lewd laughing, and smut, ranting and buffoonery? In a word, it is all Scandal and Confusion. Observe me—I speak to you all: let none who partake of this Holy Table, disqualify themselves with such Mortal diversions.

Earlier, St Cyprian condemned an actor who was also a drama teacher:

This man it seems continues in his scandalous profession, and keeps a Nursery under him. He teaches that which it was a crime in him to learn, sets up as a Master of Debauch, and propagates the lewd Mystery.

As for St Augustine, he had definite views too:

The Theatres—those Cages of Uncleanness, and public schools of Debauchery!

Royalty could get very sensitive about the treatment of royal themes, and Charles I made his own changes in the texts of plays where he thought it necessary. In one play he suggested two new speeches to make a king and his court seem less gullible. In another, Massinger's 'The King and the Subject', a risky kind of a title to start with, his own activities in the field of illegal taxation and forced loans led him to object to the lines:

Moneys? We'll raise supplies what way we
     please.
We'll mulct you as we shall think fit. The
     Caesars
In Rome were wise, acknowledging no laws
But what their swords did ratify, the wives
And daughters of the senators bowing to
Their wills, as deities . . .

The King's terse comment in the margin of the text was:

This is too insolent, and to be changed.

Less political matters were worrying the authorities in New York at the turn of the century, according to 'Broadway', by Brooks Atkinson:

Clyde Fitch's 'Sapho' was arousing the libido of the populace at Wallack's Theater at 30th Street. At the end of the second act, Hamilton Revelle, a manly actor, carried the voluptuous Olga Nethersole upstairs to an unseen bedroom where, many people thought, a terrible sin occurred at every performance. One critic with twenty-twenty vision and personal enthusiasm said he could see Miss Nethersole's dimples through her gauze nightgown. Despite her amorous beauty, or perhaps because of it, the police closed 'Sapho' after the first performance, although they permitted it to reopen later by popular demand. In New Haven, the police had been more constructive. They closed 'Sapho' until Mr Revelle could learn how to carry Miss Nethersole upstairs 'in a chaste and orderly manner' in which the implication of sin would be totally eliminated.

The first-ever plays performed in the USA were done in New England and met with hostility in certain quarters, described here in Bogard, Moody and Meserve's 'American Drama':

It is unfortunate that the Christian's traditionally uncharitable view of the theatre was strongly upheld in New England. But it was. Ministerial arguments against the theatre as a place of sin and against actors and actresses as conspirators of the devil have persisted in a long line of mainly repetitious abuse to the present day in America. That there were those in early New England who rebelled against the church's anti-theatre scruples is, however, equally true, as the activities of Thomas Morton and the Maypole at Merry-mount so well illustrate.

Yet for the real if meagre beginnings of American drama one must look to the south of New England where both a tradition of Cavalier England and a few culture-conscious rebels stimulated some interesting 'firsts'. The first known American play written in English was 'Ye Bare and Ye Cubb' by William Darby. The history of Accomac County, Virginia, notes a production of this play on 27 August 1665. In his theatrical venture Darby was aided by Cornelius Watkinson and Philip Howard with the result that all three were sued by the King's attorney for immoral or illegal activity. Upon inspection of the play, however, the court found the playwright and players 'not guilty of fault'.

A play called 'The Hustings' was refused a licence for performance in 1818 with the comment that people had no need to go to plays about elections 'while every Hustings gives them a farce for nothing'.

Bernard Shaw said:

. . . the first condition of progress is the removal of censorship.

And Leo Tolstoy commented:

What matters is not what the censor does to what I have written, but to what I might have written.

When Richard Findlater was writing his book, 'Banned!' he culled from authors a number of ludicrous examples of the Lord Chamberlain's comments on their work. David Mercer said:

The humiliating thing is to have to go to St James's Palace and haggle—e.g. 'bugger' disallowed, but a 'fart' or two handed back by way of consolation. Perhaps most sickening of all—a scene in which a man beats his mistress, of which the Lord Chamberlain's representative said: 'We'll allow that if it takes place behind the furniture.'

John Osborne recalled that in 'The Entertainer' the Lord Chamberlain asked him to omit 'rogered', 'screwed', 'shagged', 'turds', 'balls' and 'had' (in the sexual sense)—and to change 'the vicar's got the clappers' to 'the vicar's dropped a clanger'. In 'The World of Paul Slickey' there were objections to the words 'fairy', 'queer' and 'crumpet', which Osborne then changed to 'swishy', 'queen' and 'muffin'.
The Chamberlain used to check up on plays in performance too. He inspected 'The World of Paul Slickey' in Leeds and remarked:

Requirement: Jack and Deirdre must sit on the bed as allowed. They may not lie. Jack must be fully clothed, not in déshabillé, and Deirdre's slip must be inside her breeches.

But even the Lord Chamberlain had his moments of humour. When a member of the public in the 1950s complained to him about the use of the word 'maidenhead' in a revue, the Lord Chamberlain's office wrote back in reply:

Dear Sir,
Maidenhead is a town in Berkshire, in which over 17,000 people contrive to live without embarrassment.

Characters

19. Mrs Patrick Campbell and Sarah Bernhardt in 'Pelléas and Mélisande'

Sarah Bernhardt wrote in 'Memoirs':

Every time that I have had a rôle to create I have first endeavoured to evoke the outward form of the personage. I then dress it from head to foot; I make it walk, bow, sit down, and stand up; I try to find out its own particular grace, its chief defect, its habits, its pet fad. In short, I make a point of trying to present to the public the personage in flesh and blood, just as history presents it to us if it be any historical character, and such as the novelist describes it if an invented personage. I have sometimes endeavoured to force the public to return to the truth and so do away with the legendary side of certain personages, which our present-day history, with all its documents, represents just as they were in reality. The public, however, would not second me, and I soon realized that legend must remain victorious in spite of history; and perhaps it is an advantage for the mind of the people that such characters as Joan of Arc, Shakespeare, the Virgin Mary, Mahomet, and Napoleon I have entered into legend.

Paul Scofield described how he gradually developed the voice he used for Sir Thomas More in 'A Man for All Seasons':

Of the things I've done it was the least well represented at the opening. I was hovering in the wings, so to speak. I couldn't quite see where I should commit myself. The voice was a great problem to me because the strength of conviction involved in that character was such that at one point in rehearsal I was sounding like Tamburlaine the Great. Putting that amount of strength, vocally, one sounded like a booming, bellowing hot-gospeller, just trying to put the full force into the man's convictions. This was clearly quite wrong: what was missing was the total discipline and restraint of the man. In the end we found a balance. I attempted to interpret the legal way of thinking in terms of a kind of dryness. I think this was the only way to arrive at the right voice for Thomas More—through the way he thought, as a man of law. Then the humanity of More will be added to it and the appetite for life will be added to that and finally, hopefully, all the colours will be there in the voice.

South African dramatist Athol Fugard, on actors creating characters:

It's almost as if they come into a rehearsal room without a soul—soulless—and are terrified of that fact, and then set about trying to find the soul of the particular character that they're going to act in order to fill an aching void inside themselves—an absolutely aching void—and that they will go to any lengths in order to find that soul.

Committee meetings would hardly seem like good material for superb comedy—until Alan Ayckbourn came along with 'Ten Times Table'. And it was based, he wrote, on his own experience:

'Ten Times Table'...undoubtedly draws for its subject matter on experiences gained during 1976. We were due in October of that year to transfer from our present theatre home, the first floor of the Scarborough Public Library, to our new temporary housing, the far more commodious ground floor of the old Boys' Grammar School. For me, this entailed attending an interminable series of repetitive (and largely non-productive) committee meetings to finance and facilitate the move. Up till then, I had had little to do with committees. Little by little, their procedures and protocols began to intrigue me. And particularly the people involved and the way they used these procedures. Put a man behind the wheel of a car, they say, and his personality really starts to show itself. Similarly, a committee soon separates the goats. Apparent strong men weaken. Nonentities inherit the floor. Silent men gabble on inarticulately and to no point. Talkative men grow silent and merely emit low indecipherable moans of dissent and agreement. 'Ten Times Table' is a study of the committee person. It breaks a pattern for me in that I leave my usual domestic setting for the more public surroundings of the ballroom of the quite awful Swan Hotel, where everyone at some time must have stayed, much against their better judgement. The play could be described, I suppose, as a predominantly sedentary farce with faintly allegorical overtones. In more innocent days, it would probably have been sub-titled a romp.

J. M. Barrie once gave a talk at Eton College, in which he discussed his 'Peter Pan' character, Captain Hook, the pirate who went to Eton. Later, an elderly teacher was heard ruminating: 'Hook? Hook? Hmmm—can't say I remember any boy of that name....'

Child Actors

Mysie Monté can probably claim to have made the youngest debut in theatrical history:

I was three weeks old, and Mummy brought me to the theatre to show the company, and one of the girls took me and said, 'Wait a minute,' and she carried me across the stage. It was supposed to be over the ice, escaping—she was a slave, escaping. And my mother of course said, 'Oh, my baby! Here, you give me back my baby! and rushed round to the other side. And the girl said: 'There you are, she's an actress!' And ever since then, I've been one.

The nineteenth-century opera singer Maria Malibran also started young, according to Peggy Branford:

When she was five she made her stage debut in Naples in an opera 'Agnese' by Ferdinando Paer. She had to hand her father a letter while he was singing a duet with the heroine. But at one of the performances when the heroine suddenly felt unwell and was unable to finish the duet, Maria, standing on tiptoe, finished it for her, to the huge delight of the audience.

When women were first permitted on the stage as professional actresses in the late seventeenth century the companies of boy players, as well as the men who specialised in women's roles, found themselves more or less redundant. But there were still some child stars who created an occasional sensation. One of them was William Henry West, known as Master Betty: his 'Hamlet' at the age of thirteen, was such an attraction that one day the House of Commons adjourned so as to be in time to go and see it. But his fame was brief: he came to grief when he attempted the role of Richard III. He was hissed off the stage and was never to make any kind of comeback in the theatre though he lived into his eighties.

Even today, appreciation of child actors can turn out to be remarkably superficial.

A boy at the expensive and prestigious public school, Millfield, in Somerset, was delighted and proud to receive a trophy for acting—a small silver cup on a stand, bearing the legend: House Plays 1980— Best Actor. He did think it a little odd that the words were printed on plastic tape which had been stuck on to the cup. He thought it even more odd when he decided to peel the tape off: underneath, engraved on the actual cup, were the words: T. Fattah—Track Events 1956.

Collaborators

Sullivan was working hard on the music for 'The Yeomen of the Guard' when he struck a problem, wrote Hesketh Pearson in 'Gilbert and Sullivan':

He experienced considerable difficulty over the setting of 'I have a Song to Sing O' and tried in vain for a fortnight to get the right tune. Gilbert offered to recast it, but he was so pleased with it as it stood that he would not allow it to be altered. At last he gave it up in despair and said to Gilbert:

'You often have some old air in your mind which prompts the metre of your songs; if anything prompted you in this one, hum it to me—it may help me.'

This was quite true, because Gilbert frequently achieved a particular rhythm with the aid of a tune he had heard, but as a rule Sullivan would say: 'Don't tell me what the tune is, or I shan't be able to get it out of my head.' However, the present situation was desperate, and though, as Gilbert said, 'only a rash man ever asks me to hum,' he did his best to reproduce the air of a sea shanty that the sailors on his yacht used to sing in the 'dog-watch' on Saturday evenings. He had not hummed a dozen bars before Sullivan exclaimed: 'That will do—I've got it!'

Gilbert wondered whether his humming

had proved too much for Sullivan, whose sudden exclamation might have been a cry of pain. But Sullivan assured him that for once he was responsible for the music as well as the words.

In 'Act One', Moss Hart described George S. Kaufman's manner during his first collaboration with him on 'Once in a Lifetime':

I turned in my chair and looked at him as he stood by the wash basin and slowly and meticulously washed his hands, and I was struck then and forever afterward by the fact that his hands were what one imagines the hands of a great surgeon to be like.

This impression was further implemented by the odd circumstance that he invariably began the day's work by first washing his hands—a ritual that was, of course, unconscious on his part, but which he would sometimes perform two or three times more during each working session, usually at the beginning of attacking a new scene, as though the anatomy of a play were a living thing whose internal organs were to be explored surgically. I watched him dry his hands and forearms carefully—he took the trouble, I noticed, to undo the cuffs of his shirt and roll them up—and as he came back into the room, walked briskly toward the desk and selected a pencil with just the right pointed sharpness, I was again startled by the inescapable impression that the pencil held poised over the manuscript in those long tensile fingers was a scalpel.

The pencil suddenly darted down on to the paper and moved swiftly along the page, crossing out a line here and there, making a large X through a solid speech, fusing two long sentences into one short one, indicating by an arrow or a question mark the condensation or transference of a section of dialogue so that its point was highlighted and its emphasis sharpened; the operation was repeated with lightning-like precision on the next page and the next, until the end of the scene. Then he picked up the manuscript from the desk and brought it over to me.

'Just cutting away the underbrush,' he said. 'See what you think.'

And this is how Richard Rodgers described Lorenz Hart and the way they worked together in the introduction to their 'Songbook':

Larry had only one pride that I was ever able to discover. That was his work. He didn't care about the way he looked or where he lived. He wasn't concerned with the social or financial status of his friends or what row he sat in at an opening. He did care tremendously, however, about the turn of a phrase and the mathematical exactness of an interior rhyme. . . .

Our work habits were almost as diversified as the subject matter. We always had a distaste for artistic self-pampering, as I still have today, and only rarely did we ever take one of those hide-out trips so popular with writers. It was when we were preparing 'On Your Toes' for rehearsals. Our writing had been interrupted by extra-curricular pressures so often that we took a suite at the Ritz in Atlantic City for a weekend in the hope that we could finish one of three important songs that remained to be done. We returned to New York on Monday with all three completed, and I remember that we felt happy and rested.

Only one thing remained constant in Larry's approach to his job. He hated doing it and loved it when it was done. There was the never-ceasing routine of trying to find him, locking him up in a room, and hoping to fire his imagination so that actual words would get down on paper. It wasn't wise to leave him alone for a moment because he would simply disappear and have to be found all over again. His pencil would fly over the paper and soon the most difficult part of all would begin: the material had to be edited and he loathed changing any word once it was written down. When the immovable object of his unwillingness to change came up against the irresistible force of my own drive for perfection, the noise could be heard all over the city. Our fights over words were furious, blasphemous, and frequent, but even in their hottest moments we both knew that we were arguing academically and not personally. I think I am quite safe in saying that Larry and I never had a single personal argument with each other.

Comedy

David Garrick once said to a young actor: 'You may humbug the town as a tragedian, but comedy is a serious thing, my boy, so don't try that just yet.'

In Joseph Holloway's journal, he wrote:

To see a farcical comedy more than once is like drinking stale champagne.

And Noel Coward said:

It is not only getting laughs in comedy that is important—it's stopping them. There are certain laughs that have to be quelled in order to get a bigger one later. If you have a sentence, for instance, in which there is a titter in the first part of the sentence and probably a big laugh at the end of it—a technical comedian will see to it that he hurries the first part so that they hear it but haven't time to laugh so that he'll get the full laugh at the end. Many inexperienced comedians will get the first laugh and lose the rest of the sentence in the laugh. The whole of comedy depends on timing—and if you are really on your toes, you play the audience and you control the laughter. You mustn't ever let the audience get out of hand.

Trevor Griffiths' character, Waters, had this to say in 'Comedians':

A joke that feeds on ignorance starves its audience. We have the choice. We can say something or we can say nothing. Not everything true is funny, and not everything funny is true. Most comics feed prejudice and fear and blinkered vision, but the best ones, the best ones . . . illuminate them, make them clearer to see, easier to deal with. We've got to make people laugh till they cry. Cry. Till they find their pain and their beauty. Comedy is medicine. Not coloured sweeties to rot their teeth with.

22. David Garrick between tragedy and comedy, after a painting by Sir Joshua Reynolds

Corpsing

'To corpse' could mean 'to kill' in nineteenth-century slang, but in theatrical terms it is less lethal. It simply means to cause someone on stage to giggle or laugh uncontrollably. Some accidental blunder can 'corpse' an actor, but sometimes people go to elaborate lengths to get the reaction deliberately....

Lewis Casson's love of practical jokes was given full rein when he played in the Australian production of Enid Bagnold's play, 'The Chalk Garden', with his wife Sybil Thorndike also in the cast. Elizabeth Sprigge described it in her book 'Sybil Thorndike Casson':

His arrival at the front door as the judge in 'The Chalk Garden' could not be seen by the audience, but only by Gordon Chater, who as the manservant ushered him in. Lewis would appear at the door wearing a flower pot on his head or carrying Sybil's handbag and wearing a grotesque nose, only to assume his proper appearance at the last possible second.

On one occasion worse mischief took charge. Discussing the play with his colleagues during an overnight train journey, Lewis said he thought he was playing the judge a little young. That night he gave a completely different performance: the judge had become a slow, decrepit, almost unintelligible old man. At a reception after the play one of the guests asked Gordon Chater if he did not think Sir Lewis was 'a little old to be doing it still'.

In the morning Chater, knowing that Sybil was the only person who could deal with this situation, told her what had been said. That afternoon at the matinee, when Gordon Chater went to the door to let the judge in, he nearly collapsed. A dapper young man stood there with fair hair, blue eye shadow, pink cheeks and cherry lips. Gordon had painfully suppressed giggles, Jane had a nose-bleed, the imperturbable Patricia Kennedy quivered from head to foot and Sybil was struck dumb.

She was absolutely furious and did not hide her wrath, although it is only fair to record that she herself was capable of mild unprofessionalism. For example, Jane tells of her grandmother crossing her eyes at her just as they were to play a scene together, or tickling the palm of the hand she was holding, making it an ordeal for Jane not to giggle. However, Sybil would never have behaved as outrageously as this. Even if she had not protested, Lewis would have made amends in his own incomparable way. Before the evening performance he called on the management to apologize for his lapse, and then at each dressing-room in turn.

In a Stratford-upon-Avon production of 'Henry IV, Part Two', the assistant stage manager decided to play a practical joke on the last night. She took the ceremonial drinking bowl passed around in one scene and filled it with water—and several live goldfish. Each actor in turn tried to conceal his horror or mirth. The last one to drink was in on the joke, and pretended to take a monumental gulp and swallow, followed by a bow and a smile to the others, who stood watching him in stunned silence.

Noel Coward

Noel Coward's much-quoted advice to an actor who was agonising over motive and interpretation is said to have been:

'Learn your lines—speak up—and don't fall over the furniture.'

But he could also be more serious about the actor's craft:

There's an old theatrical saying: 'Lose yourself, you lose your audience.' And even in an emotional part you've got to be aware with one part of your mind that the audience is there and that they are attentive. You have got, with a little extra sense, to listen for those coughs which might start— which means that you've either got to play more softly or hurry the scene a little bit or something. You've got to, in fact, regulate your audience as well as be the character— as well as consider the other people on stage with you.

His first professional role was in a play called 'The Goldfish' in which all the performers were children. His mother took him to audition for the producer, Lila Field, and he described it in his book 'Present Indicative':

We left the house in a flurry of grandeur, Mother very impressive in grey satin with a feather boa, and me burning bright in a new Norfolk suit with an Eton collar. Miss Field received us in a small bare room in George Street, Baker Street. She was smart and attractive with a charming voice, and her large brown eyes smiled kindly at us over highly-rouged cheeks and a beauty spot. My heart sank when I noticed that there was no piano, but after a little polite conversation we surmounted that difficulty and I sang 'Liza Ann' unaccompanied, and mother la-la'd for the dance. Miss Field was delighted and said that she would engage me for the part of 'Prince Mussel' and that the fee would be a guinea and a half a week, upon which Mother became sadly red and said that she was afraid we couldn't afford to pay that. Miss Field laughed and said that the guinea and a half a week was what I would receive, and that she'd let us know soon when rehearsals started. Mother and I floated down the narrow staircase and out into the street. The moment was supreme, and we could scarcely breathe for excitement. We went straight to Selfridge's and celebrated our triumph with ice-cream sodas over which we calculated how much a year I should be earning at a guinea and a half a week.

23. Noel Coward by Clemence Dane

The Noel Coward 'image' started to build up early in his career—in fact just after his first big dramatic triumph in his play 'The Vortex', which opened in London in 1924:

With this success came many pleasurable trappings. A car. New suits. Silk shirts. An extravagant amount of pyjamas and dressing-gowns, and a still more extravagant amount of publicity. I was photographed, and interviewed, and photographed again. In the street. In the park. In my dressing-room. At my piano. With my dear old mother, without my dear old mother—and, on one occasion, sitting up in an over-elaborate bed looking like a heavily doped Chinese illusionist. This last photograph, I believe, did me a good deal of harm. People glancing at it concluded at once, and with a certain justification, that I was undoubtedly a weedy sensualist in the last stages of physical and moral degeneration, and that they had better hurry off to see me in my play before my inevitable demise placed that faintly macabre pleasure beyond their reach. This attitude, while temporarily very good for business, became irritating after a time, and for many years I was seldom mentioned in the press without allusions to 'cocktails', 'post-war hysteria' and 'decadence'.

John Gielgud made a discovery about Noel Coward's talent as a pianist, according to 'Gielgud' by Ronald Hayman:

He was amused, years afterwards, to find that Coward's piano playing was almost as limited as his own. They sat down at two pianos in Coward's home in Switzerland, trying to harmonize together in tunes they both knew, but as each could only manage his pet keys, they had little success.

Critics

Treplev, in Chekhov's 'The Seagull', says that unlike his mother he has no belief in the theatre:

She loves the stage, she fancies she is working for humanity, for the holy cause of art, while to my mind the modern theatre is nothing but tradition and conventionality. When the curtain goes up, and by artificial light, in a room with three walls, these great geniuses, the devotees of holy art, represent how people eat, drink, love, move about, and wear their jackets; when from these commonplace sentences and pictures they try to draw a moral—a petty moral, easy of comprehension and convenient for domestic use; when in a thousand variations I am offered the same thing over and over again—I run away as Maupassant ran away from the Eiffel Tower which weighed upon his brain with its vulgarity.

The first meeting of two of the leading drama critics of their own generations happened in July 1945, when one of them, Kenneth Tynan, was still a schoolboy. The other, James Agate, was guest speaker at the school's Sixth-Form Conference. He described it in 'Ego 8':

The conference may or may not turn out to be a feast of reason; at lunch the only flow was soul! This annoyed me so much that when K. P. Tynan, my boy-chairman, told me that the programme included a concert, a cricket match, and a performance of 'Hamlet' with himself in the title role, I said, 'And how, pray, will visitors know which entertainment is which?'

In 'What is Theatre?' Eric Bentley said that for the journalist-critic, the only alternative to a sharp tongue is a mealy mouth:

The critic cannot do his work without

hurting; he resembles the dentist. Even to say that artist A is very good is to spread the rumour that artist B is not so good. Motive mongers will say the critic has a grudge against B's wife.

Bentley had a poor opinion of critics' judgement:

Badness in acting is often not spotted these days, and even oftener not mentioned. Because the press is much harsher with playwrights, it is a common occurrence in New York that a bad performance of a good play is called a good performance of a bad play.

RAB "HIS FRIENDS"

GHOSTS IBSEN

THE DRAMATIC CRITIC

24. A cartoon of a dramatic critic in 1893

Curtain Calls

Jane Austen wrote in 'Mansfield Park':

'You had better stay till the curtain is hung,' interposed Mrs Norris. 'The curtain will be hung in a day or two—there is very little sense in a play without a curtain—and I am much mistaken if you do not find it draw up into very handsome festoons.'

It used to be the practice for the cast to take a curtain call at the end of each act of a play. The first major London production to break with this custom and have a curtain call only at the end was Noel Coward's 'The Vortex', in 1924.

A veteran actor-manager was making his curtain speech at the end of that week's play.

'Next week,' he declaimed, 'we shall perform "Hamlet" by the Immortal Bard. I myself will play the Gloomy Dane, and my lady wife will play Ophelia.'

A voice from the gallery shouted: 'Your wife's a whore!'

The old actor paused, stared up towards the gallery and said: 'NEVERTHELESS my wife will play Ophelia. . . .'

The actor John East remembered how his uncle, Charles East, once went a little too far with his realistically gory effects:

He used to put some red greasepaint under his nails, and he said: 'Unless you will be mine, my dear, I will scar you so you will never ever get another man!'

He pulled his fingers down the girl's face, and it gave the most realistic impression of gore and blood. . .and there was a riot in the theatre, and they had to bring down the curtain. But he made one fatal mistake: he snarled at the audience on the curtain call . . .and then there was an absolute riot!

Australian audiences in earlier and more boisterous theatrical days used to shout impatiently as they waited for the curtain to rise: 'Up with the rag! Up with the rag!'

Less welcome to the actors' ears was the cry that went up if the audience didn't like the show: 'Down with the rag!'

Death

The following extract is taken from Tom Stoppard's 'Rosencrantz and Guildenstern are Dead':

PLAYER (to GUIL). Are you familiar with this play?

GUIL. No.

PLAYER. A slaughterhouse—eight corpses all told. It brings out the best in us.

GUIL (tense, progressively rattled during the whole mime and commentary). You!—What do you know about death?

PLAYER. It's what the actors do best. They have to exploit whatever talent is given to them, and their talent is dying. They can die heroically, comically, ironically, slowly, suddenly, disgustingly, charmingly, or from a great height. My own talent is more general. I extract significance from melodrama, a significance which it does not in fact contain; but occasionally, from out of this matter, there escapes a thin beam of light that, seen at the right angle, can crack the shell of mortality.

ROS. Is that all they can do—die?

PLAYER. No, no—they kill beautifully. In fact some of them kill even better than they die. The rest die better than they kill. They're a team.

ROS. Which ones are which?

PLAYER. There's not much in it.

GUIL (fear, derision). Actors! The mechanics of cheap melodrama! That isn't death! (More quietly.) You scream and choke and sink to your knees, but it doesn't bring death home to anyone—it doesn't catch them unawares and start the whisper in their skulls that says—'One day you are going to die.' (He straightens up.) You die so many times;

how can you expect them to believe in your death?

PLAYER. On the contrary, it's the only kind they do believe. They're conditioned to it. I had an actor once who was condemned to hang for stealing a sheep —or a lamb, I forget which—so I got permission to have him hanged in the middle of a play—had to change the plot a bit but I thought it would be effective, you know—and you wouldn't believe it, he just wasn't convincing! It was impossible to suspend one's disbelief—and what with the audience jeering and throwing peanuts, the whole thing was a disaster!—he did nothing but cry all the time—right out of character—just stood there and cried.... Never again.

The American melodrama, 'Nick of the Woods', gives opportunities for some really bravura struggles to the death:

WENONGA. I have heard the voice of the dead, and am not afraid of the living. (Cuts Nathan loose.) Let me see the Jibbenainosay.

Music. Nathan springs forward, throws off Indian disguise, and appears as Reginald Ashburn.

NATHAN. Behold him here! Look, murdering villain, upon the destroyer of thy race— the avenger of his own! Die, thou human wolf, infuriate tiger, die! Die! (Hurry. Grapples with Wenonga, wrests hatchet from him, and kills him.) And with thy dying glance behold the fearful fiend, the Jibbenainosay, in Reginald Ashburn! Ha, ha, ha! Mother, sister, wife—at last ye are revenged!

(Laughs wildly and exits, dragging the body.)

25. Robert Coates, 'The worst actor ever . . .'

'The worst actor ever to appear on a stage anywhere' is how Stephen Pile describes Robert 'Romeo' Coates in 'The Book of Heroic Failures':

His total incapacity to play any part whatever, combined with his insistence upon wearing diamonds from head to foot, regardless of role, and his tendency to 'improve' upon Shakespeare as he went along, made him immensely popular with astonished audiences up and down Britain.

His specialization was death scenes, which he used to preface by spreading a white silk handkerchief on the stage. These scenes were so protracted and so deliriously received that he frequently did encores, dying again.

Coates made his first appearance on the professional stage in 1807—and rumour got around that here was entertainment not to be missed. The play was 'Romeo and Juliet':

It started quietly enough, but when he entered the audience gave way to ecstatic cheers (which he stopped to acknowledge). Visually, Coates was always surprising and, on this occasion, he chose to dress his Romeo in a spangled sky-blue coat, bright crimson pantaloons and a white hat, excessively trimmed with feathers. Over all this was spattered a multitude of diamonds and the total effect ran quite counter to Shakespeare's description of the character as a 'quiet, virtuous and well-governed youth'.

The play continued in a hail of orange peel and whenever the audience crowed 'cock-a-doodle-do' at Coates he would break off, regardless of Juliet on the balcony, and crow back at them.

At one point the audience joined in a delighted chant of 'Off! Off! Off!' at which Coates, the gifted amateur, crossed his arms and stared at them with scorn and withering contempt.

That night the play got as far as the last act, but ended in riot when Coates suddenly re-entered with a crowbar, which was quite unnecessary and not mentioned in Shakespeare's text, to prize open the Capulets' tomb.

Of course, an actor of this calibre was soon in demand by London theatres and he arrived at the Haymarket Theatre on 9 December 1811. Here, playing Lothario in the first night of 'The Fair Penitent', Coates took longer to die on stage than anyone before or since. The audience sat politely, as his writhing figure was gripped by spasm after spasm, happy in the knowledge that it was only Act IV and that Coates would soon be dead, leaving a clear act to run without him. He died and the curtain fell.

After the interval, the gifted amateur came out before the curtain, dressed in regimental uniform, and announced that there would not be a fifth act that night. He would instead be reciting his favourite monologue.

After delighting London audiences for a further few years he retired from the stage due to bankruptcy.

65

Deities

Clive Swift wrote in 'The Job of Acting':

There are two Gods in the profession—Dionysus (the Greek God who started it all) and Punctuality. These days you are fortunate to work—to work and be late is suicidal.

The Elizabethans went in for some spectacular stage effects: Heywood's 'Brazen Age' ends with Hercules sitting on top of his funeral pyre, and saying he will die by no hand but his own. However, he is soon proved wrong. The stage direction says:

JUPITER ABOVE STRIKES HIM WITH A THUNDER-BOLT, HIS BODY SINKS, AND FROM THE HEAVENS DESCENDS A HAND IN A CLOUD, THAT FROM THE PLACE WHERE HERCULES WAS BURNT, BRINGS UP A STAR, AND FIXETH IT IN THE FIRMAMENT.

How was it done? Irwin Smith explained in his book, 'Shakespeare's Globe Playhouse':

Translating the direction into terms of the physical stage, it would appear that the pyre was built upon the large trap in the middle of the platform; that to an accompaniment of Jovian thunder, the trap dropped, and Hercules with it; that from the forward trap in the heavens a hand was let down by a cord or wire, and disappeared after Hercules; and that someone in the hell affixed a star to the hand, and sent it back to heaven again.

26. The Temple of Hymen from 'Atalanta, or The Three Golden Apples'

Disasters

27. The Globe Theatre, 1579

The thatched Globe Theatre caught fire and burned to the ground during a performance of Shakespeare's 'King Henry VIII' in 1613. Sir Henry Wotton described the scene:

Now, King Henry making a masque at the Cardinal Wolsey's house, and certain chambers being shot off at his entry, some of the paper, or other stuff, wherewith one of them was stopped, did light on the thatch, where, being thought at first but an idle smoke, and their eyes more attentive to the show, it kindled inwardly, and ran round like a train, consuming within less than an hour the whole house to the very grounds. This was the fatal period of that virtuous fabric, wherein yet nothing did perish but wood and straw, and a few forsaken cloaks; only one man had his breeches set on fire, that would perhaps have broiled him, if he had not by the benefit of a provident wit put it out with bottle ale.

In the early days of theatre in Australia in the first part of the nineteenth century Barnet Levy built a theatre in Sydney, but it finally made him bankrupt. Perhaps it had something to do with the quality of the productions; a reviewer described one of them thus:

It was rather run through than acted. The burning of the mill failed; pistols were fired off...and the curtain fell to hide the confusion of those behind it.

Short-sightedness was—literally—the downfall of Robert Browning at the Connaught Theatre, Worthing. In 1972, Gordon Clyde was playing the part of the poet in 'Robert and Elizabeth' there; he said the stage had no footlights, but simply ended in a three-foot drop straight into the auditorium:

Towards the end of the show Robert was pacing furiously up and down the station platform, waiting to elope with his beloved Elizabeth. He paced with such enthusiasm that he walked right off the front of the stage and landed in the laps of two very startled old ladies in the front row. He clambered back on to the stage, bruised and shaken, to roars of applause.

As it happened, the next part of the action was the entry of Elizabeth, greeted by the line from Robert: 'Thank Heaven! I was afraid there'd been an accident....'

In 1888 in Boston, the American actor George R. Parkes was becoming so depressed about his acting career that he put on a suit of stage armour and drowned himself in the river.

Drag

Danny la Rue had this to say:

I never really think of myself as a female impersonator: I'd rather look at myself as an actor that happens to portray many types of women—glamorous and funny women. You see, I like women very much. I never knock them at all, I make fun of them because, you see, women have a marvellous sense of humour, and they like fun against themselves.... My satire is a warm sort of satire; my women are all glamorous apparitions, and the fun comes from within, the giggle comes from within, and I'm happy to say that nobody takes offence at my characterizations.

Tyrone Guthrie on the past—and likely future—of men in women's roles and vice versa:

All the greatest actresses felt impelled—usually far too late in life—to have a go at 'Hamlet' or 'L'Aiglon' or things like that. Hitherto, in this country anyway, this has always been the nudge and scream department, hasn't it?—the principal boy, and then the dame whose drawers come down, and things like that. Now, I think, we're beginning to think this isn't just funny—that it's also serious and can in fact be rather poetic and interesting; and to see a man playing a woman isn't necessarily a vulgar or a laughable experience—it can be very sensitive and touching. And I think in a year or two, the same thing will be true the other way round: that the women will be able to do some of the men's parts. And the opposite sex can make a comment: a man playing a woman, if he isn't just being a scream, if he wants to, he can give a very interesting suggestion—perhaps a little satirical but not necessarily awfully funny—of femininity. And I think equally, a good actress if she's playing a man, she won't slap her leg and talk in a big voice and thrash about—it will be a subtle woman's comment on the male.

Pantomime principal boy, Dorothy Ward, commenting on the tradition:

A girl dressed up as a boy, making love to another girl, has always been accepted. You see, the audience looked upon the principal boy in pantomime not just as another man-in-the-street but as a beautiful fairy prince. They weren't human beings at all, they were fairy-tale characters, and of course the prince, male or female, had to be daring and rather athletic. I used to enjoy climbing that beanstalk, and my terrific fight with the giant on the table. That could be pretty strenuous once or twice a day, you know!

Social historian James Laver traced the story of women's roles in drama in a radio interview:

I suppose it would be true to say that men taking female parts is a practice as old as drama itself. In the primitive dances, from what we know about them, in general all the acting parts are confined to men, and women are mere spectators, and sometimes

Vesta Tilley as Algy

stage in Roman times, and this was regarded as a grave lapse from ancient virtue. And I think it's fair to say that part of the objection that the early Christian church had to all theatrical performances was due to their feeling that women should not excite the erotic appetites of the audience.

During the Dark Ages and the early medieval period there were no set theatrical productions at all but parties of jongleurs and entertainers went from great hall to great hall; and we know from medieval manuscripts that some of these were women. But the idea of women dressing as men or vice versa doesn't seem to have taken place in those circumstances.

With the rise of the Italian comedy, women were allowed on the stage, the most spectacular being the famous Isabella Andreini of the Jalosi troupe; but of course Harlequin was frequently called upon to disguise himself as a woman in order to deceive the inevitable cuckolded husband. Then even in the midst of the period of Italian comedy we get the strange phenomenon of the Shakespearean stage, where all the parts were played by men or boys—and there must have been a certain piquancy in seeing a boy playing a girl pretending to play a boy, like Rosalind.

It took a long time for actual women to appear on the English stage: it wasn't indeed until the Restoration, in the luxurious court of Charles II. And of course the Puritans, like the early Christians, objected to it strongly: they thought it opened up a new vista of debauchery—as of course it did—in the history of the theatre. The erotic appeal began which is exploited to this day in its final term of absurdity, in the strip-tease club.

One of the most celebrated male impersonators was Vesta Tilley, who always appeared in immaculate evening dress. James Laver said:

It is recorded that Vesta Tilley's clothes were so perfectly made and she was herself such a slim figure, that the young bloods of the day copied her outfits. And she did have her clothes made carefully by the best tailors in London. It was no travesty of male dress, it was the best that could possibly be got.

not even that. And we do know that all of the female parts in the Greek drama were actually played by men; as they were in voluminous, very ample, padded robes and on stilts and with masks, of course it was of no consequence at all.

Women were first introduced at all on the

Drying

An actor in the Frank Benson company was notorious for 'drying', but whenever he forgot his lines he had a favourite method of getting himself off-stage so that he could look them up. He did it by suddenly reciting his own 'Shakespearean' speech; he produced a purse and said:

Take thou this purse. I'll hie me to the
    market-place,
And there, in an hour hence, I'll meet with
    thee.
Until that time, farewell!

Then he would go off, leaving the other actors to flounder. But his trick became so well known that whenever he reached for his purse, the rest of the actors in the scene could be observed hastily backing away from him. . . .

John Groves was at one time stage manager for a small theatre in the Boltons in London. Alistair Wilson wrote:

John Groves was no actor, he was a superb stage manager but hated playing parts. He was forced in to being a messenger in a seventeenth-century Spanish play. Denholm Elliott was the Duke, and all Johnny had to do was to enter, in a long cloak, sweep off his hat, bow low, present a parchment and say, disguising his broad Edinburgh accent into a Spanish one, 'Ah, señor, a message from-ma my master, the Count.' Elliott would take the letter and say, 'Good. Put your horse in the stable and go to the kitchen for a meal. I shall give you my reply presently.' Whereupon Johnny bowed and went out.

No trouble during the week's run, until at one performance, Johnny entered, bowed low, said his line and Denholm Elliott froze. Dried stone dead. Johnny stared at his blank face, panicked, pushed the letter into his hand, stepped back, bowed, felt he had to say something to get off, and cried out: 'Aye, weel, ta-ta!'

29. 'How an actor sees his audience and the prompter', from a painting by A. Kamak

First and Last Lines

There is something delightful about the simple opening to Shaw's 'Back to Methuselah':

Act I: The Garden of Eden. Afternoon.

And the end of that first part has its own charm, too:

EVE (slowly taking up her distaff). If you were not a fool you would find something better for both of us to live by than this spinning and digging.
ADAM. Go on with your work, I tell you; or you shall go without bread.
EVE. Man need not always live by bread alone. There is something else. We do not yet know what it is; but some day we shall find out; and then we will live on that alone; and there shall be no more digging nor spinning, nor fighting nor killing.
(She spins resignedly; he digs impatiently.)

It might be thought difficult to make a theme like the fall of Lucifer, and the creation and fall of Man, seem absurd and banal. But Dryden succeeded in his play 'The State of Innocence, and Fall of Man'. The opening stage directions are certainly spectacular:

The first Scene represents a Chaos, or a confus'd Mass of Matter; the Stage is almost wholly dark: A Symphony of warlike Musick is heard for some time; then from the Heavens, (which are opened) fall the rebellious Angels, wheeling in Air, and seeming transfixed with Thunderbolts: The Bottom of the Stage being opened, receives the Angels, who fall out of sight.

The scene then changes to Hell, where it is left to Lucifer to speak the first words of the play:

Is this the seat our Conqueror has given?
And this the Climate we must change for
    Heaven?

At least they are not quite as flat as the first words of the newly-created Adam. For him, Dryden manages to drag in Descartes' philosophical dictum, 'I think, therefore I am'. So Adam wakes into life in the Garden of Eden, saying:

What am I? or from whence? For that I am
I know, because I think.

The Prologue to William Congreve's 'The Double Dealer', spoken by Mrs Bracegirdle:

Moors have this way, as story tells, to know
Whether their brats are truly got or no:
Into the sea the new-born babe is thrown,
There, as instinct directs, to swim or drown;
A barbarous device to try if spouse
Has kept religiously her nuptial vows.

Such are the trials poets make of plays,
Only they trust to more inconstant seas.
So does our author this his child commit
To the tempestuous mercy of the pit,
To know if it be truly born of wit.

Critics, avaunt! For you are fish of prey,
And feed, like sharks, upon an infant play.
Be every monster of the deep away,
Let's have a fair trial and a clear sea.

Nell Gwynn played St Catharine in Dryden's 'Tyrannic Love'. At the end of the play she rose from her dead pose on stage and spoke the epilogue:

Hold, are you mad? You damn'd
      confounded dog!
I am to rise and speak the epilogue...

O poet, damned dull poet, who could prove
So senseless to make Nelly die for love!...

But farewell, gentlemen, make haste to me,
I'm sure e'er long to have your company.

As for my epitaph when I am gone,
I'll trust no poet, but will write my own.
Here Nelly lies, who, though she lived a
      slattern,
Yet died a princess, acting in St Catharin.

One of the most piously optimistic final couplets is to be found at the end of the early seventeenth-century 'Tragedy of Nero', when, with the villains all slain, the First Roman says:

Thus great bad men above them find a rod:
People, depart and say there is a God.

First Nights

Peter Ustinov said:

I think that first nights should come near the end of a play's run—as indeed, they often do. . . .

The very first theatrical production in Australia was performed by convicts on 4 June 1789. A group of them at Botany Bay asked Governor Phillip if they could produce a play in honour of the King's birthday, and he agreed. The play was Farquhar's 'The Recruiting Officer' and Captain Watkin Tench, who was there, gave this account of it in his book, 'A Complete Account of the Settlement at Port Jackson':

His Excellency attended, and the officers of the garrison. That every opportunity of escape from the dreariness and dejection of our situation should be eagerly embraced, will not be wondered at. The exhilarating effect of a splendid theatre is well known: and I am not ashamed to confess that the proper distribution of three or four yards of stained paper, and a dozen farthing candles stuck around the mud walls of a convict-hut, failed not to diffuse general complacency on the countenances of sixty persons, of various descriptions, who were assembled to applaud the representation.

Some of the actors acquitted themselves with great spirit, and received the praises of the audience: a prologue and an epilogue, written by one of the performers, were also spoken on the occasion; which, although not worth inserting here, contained some tolerable allusions to the situation of the parties, and the novelty of a stage-representation in New South Wales.

The prologue Captain Tench mentioned was said to start thus:

From distant climes, o'er wide spread seas
    we come,
(Though not with much éclat, or beat of
    drum)
True patriots all, for be it understood,
We left our country for our country's
    good. . . .

In 'Theatre Guyed', A. E. Wilson had this to say:

On the whole much the same ritual is

73

performed at every first night. Whether the play is good or bad, whether the audience has been bored or enchanted, there is always the same scene at the end and the same extraordinary inability of the author to make up his mind whether to scuttle out of the theatre and to flee the country beyond the reach of an extradition order or whether to brazen the thing out and chance the consequences.

The usual formula is for the producer or the leading actor to announce 'I am sorry to say that the author is not in the house'—a demonstrable lie since a pallid and furtive-looking person has all the evening been a most conspicuous figure in one of the stalls or boxes and has frequently been detected nervously dodging between the back row of the circle and the bar of the stalls.

If, however, he is forced or cajoled on to the stage, the author invariably presents the same woebegone and scared appearance. He has probably been witnessing something which he has never contemplated or designed in his play and hearing things spoken in the dialogue entirely new to him. At the best his play has been only faintly recognizable as the creation of his imagination.

He is aghast or amazed at what he is supposed to have wrought. He looks as if he had been doped or stunned. The crumpled shirt-front, the dishevelled hair, the concertina-ed trousers, the tie askew—all speak as to the violence of his emotions and the stress of the ordeal.

He stammers out a few incoherent remarks, swallows hard, goes red, gives it up, flaps his arms about like a peculiarly helpless penguin; backs awkwardly into the cast assembled behind him, treads on the leading lady's toes, or, after nearly falling into the orchestra pit, is almost beheaded by the descending curtain.

Nobody could be such a poor fish as the author looks and feels on a first night.

However, the aplomb of the leading lady or the leading actor who chooses to make a curtain speech in spite of no encouragement whatever from the audience is equally remarkable.

The actor will thank the audience for its 'magnificent reception' even though the atmosphere in front of the footlights has been absolutely frigid all the evening, while the actress will enthusiastically and gushingly declare that the behaviour of the audience has been wonderful, that the play has been wonderful, that the producer has been wonderful, that the rest of the cast has been wonderful and that the whole thing (to summarize matters) has all been too wonderful.

After that comes the hunt for coats and hats under the seats, the exasperating ordeal of being trodden upon by impatient neighbours, the struggle to get to the cloak-room and the scramble to get out of the theatre.

The American writer and director Moss Hart was launched on Broadway with 'Once in a Lifetime', which he wrote with George S. Kaufman. The backstage scene just before the first night was hardly encouraging for the young author, as he wrote in 'Act One':

Even false cheerfulness would have withered quickly in those dressing-rooms. The atmosphere in each varied from calm to controlled hysteria, depending upon the opening-night temperature of its occupant. Jean Dixon, vacant-eyed and pale in spite of her make-up, stared at me for a long moment as if trying to focus on who I was, nodded abstractedly, and then resumed a panther-like stalk up and down her dressing-room. Next door, Grant Mills sat looking at himself in the mirror and grinning idiotically. . . . Spring Byington looked so near to being embalmed as she sat solemn and still amidst the mounds of flowers in her dressing room, that I decided to go downstairs and sit on the stage for a while before continuing my rounds. I seemed to be having a little difficulty breathing myself.

Willis Hall, in a radio interview, described Broadway first nights, soon after 'Philomena' opened on Sunday, 10 February 1980:

It's terrifying—it's something that nobody should ever be put through. It's totally different to a London first night. It gets more and more frightening: the one on Sunday night was stranger than any one I'd ever been to before in that in a London first night, you always get these people, crowds of people outside the theatre—autograph-hunters—but we found on the first night on Sunday night they really are vultures there—they crowd upon you—not me but Larry Olivier and Joan—and they get inside the theatre. And during the interval there were dozens of them, prowling up and down the aisles with cameras and autograph books. They manage to shuffle them out while the play is on, but in the interval they look at you and say, 'Are you anybody?' And you have to say that you're not anybody, and they say 'There's Diana Ross!' or 'There's Dustin Hoffman! Let's get away from this schmuck Limey....'

The 'Daily Mail' ran this report on 5 February 1980:

Firemen were besieged with calls reporting an explosion in London last night. But it turned out to be a rocket fired at the National Theatre to mark the opening of Eugene O'Neill's play, 'The Iceman Cometh'. A theatre official said: 'We do this every opening night. It's a tradition.'

At a backstage party after a first night an actor who had been in the audience said to a friend among the throng: 'I thought Jane was unexpectedly good!'
Then he noticed that the lady's husband was standing nearby and added hastily: '...considering the appalling lines she had to say....'
And then he remembered that the husband had written the play!

31. Moss Hart and Alexander Woollcott at the Boston opening of 'The Man Who Came to Dinner'

Fluffing

'Fluffing' and 'making a fluff' have nothing to do with fluff as in 'a little bit of'.... A fluff is a mistake, usually mispronouncing or stumbling over a word. So, taking out the fluffs means editing out the mistakes from a recorded programme. A producer editing an interview might alternatively say that it will be necessary to de-um the recording—that is, to edit out the hesitations: the 'ums'...and also the 'ers', 'ahs' and 'hurrumphs', not to mention the 'you knows'.

'I know for a fact that her uncle was just a sugar-baker in Bristol' is one of Mrs Candour's lines in 'The School for Scandal'. In one touring performance the actress had an attack of nerves and said: 'I know for a fact that her uncle was just a sugar basin in Buxton....'

The play seems to have been a tricky one for that particular company. In its opening scene, planting gossip, Lady Sneerwell is supposed to say: 'The paragraphs, you say, are all inserted, Mr Snake?' and to get the reply, 'Yes, your ladyship.'
In one performance both actors got flustered, and the exchange went like this: 'The snakes, you say, are all inserted, Mr Paragraph?' 'Yes, your majesty....'

32. A scene from 'The School for Scandal'

Flying Tonight

A team of acrobats was featured in a nineteenth-century Australian play, staged in Melbourne, called 'The Span of Life'. In it the heroine, clutching her baby, was fleeing from the villain when she found herself at the edge of a wide chasm. Three of the helpful acrobats climbed up and stood on each other's shoulders, then fell forward, spanning the gulf and allowing the heroine to run across the human bridge, to ecstatic applause. . . .

Sir Herbert Beerbohm Tree regarded stage flying machinery as simplicity itself and expected his daughter Viola to feel the same way. She remembered:

As his prospective Ariel. . .I had to try the wires. . .and was timidly discussing with the professional on which foot to take off. The wire was, I remember, uncomfortably hooked into my strait waistcoat when he walked on to the stage. 'I always know about these things, dear; don't argue: fly!' and he gave the order to the mechanic up above to let go. Without a murmur I flew, my feet dangling high above his head, and tingling like telegraph wires at the sudden vibrations of his voice. 'Very good, dear; now sing!'

In 'The Show Is On', Beatrice Lillie went skywards above the audience, singing a 'moon' song. She described the experience in 'Every Other Inch A Lady':

To deliver this item required the services of a steel crane that weighed a ton and a half; a sturdy prop moon that swung out over the audience as far as the fourth row of the orchestra; six property men clutching ropes to control the swinging; me, sitting on the moon, wearing a rather insecure safety belt (which the management considered advisable, though I disagreed) and an air of supreme nonchalance.

The nonchalance had seen me through one traumatic rehearsal, when a stage hand fumbled one of the ropes, and the moon and I collided with one of the upper boxes. The effect was so hilarious that, by my special request, we kept this bit of improvisation in future swingings.

During one performance, a stately dowager I knew socially sat at the front of the box as I chirruped my way toward the ceiling. When I approached, she reached out and shook hands, almost pulling me off my perch.

'Bea, darling, what are you doing for

luncheon on Thursday?'

Hurriedly, I asked her to phone me and carried on with the number.

I was costumed like an Edwardian belle in a saucy pink silk dress with a froufrou skirt and lace-up boots. From the comparative safety of my moon, I tossed three pink garters a night down on the audience, aiming, if I could, for bald men with the pinkest pates. On opening night, one grasping customer couldn't wait until I got my first garter off. He stretched up and tried to tug it from my ankle, and almost got more than he bargained for. Don't misunderstand, please; I very nearly fell on his face and into the orchestra pit.

Those blooming garters became a sort of door prize flourished all over town. I flung them at Noel and Gertie when they paid us a visit, at Bob Hope and Irving Berlin, to whom I owed something for 'When I Lost You' and countless auditions long ago. I couldn't go into a restaurant or a nightclub without someone standing up and waving a pink garter at me. Since there were more of them on display than I could have handed out in ten years, I concluded that bootleggers were busy behind the scenes.

33. A scene from an 1871 pantomime

Lovely Frocks

Writing on the first productions of the Moscow Art Theatre, Theodore Komisarjevsky said:

On the opening night...the costumes of the Tzar, of the boyards, and of the Moscow people were exact replicas of historical documents and made as far as possible of the genuine old materials. The long bejewelled brocade coats of the boyards had fur collars and were lined throughout with fur, which made them so heavy that it seemed almost impossible for the actors to breathe, let alone move in them....

In the production of 'Julius Caesar' the stage was so filled with brass armour, helmets, weapons, ample togas, and various minute details of costume and properties, that Shakespeare's play was completely drowned.

Oscar Wilde, in his essay 'The Truth of Masks':

Many young ladies on our own stage insist to the present day on wearing stiff starched petticoats under Greek dresses, to the entire ruin of all delicacy of line and fold; but these wicked things should not be allowed. And there should be far more dress rehearsals than there are now. Actors such as Mr Forbes-Robertson, Mr Conway, Mr George Alexander, and others, not to mention older artists, can move with ease and elegance in the attire of any century; but there are not a few who seem dreadfully embarrassed about their hands if they have no side pockets, and who always wear their dresses as if they were costumes. Costumes, of course, they are to the designer; but dresses they should be to those that wear them. And it is time that a stop should be put to the idea, very prevalent on the stage, that the Greeks and Romans always went about bareheaded in the open air—a mistake the Elizabethan managers did not fall into, for they gave hoods as well as gowns to their Roman senators.

More dress rehearsals would also be of value in explaining to the actors that there is a form of gesture and movement that is not merely appropriate to each style of dress, but really conditioned by it. The extravagant use of the arms in the eighteenth century, for instance, was the necessary result of the large hoop, and the solemn dignity of Burleigh owed as much to his ruff as to his reason. Besides, until an actor is at home in his dress, he is not at home in his part.

When Sybil Thorndike played Lady Macbeth in a production in Paris with the American actor, James Hackett, Edith Craig insisted that she wear her mother Ellen Terry's

34. Oscar Wilde

costumes for the part. This account was given in Elizabeth Sprigge's 'Sybil Thorndike Casson':

So I had those splendid dresses—the beetle-wing one in which Sargent painted his famous portrait of Ellen Terry, and the great cloak, and the sleep-walking blankets and everything. And Edy was quite right. Those dresses brought something of their own from greater performances, and fired me to act all-out.

I'm always very nervous on these big formal occasions, and this was the first time I had played Lady Macbeth since the Old Vic, but the instant I put on Ellen Terry's dress something happened to me—not a tremble, not a quake. In the banquet scene the splendid American star somehow lost himself—his nerve went. So often in 'Macbeth' people have accidents or dry up, but the beetle-wing dress came to his aid. I wasn't a very hefty girl then, but something pushed me on from behind, and I seized that huge man—he really was enormous—and hurled him across the stage, saying his words in his ear. 'Oh, thank you, my dear!' he said to me afterwards. 'I was lost and you saved me.' 'Don't thank me,' I said, 'it was Ellen Terry's dress that did it.'

Edy was always against cleaning costumes. She said it took the life out of them. And when a little later on I had a new dress for 'The Verge' she made me wear it for rehearsals so that it would get dirty and become part of its wearer. And my 'Medea' dress—I never had that cleaned. My dresser said, 'But it's grimy,' and I said, 'I don't care, it knows exactly what to do and it mustn't be touched'. That grime was part of me when I played Medea. It was a wonderful dress, red-purple, colours of flame, and it had a long tail to it, hung from the arms. It was magical, I only had to give it a little twist and it acted by itself.

A nineteen-year-old girl from a wealthy Edinburgh family thought it would be 'fun to do a bit of acting'—and a summer repertory company in Aberdeen gave her the chance. It was a rather ramshackle outfit, and there were rumours that the

girl's parents had paid the producer to give her the job. Anyway, she arrived with two large trunks full of clothes—and very expensive ones at that. She proceeded to hang them up all around the communal ladies' dressing-room, to the annoyance of the other actresses, who were already incensed that this newcomer was going to be given 'juvenile lead' roles.

The first time she appeared, the audience was surprised to see her go out through the French windows into the garden off-stage, then reappear a few minutes later wearing a different dress. In the second act she made an exit into the kitchen, wearing a summer frock, and came back shortly afterwards carrying a tea-tray, having effected a quick change into a long, flowing silk dress. She made these lightning costume changes twice more during the show and succeeded in parading in eight different costumes during the play, with the audience's astonished murmurs growing louder each time.

Even more astonishing was the producer's failure to tell her to alter her ways; and these baffling costume changes became a feature of every production. One night she sauntered in through the French windows, wearing an elaborate frilly blouse but no skirt. The audience and the cast gasped this time, as she stood there nonchalantly in embroidered panties.

One of the other girls on stage, thinking this extraordinary display was deliberate, crossed in front of her and hissed a savage remark as she glanced down. The girl suddenly realised she had simply forgotten the skirt in her hasty change. But she was learning to keep a cool head, if not to act. She dodged behind an armchair and remained standing there until it came to the moment for her to make her exit. Then, with great aplomb, she backed to the French windows, pulling the armchair with her. She delivered her exit line, pulled the chair right out into the garden, then dropped on to all fours and crawled off. There was a moment of stunned silence as audience and cast watched her pantie-clad behind wobbling off into the wings. It was the most spectacular exit she ever achieved.

David Garrick

David Garrick was one of the actors who helped to give the profession a measure of respectability, a fact acknowledged in T. W. Robertson's play 'Garrick' in 1864. In it, Garrick is asked: 'You give me your word, sir—as a gentleman?' And he replies proudly: 'As an Actor—precisely the same thing!'

This was how one member of the audience described Garrick's acting style in 'Hamlet', in the ghost scene:

The ghost appears almost unnoticed in an intense silence. At Horatio's 'Look, my lord, it comes' Garrick starts and turns, staggering back, his legs giving way under him; his hat falls off and his arms are stretched right out; his mouth is open....

F. E. Halliday, in 'The Cult of Shakespeare', wrote of the elaborate Jubilee celebrations organised by Garrick at Stratford in 1769. They required endurance from the public, as well as tolerance for some leaden verse:

...the town was startled out of its sleep by the roar of cannon. The Jubilee had begun. As the noise died away the most important lady visitors, and there were some very important lady visitors, found themselves serenaded by actors fantastically attired, and singing to the accompaniment of hautboys, flutes, clarinets and guitars:

Let beauty with the sun arise,
To Shakespeare tribute pay;
With heavenly smiles and speaking eyes,
Give lustre to the day.

Nor had Garrick forgotten to write an aubade for the natives:

Ye Warwickshire lads, and ye lasses,
See what at our Jubilee passes;
Come revel away, rejoice, and be glad,
For the lad of all lads was a
Warwickshire lad,
Warwickshire lad,
All be glad,
For the lad of all lads was a Warwickshire lad.

By eight o'clock the Corporation had assembled in their formalities to present Garrick with his insignia of office as Steward: a medal, carved with the bust of the bard, richly set in gold, and a wand, both made from the celebrated mulberry tree. The completion of this ceremony was announced by the ringing of bells, the firing of cannon and a public breakfast in the Town Hall, price a shilling for the holders of guinea festival tickets. Most of the guests, including those of the highest quality of both sexes, wore the Jubilee Ribbon and Medal, and while they drank their tea, coffee or chocolate, a party of drums and fifes gave much satisfaction by playing outside the Hall.

John Gielgud

At the age of sixteen, John Gielgud made a number of amateur stage appearances, including one as Orlando in a production of 'As You Like It' in a rectory garden at St Leonard's in Sussex, described in 'Early Stages':

I strode on to the lawn at the first performance, drew my sword fiercely, and declaimed, 'Forbear, and eat no more!' but unfortunately I tripped over a large log and fell flat on my face. This was only the beginning of my troubles, for in the last act, when I pointed to the path where I was expecting Rosalind, with 'Ah, here comes my Ganymede'—no Ganymede was to be seen. I said the line again, with a little less confidence this time; still no-one appeared. I looked helplessly round, to find the prompter, his hands to his mouth, whispering as loudly as he dared across the hundred yards that separated us, 'She's changed back into her girl's clothes a scene too soon!'

I had also replaced a student who was ill in a couple of performances at Rosina Filippi's school in Whitehead's Grove, near Sloane Square, in an adaptation of a novel by Rhoda Broughton, and as Mercutio in three scenes from 'Romeo and Juliet'. Miss Filippi had a broad, motherly face, grey hair and a rich, jolly laugh. She walked with an ebony cane, and wore black taffeta that rustled a great deal and a gold watch on a long chain round her neck. She conducted rehearsals with much authority and humour, but I was rather put out at the actual performance, when she sat down at a piano at the side of the stage and played twiddly bits all through my delivery of the Queen Mab speech!

In 'Ego 2', James Agate wrote:

Lunched at the Ivy with Curt Dehn, my lawyer, who asked the name of the man lunching opposite.

I said, 'John Gielgud.'

Dehn said, 'It's a rum sort of head. The profile's Roman Emperor, but the rest is still at Eton.'

'An Actor and his Time' describes how John Gielgud began preparing for his performance as Spooner in Harold Pinter's 'No Man's Land':

The part of Spooner was a complete impersonation, such as I had never had a chance to do in the theatre. It was very exciting to have a chance of doing it, and I was quick in finding a way to look and to dress. The moment I read the play I saw Spooner clearly, which was rare for me. I remember saying to Harold Pinter, 'I think Auden, don't you? Do you think sandals and socks?' and he jumped at the idea. Then I said 'Do you think we should add spectacles?' and he liked that too. About a week after we started rehearsal I came on the stage with a wig, the suit and the spectacles and everybody said 'It's exactly right, perfect!' And I said 'Yes, and now I must find a performance to go inside it!'

In 'Early Stages', John Gielgud wrote:

Of all the arts, I think acting must be the least concrete, the most solitary. One gains experience continually, both at rehearsals and in performance, from the presence of a large assembly of people, one's fellow players and the audience in front. These are essential to the development of one's performance. They are the living canvas upon which one hopes to paint the finished portrait. These audiences, with their shifting variations of quality, are the only means by which an actor may gauge his acting. With their assistance he may hope to improve a performance, keep it flexible and fresh, and develop new subtleties as the days go by. He learns to listen, to watch (without appearing to do so), to respond, to guide them in certain passages and be guided by them in others—a never-ending test of watchfulness and flexibility.

But the struggles and agonies of the actor as he winds his way through this labyrinthine process every night upon the stage are of very little interest to anyone except himself. No-one cares, or is even aware, that he works for many months to correct some physical trick, or fights against his vocal mannerisms, or experiments with pauses, emphases, timing, processes of thought. No-one knows if he is suffering in his heart while he plays an emotional scene, or if he is merely adding up his household bills, considering what he will order for dinner, or regretting what he ate for lunch. Last night's audience, which he cursed for

35. Edith Evans and John Gielgud in Chekhov's 'The Seagull'

its unresponsiveness, may have enjoyed his performance every whit as much as tonight's, with which he seems to feel the most cordial and personal sympathy.

Actors talk unceasingly among themselves of all the varying feelings which assail them during the exercise of their craft; but the experience of each one is different, and nothing really matters except the actual momentary contact between actor and audience which draws the performance through its appointed action from beginning to end. At the close of each performance the play is set aside, for all the world like a Punch and Judy show, or the toy theatre of one's childhood; and each time it is taken up again it seems, even in a long run, comparatively fresh, waiting to be fashioned anew before every different audience.

W.S.Gilbert

W. S. Gilbert's quick wit sparkled as much off-stage as it did in the opera libretti he wrote:

Asked about 'The Circus Girl'—would he call it bad musical comedy?—he replied: 'I would call it bad. I believe the manager calls it musical comedy.'

He was once taken to task for using the word 'coyful' in an opera. . . . The objector said: 'How can anyone be full of coy?'
'I don't know,' said Gilbert, 'but for that matter, how can anyone be full of bash?'

When a girl in the chorus complained to him that one of the men had put his arm round her shoulder and called her 'a pretty dear', Gilbert reassured her: 'Never mind, never mind; he couldn't have meant it.'

Saying he preferred reading hostile criticism rather than praise, he said: 'I know how good I am, but I do not know how bad I am.'

When Beerbohm Tree asked Gilbert what he thought of his 'Hamlet' he got the answer: 'My dear fellow, I never saw anything so funny in my life, and yet it was not in the least vulgar.'

The Comtesse de Brémont asked for an interview with Gilbert, and was told that she would have to pay twenty guineas for the privilege. Thereupon she wrote to him in these terms:

The Comtesse de Brémont presents her compliments to Mr W. S. Gilbert and in reply to his answer to her request for an interview for St Paul's in which he states his terms as twenty guineas for that privilege, begs to say that she anticipates the pleasure of writing his obituary for nothing.

36. W. S. Gilbert reading a play to actors at the Savoy Theatre

Alec Guinness

Kenneth Tynan described the man thus in his book 'Alec Guinness':

Alec Guinness, as Shaw once observed of Irving, has no face. You notice it—or rather, fail to notice it—as soon as he enters a room. Jeeves-fashion, he shimmers in and is amongst you: a slight man, balding and bland, with deprecating, sloped shoulders which he shrugs constantly. And above the shoulders—'A blank, my lord', impassive as an almond. From it, if occasion warrants, a caressing snicker may emerge, accompanied by a rakish tilt of the head and a twitch of a smile, resembling the crescent moon. You might easily take him for a slightly tipsy curate on the verge of being unfrocked. By staring hard, you may assure yourself that he has eyes: superficially guileless, they are in truth sly and wary, and, rather than meet your gaze, they will wander contemplatively from side to side, avoiding contact like a magnet pushed close to another of like pole.

As you watch them, noting how pale and glazed they are, you find you have forgotten the face; and vice versa. The whole presence of the man is guarded and evasive. Slippery sums him up; when you think you have him, eel-like, he eludes your grasp. Should you try to pluck out the heart of his mystery, he grows cautious; he will communicate intimacy, but always from a considerable distance, as if through a reversed telescope.

The following, by Alec Guinness, was published in 'The Spectator':

Rostrums, apart from cluttering the stage, tend to produce a one-foot-up, one-foot-down sort of acting which I find peculiarly dispiriting. I have very few conversations on the stairs in my own house, and see no good reason for making God's gift to an actor—a flat square stage—into something like the entrance to the Athenaeum.

Hamlet

Anthony Burgess discovered a film version of 'Hamlet' in Hindi, which included a dance of grave-diggers and ten songs for Ophelia. It also had English sub-titles, one of which was: 'Shall I live or do myself in? I do not know. . . .'

Jeremy Collier in the seventeenth century, thought Ophelia's mad scene was lacking in taste—certainly when compared with the behaviour of Euripides' Phaedra:

Phaedra when possessed with an infamous passion, takes all imaginable pains to conceal it. She is as regular and reserved in her language as the most virtuous Matron. . . . She keeps her modesty even after she has lost her wits.

Had Shakespeare secured this point for his young Virgin Ophelia, the play had been better contrived. Since he was resolved to drown the lady like a kitten, he should have set her swimming a little sooner. To keep her alive only to sully her reputation, and discover the rankness of her breath, was very cruel.

The ghost in 'Hamlet' can rarely have had such an effect as it did on Mr Partridge when Tom Jones took him to the playhouse in Henry Fielding's novel:

As soon as the play, which was 'Hamlet, Prince of Denmark', began, Partridge was all attention, nor did he break silence till the entrance of the ghost; upon which he asked Jones, 'What man that was in the strange dress; something,' said he, 'like what I have seen in a picture. Sure it is not armour, is it?' Jones answered, 'That is the ghost.' To which Partridge replied with a smile, 'Persuade me to that, sir, if you can. Though I can't say I ever actually saw a ghost in my life, yet I am certain I should know one, if I saw him, better than that comes to. No, no, sir, ghosts don't appear in such dresses as that, neither.' In this mistake, which caused much laughter in the neighbourhood of Partridge, he was suffered to continue, till the scene between the ghost and Hamlet, when Partridge gave that credit to Mr Garrick, which he had denied to Jones, and fell into so violent a trembling, that his knees knocked against each other. Jones asked him what was the matter, and whether he was afraid of the warrior upon the stage? 'O la! sir,' said he, 'I perceive now it is what you told me. I am not afraid of anything; for I know it is but a play. And if it was really a ghost, it could do one no harm at such a distance, and in so much company; and yet if I was frightened, I am not the only person.'—'Why, who,' cries Jones, 'dost thou take to be such a coward here besides thyself?'—'Nay, you may call me coward if you will; but if that little man there upon the stage is not frightened, I never saw any man frightened in my life.'

And during the whole speech of the ghost, he sat with his eyes fixed partly on the ghost and partly on Hamlet, and with his mouth open; the same passions which succeeded each other in Hamlet, succeeding likewise in him.

During the second act, Partridge made very few remarks. He greatly admired the fineness of the dresses; nor could he help observing upon the king's countenance. 'Well,' said he, 'how people may be deceived by faces! Nulla fides fronti is, I find, a true saying. Who would think, by looking in the king's face, that he had ever committed a murder?' He then inquired after the ghost; but Jones, who intended he should be surprised, gave him no other satisfaction, than 'that he might possibly see him again soon, and in a flash of fire.'

Partridge sat in fearful expectation of this; and now, when the ghost made his next appearance, Partridge cried out, 'There, sir, now; what say you now? is he frightened now or no? As much frightened as you think me, and, to be sure, nobody can help some fears. I would not be in so bad a condition as what's his name, squire Hamlet, is there, for all the world. Bless me! what's become of the spirit? As I am a living soul, I thought I saw him sink into the earth.'—'Indeed, you saw right,' answered Jones. 'Well, well,' cries Partridge, 'I know it is only a play: and besides, if there was anything in all this, Madam Miller would not laugh so; for as to you, sir, you would not be afraid, I believe, if the devil was here in person.—There, there—Ay, no wonder you are in such a passion, shake the vile wicked wretch to pieces. If she was my own mother, I would serve her so. To be sure, all duty to a mother is forfeited by such wicked doings.—Ay, go about your business, I hate the sight of you.'

'Hamlet without the Prince' was once literally witnessed by the second night audience at Richmond in 1787, according to 'The Book of Heroic Failures' by Stephen Pile:

'Hamlet' was performed with no-one playing its title role. It was to have been played at the Richmond Theatre by an inexperienced actor called Cubit who had previously been given only small walk-on parts. His debut as the Prince of Denmark had not been much relished by the first night audience. This so undermined Cubit's confidence that he was taken unwell on the second night just before curtain-up. With Hamlet ailing in his dressing-room, the manager was obliged to request that the audience 'suffer a production' which omitted him entirely.

According to Sir Walter Scott the play was better received than on its first night, and many of the audience felt that it was an improvement on the complete play.

In 'The Critic as Artist', Oscar Wilde decreed:

When a great actor plays Shakespeare...his own individuality becomes a vital part of the interpretation. People sometimes say that actors give us their own Hamlets, and not Shakespeare's.... In point of fact, there is no such thing as Shakespeare's Hamlet. If Hamlet has something of the definiteness of a work of art, he has also all the obscurity that belongs to life. There are as many Hamlets as there are melancholies.

When John Barrymore brought his 'Hamlet' to London he directed the production himself. This account is given in 'Confessions of an Actor':

I was explaining one day to the girls who carry on the body of Ophelia in the burial scene that, owing to the extraordinary and suggestive lighting of Robert E. Jones, they would not be recognized as having appeared in earlier scenes. I cautioned them that they should remember that in this scene they were virgins. One of them said to me: 'My dear Mr Barrymore, we are not character actresses, we are extra ladies....'

An actor-manager of the old school was reminiscing about past glories:

'When we were on tour with "Hamlet",' he said sonorously, 'I played the Moody One, my wife played Gertrude, the lady I was sleeping with at the time played Ophelia, and old Robbie Casterbridge played Polonius—and you can't get him for less than three quid a week!'

When he was touring with his company in the small towns of Ireland, Anew McMaster sometimes hadn't had time for a full technical rehearsal before the show. To the mystification of the audience, he would make comments to the electrician during his performance, and even make adjustments to the lights with the point of his sword. The comments would be in the same tone as the speech in the play, so that Hamlet would be saying:

Oh, what a rogue and peasant slave am I—
Up a bit on the blue, Paddy—
Is it not monstrous that this player here,
But in a fiction, more red Paddy, in a
　　　dream of passion,
That's it Paddy....

When James Dale had to deputise at short notice for Basil Rathbone as Laertes in Sir Frank Benson's production of 'Hamlet', he had no time to rehearse the duel scene. He recalls in 'Pulling Faces for a Living':

When we came to the fencing at the end of the play I had no idea what he might do. I parried like mad, on the defensive, cautious, cagey. He seized my foil, leaned close to me and hissed through his clenched teeth 'I've killed you eight times.' I duly fell dead, with apologies.

In the same production, the call-girl used to summon Sir Frank on-stage for the grave-digger scene by alerting him with a knock on the dressing-room door, and the words: 'Mr Nicholson's throwing up skulls, sir. . . .'

One of the classic tales about Lilian Baylis is that her secretary once looked into her office and found her on her knees, praying: 'Dear God, send me a good Hamlet—but make him cheap.'

Norah's comment on 'Hamlet' in John Osborne and Anthony Creighton's 'Epitaph for George Dillon':

Yes, I saw that a long time ago. That's a very old one, isn't it. Very good though. He dies in the end, doesn't he?

Rex Harrison

In his autobiography, 'Rex', Harrison wrote:

In Maeterlinck's 'The Blue Bird', I played the cat. Apart from my entrance, which I made as big as I could, naturally, with the immortal line, 'Mee-ow-you', I don't think I had quite as big a success. My mother had muffled me in a sort of velvet suit with a long tail and a hood with ears. The costume got in my way, and I had not yet reached the stage where I could have used the tail to advantage, by tripping over it. Still I felt rather pleased with myself, and was delighted that Cynthia Miles, as well as my family, had witnessed my triumph.

There was a lot of talk about what I was going to do with my life when I left school. Sylvia's friend David Fyfe was of the opinion that I should become a solicitor. I overheard this, and the idea filled me with icy horror, as indeed did David Fyfe for suggesting it. My mind was made up: I was going to be an actor.

I took my father and mother to one side and confided this to them. I don't think they were unduly surprised. For years I had been making them sit in chairs in the drawing room while I drew the curtains in the bow window and took curtain calls. Apparently I didn't think it necessary to give them any sort of performance, only to appear. Their patience must have been exceptional. In some measure, of course, they had themselves to blame, for taking me a lot to theatres in Liverpool.

One of Rex Harrison's most famous roles was that of Professor Higgins in 'My Fair Lady'. But at first, he had been uncertain whether he should agree to do it:

At that time there had been only one musical made from a Shaw play, and that had annoyed Shaw tremendously; it was called 'The Chocolate Soldier' and had been taken, without permission, from 'Arms and the Man'. Now Alan and Fritz and Herman Levin were all anxious for me to play Professor Henry Higgins, but I was doubtful about it, especially because I had never sung. And yet it was a marvellous part, and I knew it quite well, having seen it played a couple of times, by Raymond Massey and by John Clements. It occurred to me early on that if I could get a guarantee that the key scenes in 'Pygmalion' would be included in the musical, I would have some security, but even so it was quite a step to take, and I could not make up my mind. Of the people in London whose advice I sought, several said it would be a terrible thing for me to do, and Sir Malcolm Sargent called the musical a disgraceful notion.

In my usual way, I vacillated, while continuing to see Levin and Loewe and Lerner. We went for long walks in the park together, and I found that Alan Lerner had a very good mind and was certainly a great devotee of Shaw. I knew also that Fritz Loewe was a brilliant composer. From time to time, too, we gathered round the piano and sang passages from Gilbert and Sullivan together. Loewe and Lerner wanted to find out what was my vocal range: they told me later it was one and a half notes.

Henrik Ibsen

Like many other dramatists, Ibsen felt he had established a personal relationship with the characters he created. In September 1884 he wrote to his publisher:

I am sending at the same time as this letter the manuscript of my new play 'The Wild Duck', which has occupied me every day for the last four months, and which I part with now with some sadness. The characters in this play, despite their many faults, have become dear to me during this long daily association; but then I hope that they will also find friends well-disposed towards them in the great reading public, and not least among the acting fraternity; for they all present without exception rewarding roles. . . .

And he went on:

The critics will, I hope, find the points; in any case they will find something to argue about, something to interpret.

He was right: there were some widely contrasting reactions to 'The Wild Duck' when it was given its London premiere in 1894. William Archer wrote in 'Theatrical World':

Hardly ever before, as it seemed to me, had I seen so much of the very quintessence of life, concentrated in the brief traffic of the stage.

But Clement Scott in the 'Daily Telegraph' took a very different view:

The poor 'Wild Duck' was, as epicures would say, a trifle fishy. . . . There is no need to enter into the details of so commonplace and suburban a story. In essence it is trivial.

Peggy Ashcroft played 'Hedda Gabler' at the New Theatre in Oslo in 1955 at the invitation of King Haakon. Eric Johns wrote in 'Dames of the Theatre':

After the performance there was a knock on Peggy Ashcroft's dressing-room door.

'Who's there?' she called.

'Mr Ibsen,' came the reply.

There followed a split-second silence which had a supernatural quality about it. Then she realized Ibsen's grandson had called upon her. He congratulated her especially upon the comedy which she had managed to put across. He said the humour would have pleased his grandfather because he always wanted audiences to be amused by his characters, who were essentially ordinary people. Earlier actresses who had played Hedda had over-dramatized her and

actors generally failed to appreciate the down-to-earth quality of Ibsen's characters.

Liv Ullmann had a great success on Broadway in 1975 when she played the part of Nora in 'A Doll's House', always hailed as one of the first great feminist roles. Liv Ullmann described her own view and portrayal of the character in her book 'Changing':

When she finally sees, she also understands that the anger she feels over everything that is false between them is directed just as much against herself as against him. Her responsibility was as great as his. She hopes that the change will also take place in him—not for her sake, but for his own.

Not because he is threatened by a new Nora, who shows a strength he doesn't comprehend, and which frightens him, but because he has discovered a new human being whose motives he may learn to understand.

I believe that Nora's most beautiful declaration and act of love is leaving her husband.

She says goodbye to everything that is familiar and secure. She does not walk through the door to find somebody else to live with and for; she is leaving the house more insecure than she ever realized she could be. But she hopes to find out who she is and why she is.

In this there is a great freedom: the knowledge that I have to part with my present life. I don't know for what. For myself. To be something more than I am now.

About ten times Nora exclaims: 'Oh, I am so happy!' I choose to have her say it without joy—and the last time with sorrow, anxiety and longing. A critic states that I am trying to help Ibsen, so that the farewell in the final act will not come as such a shock. But I am sure Ibsen was aware of what he was doing. Do we need to go around repeating constantly that we are so happy if we really are?

Nora is strong, even in the first act: think of the joy with which she tells her friend about the long nights when she locks herself in and works.

Nora is lonely. When the doorbell rings she says to Kristina: 'It's no-one for me.'

In the first acts Nora is not just the songbird and the squirrel: neither is she pure wisdom and feminine strength in the last.

To me, Helmer's and Nora's last scene is not a bravura number for Nora. That would be too easy. This is not how we leave someone we have loved, and presumably still love. It is not with fanfare and the sound of drums that we walk away from the familiar and go out into a new and strange world. With so little knowledge.

It is a little girl who slams the doors behind her. A little girl in the process of growing up.

Eugene Ionesco

For me, the theatre is the projection on a stage of the interior world: it is from my dreams, from my hidden anxieties, from my obscure longings, from my internal contradictions that I draw the substance of my plays. As I am not alone in the world, and as each one of us is, deep down, everyone else, my dreams, my longings, my anxieties, and my obsessions do not belong to me alone; they are part of an ancestral heritage, an age-old depository, which constitutes the domain of all humanity. And it is that which makes all men one, regardless of outside differences, and it is that which constitutes our universal languages, our profound one-ness.

Ionesco's play 'Amédée' was performed at the French Institute in London in 1958, where the author himself introduced it. He said he would not attempt to 'explain' the play because:

A play cannot be explained or demonstrated, it must be acted, it is not a lecture but a piece of living evidence. If it fails to be this, it fails to be a play.

And he went on to criticise those playwrights whose main aim in writing a play was to put over a thesis or a message:

The writer with a thesis (the thesis which has to be demonstrated is the opposite of the evidence which does not have to be proved because it is undeniable), such a writer alienates the freedom of his characters. He tries to mould them to his own ideals and in so doing makes them appear false. He makes them into preconceived ideas. And when they do not fit into his private political framework or into a world view, which does not spring from basic human truths but is simply a borrowed ideology, he will destroy, caricature or disfigure them.

But creation is not the same thing as dictatorship. It is life, it is liberty, it can even be counter to the conscious desires (these are seldom fundamental desires) and to the prejudices of the creator. The creator is not the master of ceremonies. He has only one duty, not to interfere, to live and let live, to allow his obsessions, his sufferings, his fine sense of truth to rise up, take shape and live.

Henry Irving

Madeleine Bingham wrote in 'Henry Irving and the Victorian Theatre':

In his theatre Irving demanded obedience, sparing no-one, not even himself. Rehearsals would last all day and sometimes half the night. There were no lunch breaks or tea breaks; actors would nibble a sandwich as and when they could. The driving will demanded sacrifice, human sacrifice, in the temple of the theatre. Here everything was held in reverence, there was to be no facetiousness. The theatre was a serious matter. Ellen sliding down the banisters had shocked him—how could an Ophelia or Portia show such a lack of dignity?

This total dedication of Irving amused Ellen. 'Yes, yes, were I to be run over by a steam-roller tomorrow, Henry would be deeply grieved; and would say quietly ''What a pity!'' and then add after a moment or two's reflection ''Who is there —er—to go on for her tonight?'''

When he called the first rehearsal, the play was set in his mind. He knew what he was going to do on the first night. Ellen remarked that the company would have done well to notice how he read his own part, for he never again, until the first night, showed his conception so fully and completely. It was as if he were constrained to keep his views secret lest anyone should choose to out-dazzle him.

The first reading of the play was carried out solely by Irving. He read all the parts, never faltering or allowing the company to confuse the characters. He acted every part in the piece as he read, and in his mind the tones of his actors' voices, the moves of the characters, the processions, and the order of the crowd scenes were already set. All the actors had to do was to come up to the expectations which lay in his mind. He spent no time on the women in the play. Occasionally he asked Ellen to suggest a move or two for them, or to coach them as he coached the men. To the modern mind, it was a curious way of proceeding.

Possibly Irving regarded the women in the play solely as decorations, like flowers to be placed here and there once the room was furnished. He lived in a male-dominated society and the action of most of the plays

39. Henry Irving and Ellen Terry acting at the Lyceum Theatre

he produced was concerned with male passions. Such few plays as he produced where the female element predominated usually had Ellen as their guiding star, and he knew that she could sew the material of her part into suitably glittering raiment.

Irving had his detractors, among them the American writer Henry James, whose book 'The Scenic Art' claimed:

His voice is apparently wholly unavailable for purposes of declamation. To say that he speaks badly is to go too far; to my sense he simply does not speak at all—in any way that, in an actor, can be called speaking. He does not pretend to declaim or dream of declaiming. Shakespeare's finest lines pass from his lips without his paying the scantiest tribute to their quality. Of what the French call diction—of the art of delivery—he has apparently not a suspicion. This forms three-fourths of an actor's obligations and in Mr Irving's acting these three-fourths are simply cancelled. What is left to him with the remaining fourth is to be 'picturesque'; and this even his partisans admit he has made his speciality. This concession darkens Mr Irving's prospects as a Shakespearean actor. You can play hopscotch on one foot, but you cannot cut with one blade of a pair of scissors, and you cannot play Shakespeare by being simply picturesque.

The following account was given by George Pleydell Bancroft in 'Stage and Bar'. Speaking after Sir Henry Irving at a dinner, the actor J. L. Toole told the company of a dream he had had. He dreamed that he and his friend Henry had both died. 'Henry, with his customary complete stage management, had gone straight to Heaven,' said Toole. But *he* found himself going along a black corridor, until he came to a huge gate with a blinding light shining from behind it:

I stood stock still and wondered, and I'll tell you why. Henry was dead too, you see, and the effect of this light was really so dramatic as to be worthy of Henry and the Lyceum. I couldn't help speculating whether he had had a hand in it.

There was no bell, so I banged on the gate and tried to shake it.

An impressive figure then appeared from nowhere. No, no, it wasn't Henry. In a voice really quite kindly he asked who I was. 'Toole,' I answered. But he vaguely shook his head.

'Toole, the actor,' I added with a bit of a sting in it. Well, I was rather hurt, you know. 'J. L. Toole. Johnny Toole.' There was rather an indignant tone in that. Just vanity, gentlemen, that's all.

'Toole, the actor?' asked the imposing figure.

'That's right,' I answered. 'You've got it. But may I ask, Sir, who you are?'

'I'm Saint Peter,' he replied solemnly—very.

'Oh,' I said, and wanting to be on good terms with him at once I just muttered: 'I'm—er—very glad to meet you.'

He bowed and so gave me a little confidence. I needed it.

'But where am I?' I then asked.

'This is Heaven.'

'Heaven! It is! I mean, is it? Then I—I—er—want to come in.'

'But you say you're Toole, the actor. We admit no actors here.'

'But that's wrong.' I argued. 'There's a mistake somewhere. Why, you've admitted Irving.'

His answer came pat. 'Irving! He's no actor.'

If Irving did not like the scenery when it was shown to him, he would say contemptuously: 'Is that what you think you are going to give my public?'

George S. Kaufman

Writing for the 'New York Times', George Kaufman penned some of the most pithy and devastating comments on Broadway shows, quoted in Howard Teichmann's biography, 'George S. Kaufman':

There was laughter in the back of the theatre, leading to the belief that someone was telling jokes back there.

I saw the play at a disadvantage. The curtain was up.

I was underwhelmed....

A press agent once asked Kaufman, when he was drama editor of the 'New York Times', 'How do I get our leading lady's name into your newspaper?'
  Kaufman replied: 'Shoot her.'

The actress Ruth Gordon was telling Kaufman about a new play she was to be in:

'There's no scenery at all,' she said. 'In the first scene, I'm on the left side of the stage, and the audience has to imagine I'm in a crowded restaurant. In scene two, I run over to the right side of the stage, and the audience has to imagine I'm home in my own drawing-room.'
  'And the second night,' Kaufman said, 'you'll have to imagine there's an audience out front.'

40. George S. Kaufman and Harpo Marx

Edmund Kean

When Edmund Kean was the reigning star of the London theatre in the early nineteenth century, another actor, Junius Brutus Booth, also began to make a big name for himself and was judged by many to rival Kean. So the Drury Lane management was delighted when they succeeded in recruiting him to play Iago to Kean's Othello. The performance, on 20 February 1817, was really more of a contest than a play, as Giles Playfair wrote in 'Kean':

That night the Drury Lane stage became a kind of prize-fight ring; and the auditorium was filled to overflowing with excited, wildly cheering spectators. Booth was the challenger with everything to gain. Kean was the champion whose title was in jeopardy. Booth was the sentimental favourite. The odds were about even!

Or so the spectators thought. But the contest eventually proved a very one-sided affair. 'On entering, Mr Booth was welcomed by thunders of applause,' wrote the 'Morning Post'. 'He commenced his performance with great success. But as the play advanced he lost the high ground on which he had stood; and the comparison which the audience were increasingly called upon to make was not very favourable to him. His Iago was. . .nothing like what a too sanguine public had fondly anticipated . . .. In some of the most interesting scenes his labours were witnessed with the most perfect serenity, and a most appalling calm

prevailed where heretofore we have been accustomed to look for a storm of approbation. . . . With another actor in Othello, the Iago of the evening might have been thought great, but by the side of Kean we could discover in him nothing strikingly original in thought, vivid in conception, or brilliant in execution. . . .'

He fought with a great show of sportsmanship. At the end of each scene, he bowed and smiled and took Booth by the hand and affected to suppose that the audience's applause was meant for both of them. But while the play was on, he fought in deadly earnest. He gave no quarter. He never allowed his opponent a chance. 'Up and down, to and fro he went, pacing about like a chafed lion, who had received his fatal hurt, but whose strength is still undiminished. The fury and whirlwind of the passions seemed to have endowed him with supernatural strength. His eye was glittering and bloodshot, his veins were swollen, and his whole figure restless and violent. It seemed dangerous to cross his path and death to assault him. He was excited in a most extraordinary degree as much as though he had been maddened by wine.'

Edmund acted that night as he had never acted in his life before. His Othello was a gigantically selfish performance. But its

41. Edmund Kean as Richard II

effect was overwhelming. It swept all the other players—including Iago—clean off the stage. 'Even the actors, hardened in their art—were moved.' One comedian—'a veteran of forty years' experience'—said afterwards: 'When Kean rushed off the stage in the third act, I felt my face deluged with tears—a thing that has never happened to me since I was a crack, this high!'

Next morning the press reported Edmund's triumph with varying emphasis. A few of the critics tried to make out that Booth had only lost on points, and that he had gone down gallantly to defeat. But the majority of them stated what was true—that he had been well and mercilessly slaughtered.

At any rate he did not come back for more. Though 'Othello' was announced for repetition on Saturday, February 22nd, Booth failed to turn up and Rae played the part of Iago in his stead.

When Edmund Kean was recovering from illness, he still went on stage to play 'Richard III'—a performance which led to a touching demonstration of audience affection and sympathy. A contemporary report, recounted by Giles Playfair, said:

The best compliment was paid him when Rae came forward to announce a repeat performance of 'Richard' for Monday. Contrary to the usual practice when a play goes off well, hisses and cries of 'No, no, shame,' etc., burst from all parts of the house. In the evident puny state of his health everyone felt that Mr Kean's strength was not sufficient to enable him to repeat the character so soon, and the conduct of the audience on this occasion, highly flattering to Mr Kean, was equally creditable to their own humanity and discrimination.

Leading Ladies

One of the first women dramatists in England was the seventeenth-century author Aphra Behn, who wrote nineteen plays, as well as poems and prose works. She became used to being abused, a woman playwright apparently being regarded by some with the same kind of scorn Dr Johnson later directed at women preachers. But Aphra Behn could be scornful in her turn—though she does seem to have seen her writer's imagination as a male quality in herself:

All I ask, is the privilege for my masculine part, the poet in me . . . . If I must not, because of my sex, have this freedom, I lay down my quill and you shall hear no more of me, no, not so much as to make comparisons, because I will be kinder to my brothers of the pen than they have been to a defenseless woman.

When her play 'The Dutch Lover' was published, she prefaced it with an Epistle to the Reader, which began disarmingly:

GOOD, SWEET, HONEY, SUGAR-CANDIED READER,
   Which I think is more than anyone has called you yet, I must have a word or two with you . . . .

The word or two included a swingeing diatribe against the more stupid members of the male sex, especially one who was at the play:

. . . that day 'twas acted first, there comes me into the pit, a long, lither, phlegmatic, white, ill-favored, wretched fop, an officer in masquerade newly transported with a scarf and feather out of France, a sorry animal that has naught else to shield it from the uttermost contempt of all mankind, but that respect which we afford to rats and toads, which though we do not well allow to live, yet when considered as a part of God's creation, we make honorable mention of them. A thing, reader—but no more of such a smelt: This thing, I tell ye, opening that which serves it for a mouth, out issued such a noise as this to those that sat about it, that they were to expect a woeful play, God damn him, for it was a woman's.

   Now how this came about I am not sure, but I suppose he brought it piping hot from some who had with him the reputation of a villanous wit: for creatures of his size of sense talk without all imagination such scraps as they pick up from other folks. I would not for a world be taken arguing with such a property as this; but if I thought there were a man of any tolerable parts, who could upon mature deliberation distinguish well his right hand from his left, and justly state the difference between the number of sixteen and two, yet had this prejudice upon him; I would take a little pains to make him know how much he errs.

The first English actress to appear on the stage in London was, according to most records, Mrs Hughes, in December 1660. She appeared as Desdemona at the New Theatre

42. A scene from 'King Henry VIII', with Charles Laughton and Flora Robson

in Vere Street, with the King's Company, which later moved to the Theatre Royal, Drury Lane. To mark the occasion, Thomas Jordan wrote this 'Prologue to introduce the first Woman that came to Act on the Stage in the Tragedy, call'd "The Moor of Venice"':

I come, unknown to any of the rest
To tell you news, I saw the Lady drest;
The Woman playes to day, mistake me not,
No Man in Gown, or Page in Petty-Coat;
A Woman to my knowledge, yet I cann't
(If I should dye) make Affidavit on't.
Do you not twitter Gentlemen? I know
You will be censuring, do't fairly though.
'Tis possible a vertuous woman may
Abhor all sorts of looseness, and yet play;

Play on the Stage, where all eyes are upon
    her,
Shall we count that a crime France calls an
    honour:
In other Kingdoms Husbands safely trust
    'um,
The difference lies only in the custom;
And let it be our custom I advise,
I'm sure this Custom's better than
        th'Excise,
And may procure us custom, hearts of flint
Will melt in passion when a woman's in't.
   But Gentlemen you that as judges sit
   In the Star-Chamber of the House the Pit;
Have modest thoughts of her; pray do not
        run
To give her visits when the Play is done,

101

With dam me, your most humble Servant
    Lady,
She knows these things as well as you it
    may be:
Not a bit there dear Gallants, she doth
    know
Her own deserts and your temptations too.
  But to the point, in this reforming age
  We have intents to civilize the Stage.
Our women are defective, and so siz'd
You'd think they were some of the Guard
    disguiz'd;
For (to speak truth) men act, that are
    between
Forty and fifty, Wenches of fifteen;
With bone so large, and nerve so
    incomplyant,
When you call Desdemona, enter Giant.
We shall purge every thing that is unclean,
Lascivious, scurrilous, impious or obscene;
And when we've put all things in this fair
    way
Barebones himself may come and see a Play.

**The Great Dames of the theatre are by no
means always catty about each other. Sybil
Thorndike and Edith Evans had great mutual
admiration, according to Elizabeth Sprigge's
'Sybil Thorndike Casson':**

'From the beginning,' Dame Edith says,
'Sybil has been a great beauty, with that
fine bony structure and those exquisite
features—the eyes perfectly set in that lovely
forehead. And her voice is magical with that
wonderful diction. She's important and has a
very rich life. We couldn't be more
different. I was an only child, and now I
have no relatives. Whenever I see her I wish
I were more like her.'
  'Edith is a really great actress,' Sybil says.
'We have played a lot of the same parts and
she has always been much better than me.'

*At the age of thirty, Flora Robson went to
see a producer about a play he was casting.
  'Can you look sixteen?' he asked her.
  'I've never looked sixteen,' she replied,
'but I could act a girl of sixteen.'*

**English actor Edgar Norfolk went to New
York to act with Tallulah Bankhead:**

43. Flora Robson and Charles Laughton in 'Macbeth'

Of course a love scene with Miss Bankhead
is something you always remember. Not all-
in wrestling, but...well, quite exciting....'

And he remembered other athletic feats:

She once greeted me standing on her head,
and saying: 'Oh—there's the old bastard!'
.... And I had a dear old Yorkshire aunt,
Aunt Lucy, who'd only seen her in a very
bad film she was in. And I told her about
this, I said, 'There was Tallulah standing on
her head, saying ''There he is, the old
bastard....''''
  She said, 'Aye, well, I'd like to have seen
her that way up, she might have looked
better!'

Macbeth

'Macbeth' is surrounded by so many superstitions that it's surprising that anyone ever dares to put it on at all. It is often rehearsed without the last line being said, and it is even thought unlucky to mention the title: theatre people frequently refer to it in conversation as 'That Scottish Play'. It is particularly unlucky to quote from it in the theatre, and one explanation of this is the policy followed by the old touring companies. If they launched a new play and it didn't go well they abandoned it after a couple of nights and did 'Macbeth' instead, since that always brought in the crowds. So to quote from 'Macbeth' was thought to be an omen that the current play would fail and the company would soon be back doing 'That Scottish Play' once more.

Theatre people are never short of stories to back up their belief that 'Macbeth' brings bad luck: an actor at Oldham Rep was actually killed on stage. At Greenwich, an actor fell off a rostrum and was in hospital for months. At Salisbury, a stage manager mentioned the title backstage during the performance of another play; at that moment a piece of scenery fell on one of the people on stage. At Manchester, again when some completely different play was being performed, an actress pooh-poohed the superstitions and deliberately quoted from 'Macbeth'. That night, in a night scene, a wine bottle broke; she tripped, a piece of glass jabbed her hand and she had to be rushed to hospital for an emergency operation which only just saved the use of three of her fingers.

The play's ill omens are felt even by television people. One director would never allow the play to be quoted or even mentioned around the studios. He had been running the programme 'All Our Yesterdays' happily for months before someone tactlessly reminded him of something he hadn't realised—or had forgotten. The full quotation is:

And all our yesterdays have lighted fools
The way to dusty death.

And it comes of course from . . . 'Macbeth'.

William McGonagall, poet and tragedian, made his first stage appearance at Mr Giles' theatre in Dundee, playing 'Macbeth' while Mrs Giles played Lady Macbeth. He recalled it in 'Poetic Gems':

The way that I was allowed to perform was in terms of the following agreement, which was entered into between Mr Giles and myself—that I had to give Mr Giles one pound in cash before the performance, which I considered rather hard, but as there was no help for it, I made known Mr Giles's terms to my shopmates, who were hand-loom weavers in Seafield Works, Taylor's Lane. No sooner than the terms were made known to them, than they entered heartily into the arrangement, and in a very short time they made up the pound by subscription, and with one accord declared they would go and see me perform the Thane of Fife, alias Macbeth . . . .

When the great night arrived my shopmates were in high glee with the hope of getting a Shakespearian treat from your humble servant. And I can assure you, without boasting, they were not disappointed in their anticipations, my shopmates having secured seats before the general public was admitted. It would be impossible for me to describe the scene in Lindsay Street, as it was crowded from head to foot, all being eager to witness my first appearance as an exponent of Shakespeare.

When I appeared on the stage I was

received with a perfect storm of applause, but when I exclaimed 'Command, they make a halt upon the heath,' the applause was deafening, and was continued during the entire evening, especially so in the combat scene. The house was crowded during each of the three performances on that ever-memorable night, which can never be forgot by me or my shopmates, and even entire strangers included. At the end of each performance I was called before the curtain, and received plaudit after plaudit of applause in recognition of my able impersonation of Macbeth.

What a sight it was to see such a mass of people struggling to gain admission! hundreds failing to do so, and in the struggle numbers were trampled under foot, one man having lost one of his shoes in the scrimmage; others were carried bodily into the theatre along with the press. So much then for the true account of my first appearance on any stage.

Sybil Thorndike recalled that when Hubert Carter was in a 1926 production of 'Macbeth', he 'allowed the role to go to his head, and nightly in the duel scene, all but killed Basil Gill as Macduff until Lewis had stage-hands posted out of sight among the scenery to hiss at Carter during the duel that Macbeth was intended by the author to lose it'.

Explaining why she had never acted as Lady Macbeth, Dame Edith Evans once remarked that she could never bring herself to play the part of anyone who had such curious notions of hospitality.

44. David Garrick and Mrs Pritchard in 'Macbeth'

Michéal MacLiammóir

From 'All For Hecuba':

Far from being a copyist of life's surface tricks or a facile repeater of traditional antics, the actor should live with such delicacy, with such intensity, that he brings manner and style to all the unimportant trifles of gesture and speech, so that the eating of a fruit, the folding of a letter, the raising of the arm, the donning of a cap, all become in his hands images of significance, profound mirrors of character.

A lady from a charity was waiting outside a Dublin theatre after a matinee to collect Michéal MacLiammóir—as arranged—and bring him to a meeting where he was to give a reading in aid of the charity's funds. When he emerged, she said: 'This is very good of you, Dr MacLiammóir—and I am sorry if you had to hurry. You haven't even had time to take off your make-up.'

Michéal MacLiammóir smiled and replied: 'Oh, my dear madam, I have taken off my stage make-up. This is my street make-up.'

45. Michéal MacLiammóir

Making Up

Eighteenth-century make-up, coupled with the boisterousness of the audience, made acting a dangerous profession, as George Ann Bellamy wrote in 'An Apology for the Life of George Ann Bellamy':

The orange was thrown at Mr Sheridan who played the character of Aesop, and so well directed, that it dented the iron of the false nose which he wore, into his forehead.

In some kinds of theatre and production, the need for make-up in the traditional sense has been questioned, and in some cases its use is discarded. American actor and make-up instructor Nicholas Kepros regarded this trend philosophically in 'Understanding Make-up':

The demise of make-up on the professional stage is not a recent phenomenon.... The art of make-up began its wane when American drama moved into realism. The ordinary folk of realistic drama, together with the professional theatre's penchant for type-casting, eliminated the need for transforming an actor. It gave the theatre a generation of actors whose knowledge of make-up reached its outer limits at a Max Factor pancake shade-number and a deft method for sharpening eyebrow pencils.

Now, theatre has once more swung out of the realistic, but not back to any drama we have known before—the pendulum seems to have left the clock. In this theatre of free form, which uses the actor's body as a plastic medium—often nude, in the lap of the audience, and under vastly varying light sources—what use is there for a technique that delineates character and depends on distance and homogeneous lighting for a successful illusion? The answer is, of course, none. However, in fairness, the question should also include an examination of the possible longevity and ultimate influence of this new theatre.

Whereas a limited perspective of our present theatrical tastes would lead one to discard forever the knowledge of a classical or traditional make-up...a larger view sees the current theatrical trend as part of a general one which includes popular music, painting, and even education: this is the dawning of the Age of the Amateur.

On stage and on the school board, it once seemed to promise a breath of fresh air, but as time has gone by, the arrogant incompetence that was necessary for a release from stiff professionalism has begun to try the patience of the public. Each excursion to a garage or store-front performance leads to a rediscovery, by their absence, of the strengths of professionalism, not the least of which are dependability and a sense of structure. What we recognize is that this Age of the Amateur will not ultimately obliterate other forms of theatre, but will exist side by side with them. The salutary effects of the new theatre, such as the easy acceptance of nudity and the use of mixed media, will remain, and the professional theatre will be the lucky beneficiary.

Traditional techniques on the other hand will continue to be used, and taught, in those places not entirely tied to the exploration, or exploitation, of the latest fad. Where the word is still important to communication, the actor will concern himself with being heard; where audience involvement is understood correctly as a psychological phenomenon (and not a physical one, as with the naively literal Living Theatre), there will be an appreciation of its dependence on the separation of performer and spectator—on distance. And distance, in all senses of the word—physical, historical, and emotional—gives rise to the necessity for make-up.

American make-up artist Eddie Senz said:

Make-up is changing constantly. The direction of the changes is shaped by new ideas and new products. Make-ups used to be quite heavy with a lot of pigment and substance that gave the skin the desired color but obliterated the texture. It looked dull and was very obvious. Today, we use a lot of make-ups that go on quickly; we use a thinner foundation that doesn't cover the actor's natural colour.

We used to use lights and shadows to create certain effects for character make-ups—like hardening the labule fold line from the wing of the nose to the side of the mouth or elongating the nose. We used a lot of putties and waxes. Today, we actually make physical changes. A woman can make her eyes longer or wider by using a strip lash in the correct place. Instead of putties and waxes, we use prosthetic noses made out of light fluffy rubber. New lighting techniques, improved materials, the addition of latex and rubber have all added a three dimensional effect to make-up.

Richard Huggett learned one lesson the hard way when he had to step in as understudy to Robert Atkins and play the part of Sir Toby Belch in 'Twelfth Night':

I made rather rapidly the discovery which many actors make and which I suspect that Marlon Brando has made in his 'Godfather' performance—that you can't act with a mouth full of cotton wool. Throughout the evening I steadily got rid of it in small pieces, getting visibly thinner in the face, and ending up without any at all, so the audience was treated to the spectacle of a Sir Toby who began the evening as if he had mumps and ended it as if he had lockjaw.

Lewis Casson used to make up elaborately for his part as an eighty-year-old in N. C. Hunter's 'A Day by the Sea'. He was seventy-eight at the time.

46. A sketch on the mystery of making up on Boxing Night, 1870

Christopher Marlowe

Marlowe's death was the subject of some gleeful moralising by those who regarded him as an immoral atheist. One such moralist was Edmund Rudierde. The fact that he got the place of Marlowe's death and the spelling of his name wrong, did not deter him from launching this attack in 1618 in 'The Thunderbolt of God's Wrath against Hard-Hearted and stiff-necked sinners':

We read of one Marlin, a Cambridge Scholar, who was a Poet, and a filthy Play-maker—this wretch accounted that meek servant of God, Moses, to be but a conjuror, and our sweet Saviour but a seducer and a deceiver of the people. But harken, ye brain-sick and profane Poets and Players, that bewitch idle ears with foolish vanities, what fell upon this profane wretch, having a quarrel against one whom he met in a street in London, and would have stabbed him. But the party, perceiving his villainy, prevented him with catching his hand, and turning his own dagger into his brains—and so, blaspheming and cursing, he yielded up his stinking breath. Mark this ye Players, that live by making fools laugh at sin and wickedness.

47. Marlowe's death depicted in 'A Tavern Brawl' by John Gilbert

The Mousetrap

A group of foreign tourists hailed a taxi in London and asked to be taken to the theatre where 'The Mousetrap' was showing. When they got out, they gave the driver the exact fare without any tip. As they moved away to go into the theatre the driver shouted after them: 'The butler did it!'

For the thousandth performance of 'The Mousetrap' all the press were invited, but only one critic turned up. His comment was: 'The biggest mystery of the evening is why this play has run so long.'

As the play approached its tenth anniversary, 'Mousetrap' impresario Peter Saunders kept a cool eye on the impact of the show, both on audiences and on the media. He wrote in 'The Mousetrap Man':

Publicity was still the vital factor in achieving the longevity that almost becomes perpetual motion. Weddings were always popular with the press. Lisa Rayne was married under an archway of mousetraps. Gordon Marshall, the theatre manager, had a dog that jumped out of a top window in the theatre without injuring itself. Every anniversary meant some kind of a minor party, and every cast change made news. 'The Mousetrap' was now becoming an institution. It was so much on the tourists' lists of what to see that rather than lose a potential audience from overseas I refused to allow the play to be produced on Broadway or in Australia, and although it had been done in its early days in South Africa, I wouldn't allow it to be done again. But with the ten-year milestone in sight, something pretty spectacular had to be done, and I decided on another major party at the Savoy.

The anniversary was indeed marked by a big party at the Savoy, with a birthday cake weighing half a ton. It was so bulky, it had to be built up from a number of smaller cakes —the full-size cake would not fit into any of the Savoy's ovens. 'The Mousetrap' managed to get into the newspapers, even when Peter Saunders wasn't trying:

Publicity seems to be self-perpetuating. One piece of gratuitous publicity came when doing a good turn. I had been asked to take 'The Mousetrap' company to Wormwood Scrubs to do a performance in front of the prisoners who were serving sentences of four years or more. We took the company down, the prisoners built a set, and the play went as it has never gone before, and I mean that in every sense of the word. A simple line such as, 'You don't look like a policeman,' got a roar of laughter and applause. The most unexpected incidents found new meanings, and at the end no performance has ever got a better reception. Except, I should admit, from two of the prisoners. They took advantage of the performance to escape, and although, at the request of the governor, I refrained from letting this leak out to the press, they did in fact get it themselves and the following morning it was front-page news.

In 1977 when 'The Mousetrap' celebrated its twenty-fifth anniversary, impresario Peter Saunders wrote, in a commemorative glossy booklet entitled 'Twenty-five Years of The Mousetrap', about some of the facts and figures beloved of columnists:

To keep the cast fresh, frequent changes are made, 134 different actors and actresses in a cast of eight and seven different directors in its first twenty-five years.

'Catch' adjectives became an annual feature. And so it was the 'Ninth Incredible Year', the 'Tenth Imperishable Year', the 'Eleventh Extraordinary Year', the 'Twelfth Shattering Year', the 'Thirteenth Momentous Year', the 'Fourteenth Awe-Inspiring Year', the 'Fifteenth Unashamed Year', the 'Sixteenth Mind-Boggling Year',

the 'Seventeenth Inexorable Year', the 'Eighteenth Beautiful Year', the 'Nineteenth Breathtaking Year', the 'Twentieth Proud Year' and the 'Twenty-first Coming-Of-Age Year'. And there the adjectives stopped but 'The Mousetrap' didn't.

'The Mousetrap' has been performed in forty-one countries throughout the world. In London alone more than four million people have seen it. During the London run the scenery and all the furniture and furnishings have been replaced except for one armchair and a clock. Forty-six miles of shirts have been ironed, 160 tons of programmes have been sold and ninety-eight tons of ice-cream and half a million drinks of squash have been consumed. The only change in the script has been the deletion of references to rationing and identity cards which were in force at the time. Neither the authoress nor the producer have ever been able to give an answer as to WHY it has been running so long. When Agatha Christie was once asked 'Is ''The Mousetrap'' being kept on to beat

more records?' she replied, not boastingly but in some bewilderment 'What records are there to beat?'

Mysie Monté was in 'The Mousetrap' for more than ten years, and only left the cast when she decided to retire from the theatre:

One day when I was coming out after the matinee of 'The Mousetrap', a little boy came up to me and asked for my autograph. So I said, 'What do you want, do you want my autograph, or my stage name?'

He said: 'Aren't you Mrs Christie?' I said, 'No.'

He said: 'Give me back my book!'—and he was gone!

Agatha Christie's grandson, Mathew Prichard, got 'The Mousetrap' as a present from her. In 'Twenty-five Years of The Mousetrap' he wrote about some of the qualities which always endeared her to him:

The first was her modesty. To the outside world I suppose this appeared as shyness, but to us she was always infinitely more interested in what we were thinking and doing than in herself.

She could manage to write a book almost without one's noticing and sometimes she used to read the new one to us in the summer down in Devonshire. She did so partly I suspect to test audience reaction, but partly to entertain us on the inevitable wet afternoons when, no doubt, I was rather difficult to amuse! We all tried to guess, and my mother was the only one who was ever right. I think most of my friends who met her during those years were quite astonished that such a mild, gentle grandmother could really be the authoress of all those stories of intrigue, murder and jealousy.

Her next great characteristic was her generosity. It is by now well-known that she gave me 'The Mousetrap' for my ninth birthday. I do not, I am afraid, remember much about the actual presentation (if there was one) and probably nobody realized until much later what a marvellous present it was, but it is perhaps worth remembering that my grandmother had been through many times in her life when money was not so plentiful. It was therefore incredibly generous of her to give away such a play to her grandson as in 1952 her books were

only approaching the enormous success they have now become. It is also a mistake to think of her generosity only in terms of money. She loved giving pleasure to others —good food, a holiday, a present, or a birthday ode. She loved enjoying herself, and also to see others around her enjoying themselves.

The third thing I always enjoyed was her enthusiasm. Despite her modesty or shyness, it was never far below the surface. I think she always had a love/fright relationship with the theatre. Although I am sure she found the experience very wearing, she always enjoyed other people's enthusiasm for her plays and found it infectious. I went to 'The Mousetrap' several times with her in varying company—family parties, girl-friends and the Eton cricket team when I was captain in 1962. I would say we all enjoyed the play and my grandmother's company in equal measure. But she was enthusiastic about other people's plays as well, about archaeology, opera and perhaps above all about food! In short she was an exciting person to be with because she always tried to look on the good side of things and people; she always found something to enthuse about.

49. Agatha Christie

Birth of the National

At the beginning of the twentieth century, the campaign to give London an architectural memorial to Shakespeare got under way—some people were thinking of a structure on the scale of the Albert Memorial. A Shakespeare Memorial Committee was formed to consider various schemes and finally chose one for a monument that would incorporate a statue and stand at the top of Portland Place, where there was—and still is—a small garden with curving Nash terraces on either side. But the plan roused some formidable opposition, including Bernard Shaw, Pinero, Rider Haggard, J. M. Barrie, and William Archer, who favoured a theatre instead of a monument. Archer wrote:

What needs my Shakespeare? Nothing.
What need we?
A Playhouse worthy his supremacy.
Oh bathos!—to the Voice of all our race
We raise dumb carven stones in Portland Place.

At the Lyceum Theatre in May 1908, the supporters of a national theatre—as opposed to a statue or other building—held a rally at which Alfred Lyttelton proposed the resolution, 'This demonstration is in favour of a national theatre as a memorial to Shakespeare.' He said:

The first, and almost the last time I appeared on the stage was in a play by Racine, in which I was supposed to be 'the crowd'. I was taught to come up to the footlights and say, with great embarrassment, 'Moi, je suis I'assemblée.'

Today, I am also one man, representing a crowd, and I assure you that I am not in the least ashamed of my client. The instincts of the multitude are perfectly sane and right on the question, not necessarily of an official, but of a national theatre. I am confirmed in my belief that there are not two sides to this question at all. If there were another, Mr Bernard Shaw would be upon it. Now we have the happiness and strength of his support, Mr Shaw, I suppose, is suffering the anguish of being for once in agreement with several other human beings.

The supporters of a theatre instead of a monument soon afterwards won the day and joined forces with the original committee to form the Shakespeare Memorial National Theatre Committee. But it was to take nearly seventy years for their plan to materialise.

In 1938 the Shakespeare Memorial National Theatre Committee eventually found and bought a site in Kensington, west London. Some people were sceptical, saying that it was too far away from the main theatre area in central London or that it was not a big enough site for the right kind of theatre building. Others said with gleeful gloom that the project couldn't possibly succeed there, since it had once been a pit for burying plague victims. But Bernard Shaw was enthusiastic and was the principal figure at the ceremony when the deeds were handed over, together with a symbolic twig and a sod of earth. He spoke on behalf of the committee:

We are now seized and possessed lawfully and by right of this ground upon which the Shakespeare Memorial National Theatre will

one day stand. I have to hand this sod—it is not, as some of you may suppose, a wedding cake—over to the representative of the Trustees, Mr Geoffrey Whitworth. I suppose that I am here today as the next best thing to Shakespeare. At all events, as you now see, we are so far on the road to having a national theatre that we actually possess the land on which it is to stand. We have not only got it, but we have paid for it, and we are not yet at the end of our resources.

The way the National Gallery, the British Museum and all those places begin is always by a small group of people who understand the national importance, the cultural importance, of these institutions. They make a beginning, and after a time the beginning they make becomes an institution. Then the government comes along, or rather the government does not come along, but the created institution stands in the way of the government, and the government, which never wanted it, says, 'Here is something which for some reason or other, we have got to keep going.' We have got to carry this institution to the point at which the government will be up against it.

People sometimes ask me, 'Do the English people want a national theatre?' Of course they do not. They have got a British Museum, a National Gallery, a Westminster Abbey, and they never wanted any of them. But once these things stand, as mysterious phenomena that have come to them, they are quite proud of them, and feel that the place would be incomplete without them.

In July 1973 the old foundation stone of the National was taken from its temporary place —one of many—near the Festival Hall, to be refurbished before being finally put into the National Theatre. John Elsom and Nicholas Tomalin described the occasion in 'The History of the National Theatre':

The stone had been laid originally between the Festival Hall and the old Shot Tower. Then it was moved and laid again beside County Hall. Then moved again for safety's sake, and now it was off for a twenty-two year service. Each laying had brought another flourish of ceremony, a few more column inches in the press. The road to the National is paved with ceremonial. There was a Fleet Street choir singing Old English madrigals in 1938, for the Ceremony of the Twig and Sod in Brompton Road, when Bernard Shaw 'took seisin' of the wrong piece of land. The Boyd Neel Orchestra played for the 1951 laying, and Dame Sybil Thorndike recited some very ceremonial verses from the then Poet Laureate, John Masefield. Royalty, too, had been patient with that stone, all that hard pomp wasted, and to crown the indignity, at the very last foundation ceremony, the stone was not needed at all. The new building was to be in concrete; and so, on November 3 1969, there was a Ceremonial Cement Pouring on a windy day on the South Bank.

On this moving occasion in July 1973, any more ceremony would have attracted sardonic comment. There were no rows of politicians, no elder statesmen of the theatre, no ambassadors to watch that peripatetic stone being rolled on to a lorry. There was only a camera team from London Weekend

Television, the workers and a writer. This small group waited for about an hour, because the early morning schedule (intended to provide the correct light for the cameras) had upset McAlpine's arrangement for the lorry. Someone drove over a fork-lift truck from the theatre site, but it was waved away as too dangerous and undignified. Mr Hotson—who mentioned in passing that he never went to the theatre, didn't think much of it and had 'stopped all that kind of thing' in his wife when he married her—crouched over the stone, chipping stylishly at the remaining fragments of cement. The chipping achieved nothing useful, as all the necessary work had been done the night before, but with his round mallet and cold chisel he made a fine picture of traditional craftsmanship. London Weekend recorded him from various angles.

Harold Hobson wrote in the 'Sunday Times' in August 1976:

Denys Lasdun's ambitious building has brought off a triumph to confound the sceptics. The huge foyer, which, with its tables and its Folies-Bergère Manet bars, with its people of all ages and classes walking up and down, listening to music, talking, creates an ambiance of social enjoyment that the French find it easy enough to evoke with their café tables spreading over the Paris pavements, but which has hitherto been unknown in London.

And in the 'Guardian' Michael Billington wrote in March 1976:

After all the sniping and griping, it is a relief to be able to report that the new National Theatre feels not like a white elephant or cultural mausoleum: more like a superb piece of sculpture inside which it is possible to watch a play or walk and talk in the lobbies without feeling dwarfed by one's surroundings...a building in which... human need comes before architectural grandeur and in which everything conspires to make theatre-going a pleasure rather than a penance.

Nudity

If you move, it's rude—
But if you're static, it's ART!

That revue couplet summed up, and sent up, the curious rules that used to govern the display of nudity on stage. Girls were allowed to appear bare-breasted, so long as they remained, literally, statuesque. So all kinds of artistic tableaux were devised, an underwater scene with lounging mermaids being one of the most frequent.

Sometimes there would be a (clothed) singer who sang an appropriate song in front of the posing girls; at other times the curtains would close between each tableau, and a loudspeaker announcement would tell the audience about the next theme. One girl whose act was a series of solo poses even proffered a patriotic one during the war in Korea. She announced from behind the closed curtains:

And now I'd like to show you my idea
For a little tribute to our boys in
Korea...

The curtains opened to reveal her revealingly draped in a Union Jack; she was standing on a pedestal, with a tin hat on her head, saluting....

Some of the small variety theatres that featured touring shows with static nudes in them had their posters partly obscured by printed stickers saying that the Purity League objected to the show. The stickers were printed, and stuck on, by the theatre management....

Though the bare-breasted posing girls were only one act in an ordinary variety bill that would include tenors, conjurors, comics and acrobats too, it was the nudity that was always stressed in the show's title. There were names like: 'Eves Without Leaves', 'Yes! We Have No Pyjamas!' and 'Nudes Are News'.

Kenneth More wrote in 'More or Less':

The Windmill Theatre was owned by a widow, Mrs Laura Henderson, who had inherited a fortune through a family shipping line. This theatre was her abiding interest and somehow she had persuaded the Lord Chamberlain, who was a personal friend, that tableaux vivants with bare-breasted girls were harmless entertainment and not conducive to public immorality, as her critics sometimes claimed. Indeed, the Windmill Theatre was one of the most moral places in which I have ever worked. Mrs Henderson took a personal interest in all the staff. She would come to see the show regularly every month from a box, and frequently brought along the Lord Chamberlain as her guest, so that he could see for himself that everything was being conducted in a decorous manner.

It is always startling to realise how comparatively recent is the acceptance of nudity on stage—not only in such unclad shows as 'Oh Calcutta!' but in straight plays like Peter Shaffer's 'Equus'. The authorities were always more prudish than audiences, whom they seemed to feel it was their divine right to protect from shocking sights such as the human body. But the guardians of public morals sometimes inadvertently did theatres a good turn, as Ed Berman recalls in his introduction to 'Ten of the Best British Short Plays', writing of the start of the now-

flourishing London lunch-hour theatre movement, with his Ambiance Theatre Club in 1968:

Leaving theory aside, the simple truth is that we were lucky to have had a scandal over our first play. And what a scandal! Jennie Lee, a fine classical actress, was nude in a poetic reverie of a play, 'Squire Jonathan' by John Arden—nude for three whole seconds.

In 1968 the Lord Chamberlain (that Star Chamber superstar of yesteryear) was still in business. His business was to censor plays and license them. We were a club theatre and unlicensed: thus we were defying the entire medieval power structure of the Establishment with a three-second nude. What high drama! Thirty-five photographers showed up for the press photo-call. Subsequently we have had, on average,

larger audiences without cameras.

As if this pathetic scandal were not enough, my own play, 'The Nudist Campers Grow and Grow', appeared next. A send-up of prudes, the play had two actors in fig-leaves defying the audience to join them on stage and shed their clothes. I am happy to say that few did. The flabbiness of the average bourgeois theatregoer has to be seen to be believed.

By this time, the Arts Council of Great Britain decided to give us a tiny grant. Perhaps they felt that if we could afford costumes, we might cause less disruption of national customs.

When 'Oh Calcutta!' was first launched it got indifferent reviews. One of the critics went so far as to say that a show like this could give pornography a bad name.

51. A wartime photograph of the dressing room at the Windmill Theatre

Sean O'Casey

O'Casey on actors and playwrights:

If one wanted advice on the merits of a play newly written, it would be wiser and better and safer to ask a policeman than it would be to ask an actor . . . .

Shakespeare and Molière are, possibly, the only recorded instances of actors writing great plays, and, by all accounts, Shakespeare was a very bad actor indeed.

He was also sharply critical of the naturalistic style of theatre in his time:

Now the stage has become a picture-frame, a fourth wall, a lighted box in which the actors and actresses hide themselves as much as possible from the people . . . .

Perhaps some kindly manager will in some theatre electrify the proscenium border so that any actor that steps over it will be immediately electrocuted.

Joseph Holloway, whose journal recorded the hectic scenes at the opening and subsequent nights of Synge's 'Playboy' at the Abbey Theatre, was on hand nearly twenty years later to chronicle similar scenes that kept erupting at the Abbey during the run of O'Casey's 'The Plough and the Stars'. On 11 February 1926 he wrote:

Some of the players behaved with uncommon roughness to some ladies who got on the stage, and threw two of them into the stalls. One young man thrown from the stage got his side hurt by the piano. The chairs of the orchestra were thrown on the stage, and the music on the piano fluttered, and some four or five tried to pull down half of the drop curtain, and another caught hold of one side of the railing in the scene in Act III.

The players headed by McCormick as spokesman lined up on stage, and Mac tried to make himself heard without avail. Then a man came on and begged the audience to give the actor a hearing, and they did, and Mac said he wished the actors should be treated distinct from the play, and his speech met with applause.

Joseph Holloway had also been at the first night of 'Juno and the Paycock' at the Abbey Theatre in 1924:

As I left the theatre, cries of 'Author! Author!' were filling the air, and I suppose O'Casey had to bow his acknowledgement. He sat with a friend in the second row of the stalls with his cap on all the while, I noticed. He is a strange, odd fish, but a genius in his way.

Laurence Olivier

Noel Coward, writing about Laurence Olivier:

In addition to his initial genius for acting, his imagination and the meticulous concentration with which he approaches every part he plays, he has always had and still has the physical attributes of a romantic star. True, in his earlier, halcyon days at the Old Vic he made every effort to disguise these with acres and acres of nose paste and false hair. I cannot think of any other living actor who has used such quantities of spirit-gum with such gleeful abandon. I believe that this rather excessive determination to be old before his time was the result of an integral shyness in his character. He has never had the smallest inclination to look or be himself on the stage.

Kenneth Tynan wrote in 'The Sound of Two Hands Clapping' of Laurence Olivier's 'Oedipus' in 1944, and the final agony of the ending, when:

. . .he let out those two famous cries that all but shattered the balcony of the New Theatre in London. After a quarter of a century, there is still a sort of kinship between those who were there and heard him, as if they'd been on the Somme together. I found out later, in conversation with him, that he'd been on an ermine ranch in Canada, years before, and he'd heard the sound that an ermine made in a trap—a terrible, high-pitched wailing—and he consciously reproduced that noise. It's

reverberated in my mind ever since as the sound that people make in life's extremities. That is exactly how he operates as an actor: he's an observer of all detail, and he uses it quite ruthlessly; rather than let the noise come from inside him, he observes it outside himself, and then absorbs and hoards it. But, you see, that noise, the extravagance of it, is something that would seem absurd on film. It's only possible in a large room where one man can face his audience; and that is theatre.

52. Laurence Olivier as Henry V, with Jessica Tandy as the French princess

Plagiarism

An attempt at piracy may account for the First Quarto text of 'Hamlet', a somewhat shambling version of the First Folio one and the other Quartos. It has so many variations on the usual version that it could well have been an attempt to take it down from a performance or a series of performances. The variations are startling, not least because the other version is so familiar. This is the 'To be or not to be' speech, as given in the First Quarto, with only the spelling modernised:

To be, or not to be, aye, there's the point,
To die, to sleep, is that all? Aye, all:
No, to sleep, to dream, aye marry, there it
    goes,
For in that dream of death, when we awake,
And borne before an everlasting Judge,
From whence no passenger ever returned,
The undiscovered country, at whose sight
The happy smile, and the accursed damn'd.
But for this, the joyful hope of this,
Who'd bear the scorns and flattery of the
    world,
Scorned by the right rich, the rich cursed of
    the poor?
The widow being oppressed, the orphan
    wronged,
The taste of hunger, or a tyrant's reign,
And thousand more calamities besides,
To grunt and sweat under this weary life,
When that he may his full Quietus make,
With a bare bodkin, who would this endure,
But for a hope of something after death?
Which pulses the brain, and doth confound
    the sense,
Which makes us rather bear those ills we
    have,
Than fly to others that we know not of.
Aye that, O this conscience makes cowards
    of us all,
Lady in thy orisons, be all my sins
    remembered.

In 'Recollections of Occurrences', Thomas Snagge recalled he was working for a manager in Dublin, Mr Ryder, who had pirated Sheridan's 'The Duenna' the previous season and thought Snagge could do him a service on a visit to London.

Mr Ryder had played 'The Duenna' under some fears, for although he altered the title to 'The Governess' a lawsuit was taken against him by Mr Brinsley Sheridan, but did not succeed. Mr Ryder particularly applied to me to request a copy of 'The School for Scandal', and for that purpose to apply to Mr Gurney, which I did, and several other of the shorthand writers in London, but not one would undertake the task of writing the play from the performance. So some of my friends and I absolutely set about the labour and completed it almost literally, with the song and the epilogue.

The mode we took was by going into the two-shilling gallery a party of five. By sitting together, two on one seat, two behind and one below, we composed a group and with paper and pencils each writing down the direct words of one of the characters in a scene and regulating the whole in a committee after each performance, in four or five nights we completed the whole.

When I returned I gave it to Mr Ryder who was to pay me for my expenses to London and the cash expenses in the business £40, which I unfortunately never received.

Mr Sheridan had an idea of the impossibility of preventing his favourite comedy 'The School for Scandal' being acted in Ireland; therefore he made a merit of necessity and sent a copy to his sister who, I was told, received £100 for the manuscript. The difference in the two copies was very trifling, the fair and the pirated, but we performed it from the original one.

Samuel Butler, on the 'Character of the Play-Writer', says:

He finds it easier to write in Rhime than Prose; for the World being overcharged with Romances, he finds his Plots, Passions, and Repartees ready made to his Hand; and if he can but turn them into Rhime, the Thievery is disguised, and they pass for his own Wit and Invention without Question; like a stolen Cloke made into a Coat, or dyed into another Colour. Besides this he makes no Conscience of stealing any Thing that lights in his Way, and borrows the Advice of so many to correct, enlarge, and amend what he has ill-favouredly patcht together, that it becomes like a Thing drawn by Council, and none of his own Performance, or the Son of a Whore that has no one certain Father. He has very great Reason to prefer Verse before Prose in his Compositions; for Rhime is like Lace, that serves excellently well to hide the Piecing and Coarsness of a bad Stuff, contributes mightily to the Bulk, and makes the less serve by the many Impertinencies it commonly requires to make Way for it; for very few are endowed with Abilities to bring it in on its own Accompt. This he finds to be good Husbandry, and a Kind of necessary Thrift; for they that have but a little ought to make as much of it as they can.

When he was accused of plagiarising Molloy's 'Love's Sweet Song' for one of his own tunes, Sir Arthur Sullivan said:

'I don't happen ever to have heard the song, but if I had, you must remember that Molloy and I had only seven notes to work on between us.'

53. 'A maker of much music', Arthur Sullivan

Playwriting

One of Aristotle's famous theatrical principles was once summarised thus:

Aristotle
Took another swig from the bottle,
And remarked to a friend:
'A play must have a beginning, a middle
    and an end!'

And here is Samuel Butler striking his customary sour note, in 'Characters':

A play-writer of our times is like a Fanatic, that has no wit in ordinary easy things, and yet attempts the hardest task of brains in the whole world, only because, whether his play or work please or displease, he is certain to come off better than he deserves, and find some of his own latitude to applaud him, which he could never expect any other way; and is as sure to lose no Reputation, because he has none to venture....

Nothing encourages him more in his undertaking than his ignorance, for he has not wit enough to understand so much as the difficulty of what he attempts; therefore he runs on boldly like a foolhardy Wit, and Fortune, that favours Fools and the Bold, sometimes takes notice of him for his double capacity, and receives him into her good graces.

Alexandre Dumas (fils):

When I write a play I think it is good; when I see it played I think it is stupid; and when anyone tells it to me I think it is perfect, as the person always forgets half of it.

This was how Mark Twain began his letter replying to the manager of a travelling theatre company who had 'taken the liberty' of dramatising 'Tom Sawyer' and asked permission to use Mark Twain's name as author:

And so it has got around to you, at last; and you have 'taken the liberty'. You are No. 1,365. When 1,364 sweeter and better people, including the author, have tried to dramatize 'Tom Sawyer' and did not arrive, what sort of show do you suppose you stand? That is a book, dear Sir, which cannot be dramatized. One might as well try to dramatize any other hymn. 'Tom Sawyer' is simply a hymn, put into prose form to give it a worldly air.

Why the pale doubt that flitteth dim and nebulous athwart the forecastle of your third sentence? Have no fears. Your piece will be a Go. It will go out the back door on the first night. They've all done it—the 1,364. So will—1,365...

How kind of you to invite me to the funeral. Go to; I have attended a thousand of them. I have seen Tom Sawyer's remains in all the different kinds of dramatic shrouds there are. You cannot start anything fresh.

Jean-Paul Sartre wrote in 'Sartre on Theatre':

A book gains its public gradually. A work for the theatre has necessarily to be 'theatrical' because the author knows that he will be applauded or hissed at once. It's like an examination you can take only once and never again. More and more a play is coming to be something like an assault on the public; if it fails, it recoils on its author. In the United States and—for some time now—in France, if the criticisms are bad and the box office slack, a play is taken off after a few performances. A book can speak in a murmur; drama and comedy have to shout. This may be what attracts me about the theatre: the assault and the heightened tone and the risk of losing everything in a single night.

Joe Orton said:

Oh, the public will accept me. They've given me a licence, you see. What they'll do is say 'Joe Orton can do these things' if I'm a success. But I'm a success because I've taken a hatchet to them and hacked my way in. I mean it wasn't easy. Sloane wasn't easy. It wasn't the enormous success that people seem to think.... It's always a fight for an original writer because any original writer will always force the world to see the world his way. The people who don't want to see the world your way will always be angry.

Having started out writing a novel, Joe Orton decided that the theatre was where his words could pack more punch, according to John Lahr's introduction to 'Joe Orton: The Complete Plays':

To be destructive, words must be irrefutable. Print was less effective than the spoken word because the blast was greater; eyes could ignore, slide past, dangerous verbs and nouns. But if you could lock the enemy into a room somewhere, and fire the sentence at them, you could get a sort of seismic disturbance.

David Mercer:

I've never really properly understood what people mean by entertainment. I don't think that for me the theatre is a place for anything but the discovery and the demonstration of the truth about what's happening in a society at a given time. In so far as I understand entertainment at all, I would say 'Hamlet' entertains me, but it's not light, it's not amusing, it's not shallow—and perhaps we just don't really understand these categories very well. I think that we tend to think of entertainment as something which is necessarily not to do with reality, and I think that the theatre is concerned with reality.

Alan Plater on the playwright's source material:

In the end, we all lean on our experience. Nothing is invented, only rearranged and distorted to suit our particular prejudices. All plays are based on bedrock reality —albeit the reality of a dream in a disturbed night.

And on the choice of themes:

It is self-evident that the great universal themes—birth, death, marriage, love, war,

sex, work, religion—are what people want to write about and see plays about. We all drink to that, but I'd add a couple of footnotes: first, that the themes and the manner of dealing with them should have something to do with the life on the streets outside the theatre; second, that the noblest approach to these themes is to laugh at them. The really serious issues of our time are generally very trivial—drawing up the committee agenda, or deciding how to tell somebody not to sit in grandfather's chair. Increasingly I lean to the concept that comedy is king, because the hero has to go on living with the reality of tomorrow. The tragic hero, by definition, throws in the towel, even though he may go the full fifteen rounds.

Comments by Tom Stoppard on his methods of writing:

For me, it is such a relief to get an idea! I know there are writers who are not going to live long enough to do justice to all the ideas they have, but to me it's like being struck by lightning—and I feel just as powerless to make it happen—even, as it were, by hanging about under trees in thunderstorms.

Once I've got an idea and I've got it worked out, I do this incredible ground plan for a play, and I always end up having to create a new first-act curtain, because my intended first-act curtain is an hour further on. Stepping on the tortoise in 'Jumpers' was always, as far as I was concerned, going to be the first-act curtain. By the time my people had shut up, an hour and ten minutes had gone, and we were only halfway there. And that tends to happen with my plays.

I tend to write through a series of small, large and microscopic ambushes—which might consist of a body falling out of a cupboard, or simply an unexpected word in a sentence. But my preoccupation as a writer, which possibly betokens a degree of insecurity, takes the form of contriving to inject some sort of interest and colour into every line, rather than counting on the general situation having a general interest which will hold an audience.

Harold Pinter made the following comments on his work: its method, and, first, its 'meaning', in a speech he made when he received the Shakespeare Prize in Hamburg in 1970.

Once, many years ago, I found myself engaged uneasily in a public discussion on the theatre. Someone asked me what my work was 'about'. I replied with no thought at all and merely to frustrate this line of enquiry: 'The weasel under the cocktail cabinet.' That was a great mistake. Over the years I have seen that remark quoted in a number of learned columns. It has now seemingly acquired a profound significance, and is seen to be a highly relevant and meaningful observation about my own work. But for me the remark meant precisely nothing. Such are the dangers of speaking in public.

In what way can one talk about one's work? I'm a writer, not a critic. When I use the word 'work' I mean work. I regard myself as nothing more than a working man.

If there is, as I believe, a necessary, an obligatory shape which a play demands of its writer, then I have never been able to achieve it myself. I have always finished the last draft of a play with a mixture of feelings: relief, disbelief, exhilaration, and a certainty that if I could only wring the play's neck once more it might yield once more to me, that I could get it better, that I could get the better of it, perhaps. But that's impossible. You create the word and in a certain way the word, in finding its own life, stares you out, is obdurate, and more often than not defeats you. You create the characters and they prove to be very tough. They observe you, their writer, warily. It may sound absurd, but I believe I am speaking the truth when I say that I have suffered two kinds of pain through my characters. I have witnessed their pain when I am in the act of distorting them, of falsifying them, and I have witnessed their contempt. I have suffered pain when I have been unable to get to the quick of them, when they wilfully elude me, when they withdraw into the shadows. And there's a third and rarer pain. That is when the right word, or the right act jolts them or stills them into their proper life. When that happens the pain is worth having. When that happens I am ready to take them into the nearest bar and buy drinks all round. And I hope they would forgive me my trespasses against them and do the same for me. But there is no question that quite a conflict takes place between the writer and his characters and on the whole I would say the characters are the winners. And that's as it should be, I think. Where a writer sets out a blueprint for his characters, and keeps them rigidly to it, where they do not at any time upset his applecart, where he has mastered them, he has also killed them, or rather terminated their birth, and he has a dead play on his hands.

Sometimes, the director says to me in rehearsal: 'Why does she say this?' I reply: 'Wait a minute, let me look at the text.' I do so, and perhaps I say: 'Doesn't she say this because he said that, two pages ago?' Or I say: 'Because that's what she feels.' Or: 'Because she feels something else, and therefore says that.' Or: 'I haven't the faintest idea. But somehow we have to find out.' Sometimes I learn quite a lot from rehearsals.

What am I writing about? Not the weasel under the cocktail cabinet.

I am not concerned with making general statements. I am not interested in theatre used simply as a means of self-expression on the part of the people engaged in it. I find in so much group theatre, under the sweat and assault and noise, nothing but valueless generalizations, naive and quite unfruitful.

I can sum up none of my plays. I can describe none of them, except to say: That is what happened. That is what they said. That is what they did.

I am aware, sometimes, of an insistence in my mind. Images, characters, insisting upon being written. You can pour a drink, make a telephone call or run round the park, and sometimes succeed in suffocating them. You know they're going to make your life hell. But at other times they're unavoidable and you're compelled to try to do them some kind of justice. And while it may be hell, it's certainly for me the best kind of hell to be in.

Props

'Props' don't hold up the scenery. The word is theatre shorthand for 'properties', i.e. things that are owned, possessions—or in the Oxford Dictionary definition of a theatrical property: 'Any portable article, as an article of costume or furniture, used in acting a play; a stage requisite.' The term has been used since well before Shakespeare's time and is familiar even to his own Peter Quince, the carpenter in 'A Midsummer Night's Dream' who says: 'In the meantime I will draw a bill of properties, such as our play wants.'

Until fairly recently, actors did in fact own many of the smaller props they used, and were expected to carry around their own stock. Now, stage-managers and their assistants tend to provide and look after every detail of the props, though the actor for the duration of the run is expected to look after and keep in the dressing-room such 'personal props' as, say, a pen, a notebook, coins, a purse or a walking stick. There are many other categories of props too:

'Stage props', like furniture, curtains, carpets, doors and windows, statues, trees and shrubs.

'Hand props', used by the performers, such as suitcases, trays of drinks, tennis rackets, or banners.

And the distinction between those two categories can be a fine one. Betty Gow puts it like this:

A hand prop is on the stage for the specific purpose of being handled by an actor. If the handling is incidental, if, for example, an actor takes up a rug and shakes it, it remains a stage prop, but if he crosses the stage carrying a rolled rug it is a hand prop. This is not quite so illogical as it may seem: the rug he shakes is part of the furnishing of the set, but the one he carries is provided for his particular use.

Then there are also 'costume props', anything that is worn, such as jewellery, spectacles, watches, gloves, cloaks, overcoats, hats, masks or swords. Of course, a sword that was never worn, but simply carried on, could be redefined as a 'hand prop'.

Another category is 'ornamental props'. No-one actually uses these—they are just there, mainly as decoration for the set; things like pictures, ornaments, coffee-table books or potted plants.

And just as a prop doesn't prop things up (although strictly there could, in a mining or tent scene, be such an item as a prop prop), so a 'prop table' isn't used on the stage at all: the phrase refers usually to the table in the wings where the hand props are placed, ready to be brought on. And stage managers make sure that actors know that when they bring the prop off again, it has to be put back exactly where it was.

The art of making props is a skilled one, but as Roger Oldhamstead says in Motley's book 'Theatre Props':

No matter what the prop-maker is called on to produce, he should keep it as simple as possible; clever mechanical contrivances can, and often do, go wrong at embarrassing moments. One piece of string is worth a stage full of sophisticated machinery and if it does fail, it is easy to put right.

And he goes on to describe one of the bulkier items which a prop-maker has to know how to put together:

As dead bodies seem to appear fairly regularly on stage, some advice on their

54. Theatre props

construction is relevant here. Accuracy is important and the prop-maker should first study a reference book on anatomy to learn how a skeleton is constructed and how the bones and muscles work together.

An articulated wood or metal skeleton built to correct human proportions is a basic necessity. The shoulders and hips should move in the appropriate directions and the elbows, knees, wrists, and ankles given their limited movement (which will become obvious if the prop-maker studies his own or someone else's joints). This skeleton can be covered or bound with several different materials, from old soft rags, through cotton waste wadding, to the expensive but perfect corpse-making material, Dacron wadding. (This is normally used in upholstery, but is now increasingly used as a replacement for heavy padding in Falstaffian figures, and as an interfacing in period clothes generally, since it is very light and virtually uncrushable.) When the figure has been padded out to shape, it should be bound smoothly in strips of scrim, butter muslin, or any soft, slightly stretchy fabric. If the figure is to be handled or carried, weight, in the form of sandbags or lead shot, will have to be incorporated in the layers of padding on all the limbs, the back, shoulders, head and hips. If sand is used, fill plastic bags and seal them well before covering them in tightly woven canvas or burlap. Sand has a habit of getting out of any container, and while a trail of blood across the stage would be highly impressive, a trail of sand would not.

The head and hands he suggests can be made by taking casts from life. And there are all kinds of other tricks of this curious trade: for making swords that snap in half; windows, vases and bottles that smash without hurting anyone; bullet holes that suddenly appear in the wall when a gun is fired. Or, for the illusion that the arrow or dagger has been flung and hit its target:

For arrows or thrown knives the traditional method works well. The knife or arrow is hinged to a small plate, with a spring attached to the underside and a stop to the top side. This plate is glued or sewn to the target, which may well be human, and the

arrow or knife is then pulled down against the spring and held flat against the surface or body with a breakable cotton thread or a small strap held with a snap fastener (press stud). When this is released the arrow or knife springs up to a horizontal position and quivers most convincingly. Care must be taken, of course, to camouflage the weapon before it is sprung.

Browsing through such technical works can be a surprising experience for the lay reader, stumbling across such statements as:

Both polystyrene and foam plastic are ideal for cakes and desserts.

or:

Tiered wedding cakes and other iced confectionery are improved by applying Polyfilla with a spatula over the basic shape and then painting with white emulsion.

And you can even learn how to make a stage baby, using the following ingredients:

A rubber ball, a stockinet dishcloth, two feet of wire, half a yard of thin unbleached calico, or part of an old sheet or pillow case, three or four pounds of butter beans, two yards of soft string, and a small roll of wadding or cotton wool.

A 'practical' prop or piece of scenery (sometimes abbreviated to 'prac') is one that has to be able to function: a practical table-lighter, spinning-wheel, candle, pin-table, scent-spray, or a shelf of books.

There is a story that two old and usually unemployed actors met one day in the park. One told the other the glad news that he had just got a part in a play.

'Well, congratulations, old boy,' said the second actor. 'A big part is it?'

'Afraid not, old boy—a very small part. But there's a practical meal in the second act!'

Provincial Tour

The Midland town of Mansfield proved to be one of the less successful venues when Thomas Snagge went to join other members of a touring theatre company there. He wrote in 'Recollections of Occurrences':

I then enquired for the theatre. There was no regular house at present, but if the company pleased their spectators the Squire of the place had promised to supply that deficiency by having one built. To be sure, for the moment, we might be a little inconvenienced, but there was a large unfinished mansion that would, with a small expense and time, be properly converted for our performance.

I went to explore and see the theatre, but behold! It was two old empty houses that a country carpenter had promised to metamorphose into a most elegant Theatre. Day after day passed and only three or four wretched strollers had I seen, who looked very like half starved mendicants, but shortly a Mr and Mrs Fowler arrived and by chance, a Mr Harper, a Gentleman of the Profession, who was travelling thro' that town on foot on his way from Dublin to Bath. He was prevailed upon (without much difficulty) to stop a few nights to assist us. He was an acquisition, being a bold bustling man, confident of his abilities, and from his travels knew the world, had great experience in the strolling line and would undertake any character to Turn the Penny and shew his Parts and Utility.

The stage being elevated, that is whole deals being laid together for that purpose, and some old boards being knocked up for seats, composed pit and gallery. These were joined sloping and divided by a board drop to separate the Quality. The scenes were unrolled, which with the clothes and whole apparatus, when laid out for view, were the most miserable sticks and rags that really any Nagozian or Dapperwit would have been ashamed of.

The comedy of 'The Beaux' Stratagem' was fixed upon for the opening performance, and as appropriate and a compliment to the town, 'The King and the Miller of Mansfield'. I was to enact Archer and to strut in 'The King', Mr Fowler the Boniface, and our Manageress the Lady Bountiful. With doubling the parts and getting the carpenters and workmen to personate the highwaymen, etc. etc., we contrived to murder the play, which was of no great consequence, for except a few shopkeepers, journeymen and apprentices, two or three milliners, mantua makers, women or servants in the gallery, we exhibited to Empty Benches, there being only some few shillings in the house.

A member of a nineteenth-century touring troupe of actors told Henry Mayhew about their life. He recounted in 'London Labour and the London Poor':

Mumming at fairs is harder than private business, because you have to perform so many times. You only wear one dress, and all the actor is expected to do is to stand up to the dances outside and act in. He'll have to dance perhaps sixteen quadrilles in the course of the day, and act about as often inside. The company generally work in shares, or if they pay by the day, it's about four or five shillings a day. When you go to get engaged, the first question is, 'What can you do?' and the next, 'Do you find your own properties, such as russet boots, your dress, hat and feathers, etcetera?'

Of course they like your dress the better if it's a showy one; and it don't matter much about its corresponding with the piece. For instance, Henry the Second, in 'Fair Rosamond', always comes on with a cavalier's dress, and nobody notices the difference of costume. In fact, the same dresses are used over and over again for the same pieces.

The general dress for the ladies is a velvet skirt with a satin stomacher, with a gold band round the waist and a pearl band on the forehead. They, too, wear the same dresses for all the pieces. A regular fair show has only a small compass of dresses, for they only goes to the same places once in a year, and of course their costumes ain't remembered.

Touring with her magician husband in the USA in the early years of the twentieth century, Louella Houston collected the money at the door and also sang in the show. They played for a week in the Oddfellows Hall in a small western town in the gold-fields, called incongruously Manhattan:

When I went across to the Oddfellows Hall, the Sheriff was standing at the door and he said, 'I'll stay here, lady,' he said, 'stand alongside you, because some of these chaps, they get funny ideas.'

So they came. They start coming in, and they were throwing what looked to me like pebbles on the table, and I said, 'Excuse me, you can't...I can't take this—I want a dollar.'

And the Sheriff picked it up and looked at it, and he said, 'That's all right, go on in, Jim, go on in, Bill....' And I said, 'What?'

He said, 'Those are gold nuggets, lady.'

I said, 'Real gold?'

He said, 'Of course they are!'

So anyway, I had a bag full of gold when I went back to the stage. I told my husband, I said, 'We've got a gold-mine!'

He said, 'Yeah, I've heard that before!'

And I said, 'Look!' And I opened the case and there was all the gold.

He said, 'How do you know that's gold?'

I said, 'The Sheriff says it's gold, so it must be gold!'

So in the morning, we took our gold down to the bank and they exchanged it for money for us.

Long before it became famous for televised Victorian Music Hall entertainment with 'The Good Old Days', the City Varieties Theatre in Leeds was featuring touring variety shows. A Leeds friend was at one of these and was highly entertained by a cockney comedian. But in the seat beside him was a stranger, a fellow Yorkshireman, who was clearly not amused: he was sitting with arms folded, cap still on his head, staring glumly at the comic on stage.

Finally the man who found the jokes very funny could bear it no longer. He turned to his dour neighbour and asked: 'Don't you think this lad's bloody funny?'

The man in the cap, still unsmiling, replied: 'Well—he's getting paid for it, isn't he?'

When John Gielgud went to Boston, Massachusetts, in 1959, with his production of 'Much Ado About Nothing' there was certainly much to contend with: they were playing for a summer festival in a huge tent, twenty kilometres outside Boston. He described the ordeal in 'Stage Directions':

A bulldozer breaks a water pipe which is laid on for our water supply, and we can neither drink nor wash (on a matinee day too, when we are in the place for a full eight hours). After a great deal of confusion, the local fire brigade arrives to pump in a supply out of the river.

I am asked to sign autographs between the performances for a visiting party of blind people, and demur, as there will be little time to rest. The curtain then rises on the matinee to a half-empty house. Ten minutes later the blind people arrive and are escorted to their seats. This done, the usherettes sink wearily into the empty chairs in the front row and yawn at us and buff their nails. People whose seats are in the direct rays of the sun, shining remorselessly through the gaps in the canvas sides, move about, changing their chairs to get into the shade. The actors keep escaping out of their dressing-rooms to gasp for air on the river bank, some half-naked, some half in costume. The girls' elaborate dresses are soiled as they drag their trains in the long grass, and people cannot be found and miss their entrances. One of the actresses slips in front and outrages me by trying to photograph the play from the front in a scene in which she does not appear herself. . . .

A cloudburst descends during the last act, and the open passage behind the stage is deep in water. We pick our way from dressing-rooms and battle on with the final scene, not a word of which can be heard, as the rain is crashing down on the sagging top of the roof where it drums and reverberates unceasingly and drips through the gaps in the canvas. The aisles are running with water, and the audience sit, with their feet tucked under them, preparing to plunge out at the earliest opportunity, with umbrellas at the ready.

An opera singer who was performing in the city of Cork sampled rather too much of the local hospitality one afternoon before the show. His voice and his legs seemed distinctly wobbly during the first act. Since he did not have to appear again until the third act, the theatre manager hoped he would have had time to recover.

But during the interval before the third act the singer was found snoring in his dressing-room, and no amount of shaking or shouting could wake him.

The manager stepped in front of the curtain with an imaginative apology:

'Unfortunately, Mr ---- will be unable to continue his performance tonight, owing to a sudden attack of malaria.'

A voice from the gallery called: 'Bejaysus, I wouldn't mind a bottle of that myself!'

A genteel lady who kept a boarding-house in Ballater, Aberdeenshire, was approached about accommodation for some of the actors arriving with a touring repertory company the following week.

'Actors?' she said. 'Yes, I imagine I could accommodate a few of them. What do they eat?'

Victor Borge on suiting the show to the audience:

You know, I wouldn't go out to Greenland and perform for the Eskimos and do a Mozart opera, because I don't think they have heard one—but if I were to go out in a kayak and turn upside down and stay underwater for ten minutes, I think they would die laughing.

Public Faces

One star with an astute eye for publicity was the Australian singer, Dame Nellie Melba. Claude Kingston, who worked for the J. C. Williamson theatre management—known as 'The Firm'—was in charge of publicity in Sydney during Melba's 1924 tour. He travelled with her from Melbourne, bearing a carefully prepared press release. Dame Nellie tore it up: she had her own ideas of how to get publicity, as he wrote in 'It Don't Seem a Day too Much':

The express stopped at Moss Vale and the reporters crowded into Melba's compartment. She received them with royal graciousness. One of them asked a leading question about the opera season but Melba brushed it aside. 'Bother the opera!' she said. 'What I want to talk about are the fleas on this beastly express. It's alive with them.'

She then told the hard-scribbling reporters that she had not slept a wink because of these voracious fleas. 'I'm bitten all over,' she exclaimed. 'Would you like me to lift my skirts to prove it?'

Nobody was ungallant enough to make her do that. It was just as well, I suspect. No fleas had bitten me and if they had attacked Melba she had not mentioned it until then.

The reporters scuttled away and wired off vivid accounts of Melba's battle with the fleas of the Melbourne-Sydney express. Every newspaper featured the story and plastered Sydney with posters about it. The railway authorities protested that nobody else had complained and said they were mystified why their fleas had singled out Melba, but they undertook to purify the train at once.

Was it legitimate publicity? I prefer to let moralists answer that. All I know is that the talk about Melba's fleas reached a thousand people for every one who would have bothered to read of Toti Dal Monte's dazzling coloratura and that practically not a soul in Sydney or New South Wales was unaware that we had arrived to launch a grand opera season.

But Claude Kingston discovered there was a less showy side to Melba, too:

. . .she had one uncanny gift which I have never met in any other woman or any man. She could work through a sheaf of begging letters quickly and separate the genuine from the bogus without faltering. Being in the public eye, she was a natural target for

both professional cadgers and decent people down on their luck who did not know where to turn for help.

Every morning she would come to my office with the day's collection of letters pleading for aid. She would read them with care, tearing up one with some such remark as, 'I don't like this handwriting or the person behind it. No!' Then perhaps tossing the next one across my desk and saying, 'This woman's in real trouble, Claude. We must help her.' The money she distributed, anything from five to fifty pounds, came out of her own pocket. One day, I remember, the total was more than £400.

I knew better than to gossip about her generosities. 'If you ever mention this to anyone,' she warned me once, 'I'll never speak to you again.'

In 'Life is a Cucumber', Peter Bull wrote:

Being an actor, one is frequently accosted by total strangers who are convinced that they know you personally, having met you on midget screens in lounges, bedrooms or mother-in-law's houses. Usually the encounter starts with a penetrating stare which induces one to think that one may not have adjusted one's dress properly, as is de rigueur in some of the better-class conveniences. After this the braver specimens advance for a verbal attack.

'I know you, don't I?' is a familiar approach. I tend to remain impassive and totally unhelpful, favouring them nonetheless with a quizzical but wry smile.

After several floundering sentences they usually give up and say, 'I know the face but . . .' and their voices trail off, leaving them temporarily at a loss. If they look nice or, I'm afraid, beautiful, I come to their rescue and volunteer my name, but frequently this step is a disaster for both parties. They look even more puzzled and are, I think, convinced that I've given them an alias, and I might tell you that the whole incident isn't inclined to give my morale much of a boost. So I just look sadly at them and slink away, hoping that they may imagine that I'm one of those lovely wrestlers who bite each other on Saturday afternoons, while I am waiting to check my football pools. Funnily enough I did tell one enquirer that I was Tom Jones and he didn't seem in the least surprised. So anything is possible.

In our profession we really are up against it when it comes to the layman (or laywoman if there is such a word) and their idea of what the actor does. 'Do you have to do it every night?' (If it happens to be a West End play.) 'Does the make-up hurt?' and 'How do you know when it's your turn to speak?' are typical examples of the questions one is asked at parties and things. Which reminds me of what Dan Massey said to the silly young girl who asked him at a party, 'Don't you get tired of saying the same thing every night?' Replied Mr Massey, 'Yes, don't you?'

Bruce Forsyth, Sean Connery and Dickie

Henderson were once travelling in a taxi to see a boxing match at Harringay in London. The driver was sure he knew Bruce Forsyth's face and at every halt in traffic or at lights he would turn round and say, 'I know your face. Why don't you tell me who you are? I know your face; I know I've seen you somewhere . . . .' But Bruce Forsyth kept him guessing, saying, 'Never mind about that, we want to get to the fight . . . .'

Eventually they reached Harringay, got out and were paying for the taxi, and the driver was still puzzling: 'I know your face,' he said, 'I've seen your face . . . who are you?'

Bruce Forsyth said, 'Oh, well, all right—I'm Bruce Forsyth.'

The driver said: 'Bruce Forsyth?! That's a laugh—you might just as well say I'm James Bond!'

Sean Connery leaned forward and said: 'No, I'm James Bond!'

Playwrights Ted Willis and Willis Hall are used to confusions about their names, but it must have been a tricky moment for Ted Willis when he attended the opening of a local hall and was expected to react with delight when the surprise announcement was made that the place was going to be named after him: Willis Hall.

When Charles Laughton was starring in 'The Party' at London's New Theatre (now the Albery), the queue for the gallery was entertained one night by a busker doing a very deft soft-shoe shuffle. It was Laughton himself: in spite of his bulk, he was a neat and light-footed dancer and had learned the routine for a Rosemary Clooney TV special. There is no record of how much he earned from the theatre queue.

An elderly and distinguished-looking actor was walking down the street in a small town where a touring company was playing. A man stopped him, peered into his face for a few seconds, then said: 'Weren't you Ernest Milton?'

Punch and Judy

In 1872 Gustave Doré and Blanchard Jerrold published 'London: A Pilgrimage', and Jerrold described a show that rivalled the barrel-organ in popularity.

It is equalled only by the stir and bustle, and cessation of employment, which happen when the man who carries the greasy old stage of Mr Punch, halts at a favourable 'pitch'; and begins to drop the green baize behind which he is to play the oftenest performed serio-comic drama in the world. The milk-woman stops on her rounds: the baker deliberately unshoulders his load: the newsboy (never at a loss for a passage of amusement on his journey) forgets that he is bearer of the 'special edition': the policeman halts on his beat—while the pipes are tuning, and the wooden actors are being made ready within, and dog Toby is staring sadly round upon the mob. We have all confessed to the indefinable witchery of the heartless rogue of the merry eye and ruby nose, whose career—so far as we are permitted to know it—is an unbroken round of facetious brutalities. Wife-beating is second nature to him. To be sure Judy does not look all that man can desire in the partner of his bosom. The dog, indeed, makes the best appearance; and is the most reputable member of this notorious family.

Yet how would a 'goody' Punch and Judy succeed? Make the Mr Punch of the street corner—the high-minded, amiable, distinguished, and elegant gentleman, we have known so many years in Fleet Street. Turn him into a sounding moralist, and give a serious purpose to his shrill voice. Gift his wooden tongue with the unsleeping wit of Shirley Brooks. I believe the milkmaid would hook her pails, at the first passage of the play: the newsboy would deliver the special edition forthwith.

. . . surely he is the very merriest fellow—the truest benefactor—that has ever paced the hard streets of London! We should call blessings down upon the man who wakes those shrill pipes, and sounds the rub-a-dub that quickens the pulses of the infant poor—of this ragged nurse of nakedness, dreaming in the street! He is comedy, farce and extravaganza to his audiences—
Shakespeare and Molière, Morton and Planché. Many strangers with whom I have lingered over the great street comedy, have surveyed the tiers of pale faces, from the babes pushed to the front to the working men and women in the rear, and have exclaimed that it was a terrible sight. Laughter sounded unnatural from the colourless lips. To take the cause of this smile from them, because there are fastidious ears which shrink at the sharpness of the street pipes, would be a downright cruelty and shame.

57. A Punch and Judy show in a London street, 1900

Radio Dramas

In the days when radio plays were broadcast live, actors had to be as ingenious as they must be on stage in covering up mistakes such as sound effects that don't materialise at the right moment. This was what the listening audience heard at a dramatic moment in an American gangster play:

'No, no. Spike—don't shoot! I didn't tell the cops, Spike, honest I didn't. Put that gun away, Spike....'

'Shut up, you dirty double-crossing little rat! This is curtains for you. Take that!'
(Silence)
'I said, take that, you dirty rat!'
(Silence)
'OK, now I've got the safety catch off. So—take that!'
(Silence)
'OK, I changed my mind. I'm gonna stab you with my knife! Take that!'
(Sudden gun-shot)
'Ah, the hell with it!'

And in those days of live broadcasting, it was often the practice to allow an actor who was only in one of the early scenes to go off home after doing his bit. One actor with a small part in 'Saturday Night Theatre' finished his scene, looked enquiringly at the producer through the glass of the control room, and saw the producer smile and nod at him. He duly left the studio, got into his car and set off home, listening to the remainder of the play on the radio as he drove.

Suddenly he heard the cue coming up for his one line in the last scene....

Martin Esslin, former head of BBC radio drama, commented on the musical structure of drama on radio in 'The Mind As A Stage':

The radio play approximates musical form—which is not surprising as both have sounds in time as their raw material. A good radio dramatist will have an over-all formal concept of his piece: he will know where his slow movement will be and where his scherzo, where he can pull out the stops and where the soft passages will come.

Equally, in approaching his characters, the radio dramatist must think musically: their voices are the instruments at his disposal, how will he orchestrate them? In the BBC's archives there is a long letter from Bernard Shaw in which that old music critic advises a producer how to cast a radio performance of 'St Joan': this character is a baritone, that one a light tenor, a third a contralto, etc. And there is good practical sense in that approach: nothing will confuse the listener more than two characters with very similar voices.

Of course, there are other and subtler ways of characterization as well: in radio more than in any other kind of dialogue the speech patterns, vocabulary, accent and linguistic idiosyncrasy of each character is the hallmark of the good writer. The most primitive way to achieve such linguistic characterization is the introduction of regional accents: hence the Scottish housekeeper, the cockney bus-driver, the exaggeratedly well-spoken butler are the clichés of radio drama. But in the hands of the best writers, like Pinter or Arden, the differentiation of characters by their language is on an altogether different level. Certainly, writing for radio is an excellent training for any dramatist: it prevents him from relying lazily on his actors' appearance or personality to save him from characterizing his creatures by endowing each of them with his own peculiar way of speaking.

And on the use of sound effects:

Excessive reliance on sound effects is a sure indication of radio drama at a fairly primitive level. The trouble with the sounds we hear in nature or in daily life is that, being often associated with visual impressions, they are not always easy to recognize when merely heard. One often comes across radio scripts from beginners which try to locate the action of a play by, for example, starting with: 'Sounds of a cotton mill.' The author thinks that this will be sufficient to tell all his listeners that the action takes place in such a factory. Yet a cotton mill probably sounds exactly the same as a toy factory or, indeed, a threshing machine, or the engines of an ocean liner. Most sound effects of this kind only come to dramatic life after the listener has been told what they represent.

There are exceptions, of course. Seagulls always suggest the sea (but probably only because repeated use in radio plays has made them into an aural cliché, an acoustic ideogram!) Curiously enough, so strong is the suggestive power of the word, that a hint in the dialogue often does more than the actual sound effect. It has happened to me that listeners have complimented me on the marvellous sound effects of the sea or the woods in a play I produced, when in fact I had not used any sound effects at all, but the dialogue had referred to the roar of the waves or the song of the birds.

Although it is a young medium, radio, like the theatre, has its quota of classic anecdotes and incidents. One of them concerns the large room where the spot effects equipment was kept. These effects are ones made by a technician in the studio, 'on the spot', instead of being played in from recordings: they could be anything from creaking doors to footsteps or champagne bottles being opened—by means of a cork stuck in the end of a bicycle pump. Among the items in this Aladdin's cave of noise-making bric-a-brac were all kinds of locks, hinges, latches and door-knobs, attached to bits of door-frame and kept lovingly in rusty condition so that they would creak and groan convincingly whenever required to do so.

One night, a keen new security man was doing his rounds and looked into this room. Having some time on his hands, he decided to be helpful and carefully oiled all the locks and hinges.

His sense of a job well done would have been shattered next day had he been there to see an enraged and distraught studio manager, trying to select the right gear for eerie creaking doors and ghastly noises in the 'haunted castle' play for which he was making the spot effects.

Michael Redgrave

Michael Redgrave made his first London appearance at the Old Vic:

In those early days I know I often took too much for granted. After two years at the Liverpool Repertory Theatre I was 'spotted' by Tyrone Guthrie and found myself at the Old Vic, playing parts like Laertes and Orlando.

If anyone should claim to have witnessed a tall young man wearing a raincoat, green tights and a flaming red wig, jogging across Waterloo Bridge about eight o'clock of a December Saturday evening in 1936, I would willingly believe him.

I had discovered that in the uncut or 'eternity' 'Hamlet', Laertes has about two hours' wait between his departure for England in Scene Two and his return leading the rebellion in Act Four. At first I tried to keep 'in the mood'. I found I could do this for about twenty minutes. Reading a book or writing letters didn't help much—I suppose I was itching to get on with the play. I drank cup after cup of coffee in the cabmen's shelter across the road from the stage door. This gave me sleepless nights. Then I remembered that at the end of the Waterloo Road was Waterloo Bridge and beyond Waterloo Bridge stood the Gaiety Theatre where Leslie Henson—one of our great comics—was playing in 'Seeing Stars'. I took careful note of the time and then started off at a trot for the Gaiety. I reached the gallery entrance door which was open and I slipped inside, climbed the long staircase and was watching the great Leslie. A surprise visitor in 'the gods'. I did this several times and never suffered a jot of conscience since I was never caught.

But what if I had been? I would rather not think of it. I recount the story as an example of extremely unprofessional behaviour. Perhaps the worst aspect of the whole escapade was that I was putting my fellow actors in a terrifying situation. What would have happened?

I don't think I should have been long at the Old Vic.

Michael Redgrave also wrote in 'The Actor's Ways and Means':

. . . so often the actor who excels in certain aspects of his craft is tempted to rely more and more on what comes most easily to him. A well-placed, resonant and pleasing voice has been the downfall of many. It can be almost as fatal as an exquisite face and a beautiful body. When the actor has gained some mastery of the essential qualifications, his difficulties have only just begun. He must in the first place strengthen his mastery of all these things so that in each of them he can feel a great reserve of power and then he must, by his intelligence or taste, know how not to use these powers to the full. He must know, in fact, what to leave out.

58. Michael Redgrave and Wanda Rotha in 'Hamlet'

Rehearsals

59. A nineteenth-century illustration of a theatrical rehearsal

Thomas Snagge, in 'Recollections of Occurrences':

To avoid rehearsing at the Inn and making my abilities a laugh for the waiters or chambermaids, I retired to the convenient fields in the neighbourhood and most opportunely discovered a delightful covered (tho' the sides were open) cow-house, where I thought I might bellow like any bull without the least disturbance to anyone.

Here, with becoming consequence, I drew forth my book, studied, rehearsed and practised attitudes with dignity, secrecy and a striving emulation to excel. I had done this once or twice and been only observed by a cow-boy, who, when he saw me, bowed and retired. Again I essayed, and really grew in my own estimation, thus proceeding the third day through that long part of Archer and had arrived at the Robber's scene and

roaring to protect Mrs Sullen, when turning my head around, at a little distance behind a beech I espied a knot of boors, cottage wenches and clodpoles. Heaven knows how long they had been spectators, but so unexpected a discovery discomposed and threw me into amazement.

In Henry Mayhew's 'London Labour and the London Poor' an actor describes the manager of a touring troupe dishing out the parts for a play called 'The Floating Beacon, or the Weird Woman of the Wreck'. He sketches out the plot and characters, and the actors are expected to improvise their lines:

Then the manager turns to Ormaloff and Augerstoff, and says: 'Now, you two play the smugglers, do you hear? You're to try and poison the young fellow, and you're defeated.'

Then he says to the wild woman: 'You're kept as a prisoner aboard the beacon, where

your husband has been murdered. You have refused to become the wife of Ormaloff. Your child has been thrown overboard. You discover him in Frederick, and you scream when they are about to stab him, and also when he's about to drink. Make as much of it as you can, please; and don't forget the scream.'

'You're to play the lady, you Miss. You're in love with Frederick. You know the old business: ''What! to part thus? Alas! alas! never to this moment have I confessed I love you!'''

That's a true picture of a mumming rehearsal, whether it's fair or private business. Some of the young chaps stick in their parts. They get the stage-fever and knocking in the knees. We've had to shove them on to the scene. They keep on asking what they're to say. 'Oh, say anything!' we tell 'em, and push 'em on to the stage.

If a man's not gifted with the gab, he's no good at a booth. I've been with a chap acting 'Mary Woodbine', and he hasn't known a word of his part. Then, when he's stuck, he has seized me by the throat, and said, 'Caitiff! dog! be sure thou provest my wife unfaithful to me.' Then I saw his dodge, and I said, 'Oh, my lord!' and he continued—'Give me proof, or thou hadst best been born a dog.' Then I answered, 'My lord, you wrong your wife, and torture me;' and he said, 'Forward, then, liar! dog!' and we both rushed off.

Reviews

When John Holloway and Matheson Lang took a touring company to India, they found that their greatest success with the critics was in Bombay. There was a good reason for this, as David Holloway wrote in 'Playing the Empire':

John had an extra duty added to his many others when he contacted the newspaper offices about seats for their critics. The editors of the Bombay papers told him that as King George V and Queen Mary were in the country for the Royal Durbah all their staff men were fully occupied, but that they would be happy to print any notices that he cared to send in. So as each new production opened, and they changed the bill every other night, John had to sit down to write three different reviews which after the show he would send round to the newspaper offices, where they were duly printed in full. It was an interesting exercise in the rationing of superlatives, so that the same ones did not appear in all the papers. Lang, who was not aware of what was happening, was more than satisfied with the notices, though he did think that the critic on one Bombay paper seemed less perceptive than the others.

The 'Sydney Herald' published this in a review of 'Othello' in 1838:

We would recommend Mr Arabin to cure himself of that vile habit—so common to our colonial actors and actresses—of addressing soliloquies and dialogues directly to the audience.

Eric Bentley wrote:

At first blush Mr Capote's play 'The Grass Harp' is simply ridiculous: it is about living in trees. But it is saved from the ridiculous by the trite when, late in the evening, the conclusion is announced: 'We can't live in trees, maybe some of us would like to, but none of us can.'

Two of the briefest and most damning reviews ever published were of Broadway

61. An old macaroni critic at a new play

productions. A show called 'Wham!' drew the response: 'Ouch!' And the play 'I Am a Camera' was reviewed by one critic thus: '"I Am A Camera": No Leica.'

Some nineteenth-century pantomimes had their own 'rave reviews' attached to the title:

'Little Jack Horner; or, Harlequin ABC and the Enchanted Region of Nursery Rhymes' ...an entirely Allegorical, Beautiful, Comical, Diverting, Educational, Fanciful, Gorgeous, Hyperbolical, Intellectual, Jovial, Keen, Laughable, Merry, Novel, Original, Peculiar, Quizzical, Romantic, Splendid, Transcendental, Unobjectionable, Volatile, Waggish, X-travagant, Youthful, and Zigzaggy pantomime.

In 'Mink Coats and Barbed Wire', Ruth Kaminska describes how in 1941 she was in a revue company touring the Soviet Union. It was suddenly summoned to the Black Sea resort of Sochi and flown there by special plane. At the hotel, the company manager spoke to them with nervous excitement:

'Tomorrow, you must be excellent. Give every bit of your talent. Mobilize all of your possibilities. And now—now, please go to your rooms and try to have a good night's rest.' He was still sitting in the puddle formed by the water dripping from his clothes when the last of the company left. His jaw quivered and he began to cry.

'Adi Ignatzevich! Ruth Zigmundovna! Tomorrow will be the biggest day in my life—in all of our lives! I cannot say anything more.'

We hardly slept that night. By morning, everything was dry and the sun was shining. Our technical staff had been at the theatre for hours. We would be escorted there at 5.30. 'Be sure to bring your identification documents with you,' we were told.

That evening at the stage door, NKVD (secret police) officers and civilians checked each of us. One officer looked at the pictures on our documents and compared them with our faces. Another inspected pockets and handbags, still another checked our names on a list. When we were allowed to enter the theatre, the atmosphere was so tense that we avoided speaking to each other even in our dressing-rooms.

Curtain time. The lights went on. The curtain rose. Before us was an empty theatre. Only the closed curtains of the boxes at the sides of the stage indicated that this was not some ghastly joke.

Any performer—but especially a musical revue performer—needs a live audience. We spent two hours delivering jokes without getting a laugh, two hours singing songs and playing music followed by silence. When the reverberations of our imposing brass and tympani sections finally subsided and the curtain rang down, there were no curtain calls. We left the theatre in dispirited silence.

None of us slept that night. Some timidly knocked on colleagues' doors and tried to make jokes to break the sombre mood, but their humour fell with a thud.

Our manager, who had not bothered to reserve a room for himself, sat in our room, still wearing his raincoat and hat. His fingers drumming on the desk, he got more on our nerves every moment. From time to time, he rose and paced the floor with his hands behind his back, occasionally taking off his hat to scratch his head.

'If only I could get drunk,' he said, hollow-voiced. Two minutes later he repeated, 'If only I could get drunk.'

At 6 a.m., the funereal atmosphere was shattered by the telephone's ring. We jumped. Our manager reached for it with a shaking hand. His first 'hello' stuck so deep in his throat that he coughed and started again.

Then he removed his hat, wiped his forehead and the back of his neck with his handkerchief, and stood stiffly as he spoke.

'Yes, Comrade,' he whispered.

'Yes, Comrade.'

'Thank you, Comrade.'

'Thank you!'

'Thank you! Many thanks!!'

After he hung up, he remained silent, staring at the phone. Then he said softly, 'I have been told the Boss liked the performance.'

Then, seeming to grow taller, he said loudly, 'Now, we are really in business!'

Nobody to this day has told us that we had performed for Josef Vissarionovich Stalin—the Boss.

Royal Command

Charles II was a frequent visitor to the public theatres, helping to make the stage fashionable as an entertainment for the gentry, according to Arthur Bryant in 'King Charles II':

In July Charles took his aunt of Bohemia—who had once seen Shakespeare's plays acted in his own lifetime for her girlish delight—to witness Davenant's 'Siege of Rhodes', at the new Opera House in Lincoln's Inn Fields. The theatre was packed, and the long wait before the royal party arrived was enlivened by the breaking of a board overhead, which precipitated a great deal of dust down the ladies' necks, making, as one present records, good sport. The show itself was magnificent and well acted, all but the eunuch—a naturally unpopular part—who was hissed off the stage.

When Dryden's play 'The Spanish Friar' was revived for Queen Mary in 1686, her reaction was troubled at times:

Some unhappy expressions put her into the greatest disorder, and frequently forced her to hold up her fan and often look behind and call for her palatine and hood, or anything she could think of.

During the period of mental illness suffered by George III, the theatres tactfully refrained from putting on any production of 'King Lear'.

Sarah Siddons:

The Royal family very frequently honoured me with their presence. The King was often moved to tears which he as often vainly endeavoured to conceal behind his eye-glass, and Her Majesty the Queen, at one time told me in her gracious broken English that her only refuge from me was actually turning her back upon the stage at the same time protesting, 'It is indeed too disagreeable.'

In 'Queen Victoria was Amused' Alan Hardy says Queen Victoria was a keen theatregoer, and went to see Shakespeare, French plays and even melodramas like 'The Corsican Brothers', in spite of criticism that such melodramatic fare was not seemly. She and Albert had a small theatre specially built at Windsor Castle, where they watched performances of Shakespeare and other classic plays. But she certainly had a taste for light-hearted entertainment and was more easily amused than she is often given credit for. One of her court ladies recorded:

I went with the Queen and the Prince last night to the Haymarket Theatre to see the 'Beef and Orange', a fairy tale plot, and awfully stupid, as Lady Canning and I agreed, but the Royal couple laughed very much and seemed to enjoy it of all things. It is certainly a nice thing about them that they are so easily amused.

After Albert's death in 1861 Queen Victoria

never went to a public theatre again, though she did attend musical performances at the Albert Hall and special concerts at Windsor by such composers and musicians as Grieg, Paderewski and Pablo Casals. She started bringing theatrical performances to the castle again, after the Prince of Wales in 1889 brought a company led by Henry Irving and Ellen Terry to Sandringham. The Queen wrote down her enthusiastic reaction in her diary:

The stage was beautifully arranged and with great scenic effects, and the pieces were splendidly mounted and with numbers of people taking part. . . . The piece, 'The Bells', is a melodrama and is very thrilling. The hero (Irving), though a mannerist of the Macready type, acted wonderfully. He is a murderer, and frequently imagines he hears the bells of the horses in the sledge, in which sat the Polish Jew, who is murdered. The way in which Irving acted his own dream, and describes the way in which he carried out the murder, is wonderful and ghastly, as well as the scene at his death. He had carried his secret about with him for thirteen years! . . . it was a most successful performance.

Queen Victoria's old age was enlivened by her delight in amateur theatricals, and she encouraged her grandchildren, and members of the Royal household to put on shows:

As well as extracting the maximum enjoyment from both rehearsals and actual productions the Queen took a keen interest in the plots and language of the plays. With her dislike of vulgarity and indelicacy she did not hesitate to make alterations where it suited her. Since most of these amateur productions were already English variations on the original French plays additional changes could, Arthur Ponsonby discovered, lead to ridiculous situations:

The play was a translation of a French piece called L'Homme Blasé. When the cast was made up but before they knew their parts the Queen bade them perform before her. She was amused; but finding that Princess Beatrice who had a good part in the first act did not come on again, she ordered Colonel Collins to rewrite the last act so that she might reappear. On this Major Bigge writes: 'I think Collins ought to have added to the printed description in the programme: The return and reconciliation of Mrs Ironbrace is by command!'

To begin with, the marriages in the acted version were an insertion. In the original French there were none! This much amused the Empress Eugénie who was present.

Oxford in the sixteenth and seventeenth centuries used to honour Royal visits by staging a special play or masque performed by the students. There was a bit of a gap in the tradition after Charles I's visit in 1636—a gap of over three centuries. The custom was revived in 1948 when the Queen, then Princess Elizabeth, visited University College. Neville Coghill wrote 'The Masque of Hope', an allegorical work which featured a fight between two characters called Black Market and Young Sterling, as well as more conventional figures such as Neptune, Venus and Hymen. The masque was performed by the Oxford University Dramatic Society, and in the cast were John Schlesinger as Black Market and Kenneth Tynan as Fear. Towards the end, the great age of the first Queen Elizabeth is celebrated in fawning couplets:

Under her rule this Island was secure,
Her honour bright and her religion pure.
Under her rule the roving sailors pressed.
To pearly Orient and golden West.
Under her rule LEARNING and ART arose
In Spenser's poetry and Bacon's prose.
What more is there to say in this recital?
This! She was SHAKESPEARE'S FRIEND. Her
        proudest title!

Saints and Sinners

There could hardly be a worse disaster than that which overtook the actor Genesius, as Donald Attwater wrote in 'A Dictionary of Saints':

The story told of him is that, in the course of an entertainment given to Diocletian in Rome, he played the part of a candidate in a mocking representation of Christian baptism. But the grace of God touched him, and when afterwards he was presented to the emperor he declared that he had suddenly been converted to Christ during the performance. He was therefore put to the torture; but he would not recant, and so his head was struck off. The same or a similar story is told of three other actor martyrs (Aradalio, Gelasius of Heliopolis, and a Porphyry), and in every case it is probably fictitious. Whether there ever was a martyr named Genesius at Rome has not been decided for certain. The legend has attracted and been turned to account by several dramatists and musicians, among them Lope de Vega, Jean de Rotrou, Karl Lowe, Felix Weingartner, and Henri Gheon.

God was of course a principal character in the medieval mystery or guild plays, and there were no inhibitions about representing him or Jesus as characters in the drama. (It is curious to think that centuries later, in the 1940s, the idea of an actor playing Jesus even on the radio caused quite a furore before the production of Dorothy Sayers' 'The Man Born to be King'.)

In the guild plays there are dramatic scenes like the Harrowing of Hell, when 'Jesus enters through the gates of Hell, that open before his voice'.

The plays were prestigious events for the towns that staged them, and if production or acting were slipshod, there were penalties imposed. At Beverley in Yorkshire in 1452, a weaver called Henry Cowper was fined more than six shillings for not knowing his part—a sum that would have represented more than ten times his daily wage at the time.

To encourage good performances, the actors were paid, though the sum varied according to the part. The records at Coventry show that Pilate got five shillings, and one shilling each went to Caiaphas, Annas and the two Maries. Demons were paid one shilling and four pence, and Souls, whether saved or damned, received one shilling and eight pence.

The people in charge of the stage effects were rewarded too. Four pence went to the man who imitated the cock crowing, and the same to another man 'for keeping of fire at hell mouth'. But someone else got five pence 'for setting the world on fire'. More constructively, two shillings were 'paid to Crowe for making of three worlds'. A world was destroyed at each performance, usually by fire, and the end of the world and Day of Judgement scenes were the great climax of the show.

There begynneth a treatyse how ý hye fader of heuen sendeth dethe to somon euery creature to come and gyue a counte of theyr lyues in this worlde/and is in maner of a morall playe.

62. An illustration from the first page of the morality play 'Everyman', from the Britwell copy

This is the finale of the scene in 'The Play of Coventry'—splendidly dramatic even now; and it must have been even more thrilling and chilling to the strongly believing audiences of the time:

ALL THE RISEN SOULS CRY. Ah, mercy. Lord, for
    our misdeeds,
And let thy mercy spring and spread!
But alas! we bide in dread
It is too late to ask mercy.
GOD APPEARS ON HIGH, AND SPEAKS. Venite,
    benedicti,
My brethren all,
Ye children dear,
Come hither to me to mine hall;
All my suitors and servants to be,
And all the foul worms from you fall.
With my right hand I bless you here.
My blessing burnished you as bright as
    beryl,
As crystal clear it cleanseth you clean,
All filth from you fade.
Peter, to heaven's gates wend thou and go,
The locks thou loosen and them undo,
My blessed children thou bring me to
Their hearts for to glad.
PETER. The gates of heaven I open this tide:
Now welcome, dear brethren, to heaven
    i-wis;
Come on, and sit on God's right side,
Where mirth and melody never may miss.
THE SAVED SOULS. On knee we creep, we go,
    we glide,
To worship our Lord that merciful is;
For through his wounds that be so wide
He hath brought us to his bliss.
Holy Lord, we worship thee!
GOD. Welcome ye be in heaven to sit,
Welcome, from me shall ye never flit,
So sure of bliss ye shall be yet,
To mirth and joy welcome ye be!
THE DAMNED SOULS. Ah, ah! Mercy we cry
    and crave,
Ah! mercy, Lord, for our misdeed!
Ah! mercy, mercy, we rubbe! we rave!
Ah! help us, good Lord, in this need!
GOD. How would ye, wretches, and mercy
    have?
Why ask ye mercy now in this need?
What have ye wrought your souls to save?
To whom have ye done any merciful deed,
Mercy for to win?
FIRST DEVIL. Mercy? nay, nay, they shall
    have wreck,

And that on their foreheads witness I take,
For there is written with letters black,
Openly, all their sin.
GOD. To hungry and thirsty that asked in
    my name,
Meat and drink would ye give none;
Of naked men had ye no shame,
Ye would not clothe men in any prison;
Ye had no pity on sick or lame,
Deeds of mercy would ye never do.
These works do you fordo.
For your love's sake I was rent on the
    cross,
And for your sake I shed my blood.
When I was so merciful and so good,
Why have ye wrought against my will?
SECOND DEVIL. I find here written on thy
    forehead,
Thou wert so stout and set in pride,
Thou wouldst not give a poor man bread,
But from thy door thou wouldst him chide.
THIRD DEVIL. And in thy face I here do read,
That if a thirsty man come any tide,
Drink from him thou wouldst ever hide;
On covetousness was all thy thought.
FOURTH DEVIL. The sin of sloth thy soul shall
    curse,
Mass nor matins wouldst thou none hear,
To bring the dead man thou wouldst not
    went,
Therefore thou goest to endless fire.
THE DAMNED SOULS. Ah, mercy, lord, mighty
    of power,
We ask thy mercy and not by right.
Now after our deed, so us requite;
We have sinned, we are to blame.

Some of the most sonorous and dramatic stage directions occur in those medieval mystery plays. They have a splendid finality and certainty about them:

God returns to heaven, and an angel seraph with a flaming sword drives Adam and Eve from Paradise.

All the Souls shall rise from their graves, whilst the earth quakes and the world is consumed by fire. As they rise they cry: 'Ah, ah, ah! Ah, ah, ah!'

Scenes of Splendour

Some bizarre and accidental sights could be seen sometimes in the early eighteenth-century theatres, as when Richard Steele saw a play when they forgot to change half the scenery between acts:

We were presented with a prospect of the Ocean in the midst of a delightful Grove; and though the Gentlemen on the stage had very much contributed to the beauty of the Grove by walking up and down between the trees, I must own I was not a little astonished to see a well-dressed young fellow in a full-bottomed wig, appear in the midst of the sea, and without any visible concern, taking snuff.

Like the movie moguls of Hollywood later on, the managers of Victorian theatres kept trying for more and more lavish spectacle. Augustus Harris was the co-author with Henry Pettitt of 'Pluck' in 1882, and the scenes in this play include a house on fire, a snow storm, the heroine in a carriage with real horses, a double train crash, and an angry mob attacking a bank and smashing the glass windows.

And, according to 'The Story of Pantomime' by A. E. Wilson, at Drury Lane, no pantomime was complete for Harris without the most elaborate processions:

He was never at a loss for an excuse to introduce a procession. In one pantomime there would be a gorgeous parade of 'remarkable women of all ages' from Semiramis, Queen of Babylon, to Napoleon's Josephine. In another there was a procession representing the heroines of Shakespeare's plays. Yet another introduced representatives of England's worldwide possessions, beginning with the annexation of India and ending with a general tribute to Britain from her numerous colonies and dependencies.

On one occasion there was an unending parade representing twenty-one English sports; on another a procession introducing all the Kings and Queens of England, with their courts and attendants. For this display (which must have given the children the idea that instead of being entertained by pantomime fun they were being given a history lesson) Sir Augustus had consulted every learned authority in order that the detail might be correct, for he was always insistent upon strict accuracy.

There was a procession representing twenty-four different nations one Christmastide. There were Tartar maidens in amber silk and furs, girls from Cochin China in creamy robes and feathered headdresses, Lapps in white furs, Japanese in embroidered purple, girls from China in terra-cotta and gold robes, Greek damsels in classic draperies, Spanish señoritas in black lace mantillas, Americans in stars and stripes—all this to introduce the famous Marie Lloyd as Princess Allfair in bridal array.

In 'Ali Baba and the Forty Thieves' the stage was filled with three or four hundred people representing the invasion of the robbers' den. Each of the forty thieves was

63. 'Aladdin and the Wonderful Lamp' at Covent Garden, mid nineteenth century

accompanied by a train of ten or twelve people!

This was one of Augustus Harris's spectacular sequences for 'Aladdin', starting off in a swamp:

In truth it is a dismal place. Monstrous creatures crawl about in it; great bats flap their lazy wings. The Demon who owns the freehold of this undesirable site and who appears as a gigantic frog, is disinclined to part with his rights. He has therefore to be fought and overcome by another demon and a tremendous combat ensues, the rival demons appearing and disappearing through traps with lightning speed. In the end the demon frog is vanquished and Aladdin is free to proceed with his palatial schemes.

A further rub of the magic lamp changes the swamp into a fertile plain with a lake in the background. Myriads of tiny British workmen troop in and, having erected a hoarding with the strange device 'Gusarris, Builder and Decorator', proceed to build a palace behind it. When the scaffolding is removed is seen a beautiful palace with a practicable bridge which provides a picturesque route for the brilliant procession of Aladdin's retainers.

The theatres which staged Victorian melodramas certainly spared no expense when it came to stage machinery and spectacular effects. James L. Smith gave this account in 'Victorian Melodramas':

The stage floor could be raised or sunk in sections, allowing snowdrifts to pile up over alpine cottages and giant rocks to sink into a sea of green-gauze waves. Back scenes could be flown or sunk, or divide in two and do both simultaneously. The diorama, a backcloth painted on long strips of canvas wound between two vertical rollers, enabled characters to travel from Paris to Vienna in full view of the audience. Sometimes sections of the floor were replaced by laths of wood glued on to canvas loops to form caterpillar tracks; armies could march for miles on them, and horses gallop at full stretch without stirring from the spot. Fix the track to an ascending trap, and ghosts or visions can glide sideways as they rise up through the floor. Gas lighting, introduced in the first quarter of the century, brought with it undreamed wonders. Buildings painted on transparent gauze dissolve at once by turning up the light behind them, and reappear when it is dimmed. Fog effects are made by stretching gauze across the arch of the proscenium, towers drawn on thin wooden blocks collapse in ruins when a string is pulled, and flames are red silk streamers agitated by a fan. The results were certainly spectacular. The villain in MacFarren's 'Malvina' (1826) falls into an 'extensive mountain torrent', ships sink in flames in Fitzball's 'The Red Rover' (1829), an earthquake destroys an amphitheatre in Medina's 'The Last Days of Pompeii' (1834), and in Boucicault's 'Pauvrette' (1858) an avalanche 'entirely buries the whole scene to the height of twelve or fifteen feet'. When poor Lina is trapped on a cliff-ledge in 'The Harbour Lights', the tide rises, the cliff sinks, a wave sweeps her out to sea, and she is rescued by a passing boat. 'Masaniello' shows Vesuvius in eruption: 'The crater of the volcano emits torrents of flame and smoke—forked lightnings rend the sky in every direction.... A terrific explosion ensues from the mountain, the lava impetuously flows down its side, and extends itself into the sea.—The people, awe-struck, bend in submission to the will of heaven, and the curtain slowly descends.'

But this is nothing compared to Moncrieff's 'The Cataract of the Ganges' (1823), which winds up with an orgy of fire, horses and real water:

As the scene draws, the whole of the Trees are discovered in flames.... The burning trees fall on all sides, and discover the terrific Cataract of Gangotri, supposed to form the source of the Ganges. The Emperor and the Bramin's troops appear, pouring down the rocky heights around the Cataract in every direction.... Zamine mounts the courser of Iran, and while he keeps the foe at bay, dashes safely up the Cataract, amidst a volley of musketry from the Enemy on the heights.... The contest becomes general—horse and foot are engaged in all parts.... Iran brings forward Zamine in safety—the Rajah joins their hands—and the Curtain falls on the shouts of the Conquerors.

The nineteenth-century audiences in London were well provided with spectacle. Besides the Gothic melodrama, they could see battle spectaculars, many of them staged in a circus ring and full of charging horses, thundering cannons and battling armies. One celebrated theatre concentrated on watery themes, described by Michael Booth in 'Hiss the Villain':

Sadler's Wells in the first decade of the nineteenth century called itself the Aquatic Theatre, and put on 'The Battle of Trafalgar', 'The Battle of the Nile', and other marine spectacles. For these a water tank a hundred by forty feet was constructed, and models of hundred-gun ships cannonaded one another, burned, and sank, with satisfying effect. As might be imagined, such spectacles were staged with maximum sound and action, even in small theatres. A manager of a fit-up company remembers that in 'The Fall of Sebastopol' he appeared as an English sergeant, 'and defended myself, amid shot and shell, against six of the enemy at one time'. No opportunity for noise was neglected:

During the siege there would be some fifty persons upon the stage blazing away at each other, and so filling the booth with smoke with their red-hot shot and shells, that the audience had to hopelessly abandon itself to coughing and sneezing for fully ten minutes after the ramparts of Sebastopol had been destroyed.

64. The Battle of Actium, a scene from 'Antony and Cleopatra', Drury Lane Theatre, 1873

In 'Theatre in Australia' Allan Aldous wrote that in the 1890s, Australian playwrights had great success with dramas that had Australian settings and spectacular effects:

Their plays were dotted with impressive spectacles, such as holding up a gold escort, a corroboree, bush fires, and real horse races on the stage. One play, 'The Double Event, or a Tale of the Melbourne Cup', was blurbed: 'In the Great Cup Scene no less than twenty thoroughbred horses will compete and all the accessories of lawn and paddock will be reproduced with lifelike fidelity.' Some of these early Australian plays even anticipated the Left-wing New Theatre movements by presenting plays such as 'Work and Wages', which was all about iron-workers, black-hearted capitalists and dirty blacklegs.

Bland Holt, especially, made spectacle a feature of his productions at the Melbourne Royal. On one occasion he hung a skydrop on the buildings on the opposite side of Little Bourke Street. The big doors at the back of the stage were opened and the Melbourne Hunt raced down the street in full cry and in full view of the audience. Passers-by made buckshee supers, although Holt had no worries in that direction. He frequently put a hundred of them on the stage at a bob per nob per night.

And when Richard Flanagan staged 'As You Like It' in the 1920s at the Queen's Theatre, Manchester, he had a cast of 250, a water-lily pond with real water and real deer roaming the forest.

William Shakespeare

Robert Greene, 'Greene's Groats-worth of Wit bought with a Million of Repentance', 1592:

...there is an upstart Crow, beautified with our feathers, that with his Tiger's heart wrapped in a Player's hide, supposes he is as well able to bombast out a blank verse as the best of you: and being an absolute Iohannes fac totum, is in his own conceit the only Shake-scene in a country.

John Milton, 'L' Allegro':

Then to the well-trod stage anon,
If Jonson's learned sock be on,
Or sweetest Shakespeare, Fancy's child,
Warble his native wood-notes wild...

John Milton, 'On Shakespeare':

What needs my Shakespeare for his
        honoured bones
The labour of an age in piled stones?
Or that his hallowed reliques should be hid
Under a starry-pointing pyramid?
Dear son of memory, great heir of fame,
What need'st thou such weak witness of thy
        name?
Thou in our wonder and astonishment
Hast built thyself a livelong monument.

Dr Samuel Johnson, a Prologue at the opening of the Drury Lane theatre:

When learning's triumph o'er her barbarous
        foes
First rear'd the stage, immortal Shakespeare
        rose;
Each change of many-coloured life he drew,

Exhausted worlds, and then imagined new:
Existence saw him spurn her bounded reign,
And panting Time toiled after him in vain.

William Basse:

Renowned Spenser, lie a thought more nigh
To learned Chaucer, and rare Beaumont lie
A little nearer Spenser, to make room
For Shakespeare, in your threefold, fourfold
        tomb.

Samuel Pepys:

To the King's Theatre, where we saw 'Midsummer Night's Dream', which I had never seen before, nor shall ever again, for it is the most insipid, ridiculous play that ever I saw in my life.

John Evelyn:

I saw 'Hamlet Prince of Denmark', played; but now the old plays begin to disgust this refined age.

Thomas Rymer, on 'Othello':

In the neighing of an horse, or in the growling of a mastiff, there is meaning, there is as lively expression, and, may I say, more humanity, than many times in the tragical flights of Shakespeare....

So much ado, so much stress, so much passion and repetition about an handkerchief! Why was not this called 'The Tragedy of the Handkerchief'? Had it been Desdemona's garter, the sagacious Moor might have smelt a rat; but the handkerchief

65. Shakespeare by Martin Droeshout

is so remote a trifle, no Booby, on this side of Mauritania, could make any consequence from it.

Arthur Murphy, 'The Apprentice':

Aye, that damned Shakespeare! I hear the fellow was nothing but a deer-stealer in Warwickshire. Zookers! If they had hanged him out of the way, he would not now be the ruin of honest men's children. But what right had he to read Shakespeare? I never read Shakespeare! Wounds! I caught the rascal, myself, reading that nonsensical play of 'Hamblet', where the prince is keeping company with strollers and vagabonds: a fine example, Mr Gargle!

A nineteenth-century American theatregoer:

Shakespeare, Madam, is obscene, and, thank God, we are sufficiently advanced to have found it out.

'On the Tragedies of Shakespeare'—Charles Lamb thought Shakespeare too good to be acted:

...to see Lear acted—to see an old man tottering about the stage with a walking-stick, turned out of doors by his daughters in a rainy night, has nothing in it but what is painful and disgusting. We want to take him into shelter and relieve him. That is all the feeling which the acting of Lear ever produced in me. But the Lear of Shakespeare cannot be acted. The contemptible machinery by which they mimic the storm which he goes out in, is not more inadequate to represent the horrors of the real elements, than any actor can be to represent Lear; they might more easily propose to personate the Satan of Milton upon a stage, or one of Michael Angelo's terrible figures. The greatness of Lear is not in corporal dimension, but in intellectual: the explosions of his passion are terrible as a volcano; they are storms turning up and disclosing to the bottom that sea, his mind, with all its vast riches. It is his mind which is laid bare. This case of flesh and blood seems too insignificant to be thought on; even as he himself neglects it. On the stage we see nothing but corporal infirmities and weakness, the impotence of rage; while we read it, we see not Lear, but we are Lear....

One of Shakespeare's most distinguished detractors was Leo Tolstoy. The great Russian author realised he was in a minority, and was certainly thorough in his attempts to get to know and like the Bard: he read and reread his works in English, Russian and German. But it was no good—Tolstoy said: 'I invariably underwent the same feelings; repulsion, weariness and bewilderment.'
'King Lear' was a particular target of Tolstoy's scorn, and he said he much preferred the older 'True Chronicle Historie of King Leir and his Three Daughters', which ends with Cordelia restoring King Lear to his throne. Tolstoy tries to mock Shakespeare's version by the simple device of flatly describing the action, in his own work, 'Shakespeare and the Drama':

Lear walks about the heath and says words which are meant to express his despair: he desires that the winds should blow so hard that they (the winds) should crack their cheeks and that the rain should flood everything, that lightning should singe his white head, and the thunder flatten the world and destroy all germs 'that make ungrateful man'! The fool keeps uttering still more senseless words. Enter Kent: Lear says that for some reason during this storm all criminals shall be found out and convicted. Kent, still unrecognised by Lear, endeavours to persuade him to take refuge in a hovel. At this point the fool utters a prophecy in no wise related to the situation and they all depart.

George Orwell commented on Tolstoy's antipathy to the play in his essay, 'Lear, Tolstoy and the Fool', from 'Collected Essays':

In Tolstoy's impatience with the Fool one gets a glimpse of his deeper quarrel with Shakespeare. He objects, with some justification, to the raggedness of Shakespeare's plays, the irrelevancies, the incredible plots, the exaggerated language: but what at bottom he probably most dislikes is a sort of exuberance, a tendency to take—not so much a pleasure as simply an interest in the actual process of life....

Indeed his whole theory of 'crazes' or 'epidemic suggestions', in which he lumps together such things as the Crusades and the Dutch passion of tulip growing, shows a willingness to regard many human activities as mere ant-like rushings to and fro, inexplicable and uninteresting. Clearly he could have no patience with a chaotic, detailed, discursive writer like Shakespeare. His reaction is that of an irritable old man who is being pestered by a noisy child. 'Why do you keep jumping up and down like that? Why can't you sit still like I do?' In a way the old man is in the right, but the trouble is that the child has a feeling in its limbs which the old man has lost. And if the old man knows of the existence of this feeling, the effect is merely to increase his irritation: he would make children senile, if he could. Tolstoy does not know, perhaps, just what he misses in Shakespeare, but he is aware that he misses something, and he is determined that others shall be deprived of it as well.

The composer Hector Berlioz saw an English company play 'Hamlet' in Paris in 1827 and found himself quite overwhelmed—on two counts:

In the role of Ophelia I saw Henriette Smithson, who five years later became my wife. The impression made on my heart and mind by her extraordinary talent, nay her dramatic genius, was equalled only by the havoc wrought in me by the poet she so nobly interpeted. That is all I can say.

Shakespeare, coming upon me unawares, struck me like a thunderbolt. The lightning flash of that discovery revealed to me at a stroke the whole heaven of art, illuminating it to its remotest corners. I recognized the meaning of grandeur, beauty, dramatic truth, and I could measure the utter absurdity of the French view of Shakespeare which derives from Voltaire:

That ape of genius, sent
By Satan among men to do his work
and the pitiful narrowness of our own worn-out academic, cloistered traditions of poetry. I saw, I understood, I felt...that I was alive and that I must arise and walk.

But the shock was too strong, and it was long before I recovered from it. A feeling of intense, overpowering sadness came over me, accompanied by a nervous condition like a sickness, of which only a great writer on physiology could give any adequate idea.

Berlioz reacted with equally extreme feelings when he saw 'Romeo and Juliet' a few days later, as he recounted in 'Hector Berlioz: Memoirs' (translated by David Cairns):

...to witness the drama of that immense love, swift as thought, burning as lava, radiantly pure as an angel's glance, imperious, irresistible, the raging hatreds, the wild, ecstatic kisses, the desperate strife of love and death contending for mastery—it was too much. By the third act, hardly able to breathe—as though an iron hand gripped me by the heart—I knew that I was lost. I may add that at that time I did not know a word of English; I could only glimpse Shakespeare darkly through the mists of Letourneur's translation; the splendour of the poetry which gives a whole new glowing dimension to his glorious works was lost on me. Even now I labour to some extent under this disadvantage. It is much harder for a Frenchman to sound the depths of Shakespeare's style than it is for an Englishman to catch the individual flavour and subtlety of La Fontaine or Molière. They are continents, Shakespeare is a world.

H. L. Mencken:

Shakespeare made his heroes foreigners and his clowns Englishmen.

George Bernard Shaw

Preface to 'Mrs Warren's Profession':

I declare that the real secret of the cynicism and inhumanity of which shallower critics accuse me is the unexpectedness with which my characters behave like human beings, instead of conforming to the romantic logic of the stage.

According to Elizabeth Sprigge's 'Sybil Thorndike Casson', Shaw's skill at putting over his own work impressed Sybil when she and her husband Lewis Casson went to his home in 1923 to hear him read the new play she was to star in—'Saint Joan':

We simply could not believe our ears. It seemed to me the most wonderful first scene that I had ever heard. Very daring, very startling. 'No eggs! No eggs! Thousand thunders, man, what do you mean by no eggs?' It was extraordinary—and then the way he developed the mystery in that first scene. So daring and true, with that girl who was exactly as I had imagined her. When that first scene came to an end Lewis and I didn't say a word to one another. We both just felt, 'Oh, wonderful!' We could tell that Bronson Albery had certain doubts about it, but we had none.

Shaw read divinely. Like an actor, but much bigger size than most actors. Yes, a big-size actor. I felt, 'This is too good, it can't go on and be the real Saint Joan I've always wanted.' But it did, and I got more and more excited. And then at the end of the Loire scene, where the wind changes so dramatically, Shaw said, 'Well, that's all flapdoodle. Now the real play starts', and went into the tent scene with Warwick, Cauchon and de Stogumber, the Chaplain —one of the best scenes, I think, in all theatrical literature. He got the whole argument of the play into this scene, and one could see why he had wanted so passionately to write it. He made it clear that Joan did for France then what we hope somebody may yet do for the world. All the little warring factions in France she linked together. She made the nation. Shaw called her the first Nationalist and, although she was a devout Catholic, 'one of the first Protestant martyrs'. He also brought out the fact that she was a born general—she actually invented a new way of using artillery.

As the play progressed Lewis and I were more and more thrilled. The trial—I'd read the Records of it, and Joan's lines were word for word what she said. Except for the last big outburst, which was sheer poetry and pure Shaw. His two great speeches—the loneliness of God, at the end of the cathedral scene, and the great cry against imprisonment in the trial scene, those are the ones, and when people say Shaw wasn't a poet they should just read those speeches and consider whether they could have been written by anyone except a poet.

When it came to the Epilogue Lewis and I were in tears. Bronson Albery wasn't too keen on it—hardly anybody was. They said it was redundant, when the trial scene ended so marvellously—'You have heard the last of her'. 'The last of her? Hm, I wonder.' People said that was the right finish, but Shaw said, 'No, that's not the finish. Now we've got to see what the modern world says. If she came back now it would be exactly the same.'

Shaw was so delighted with Sybil Thorndike —and with himself—after the success of 'Saint Joan' that he sent her a copy of the play, inscribed: 'To Saint Sybil Thorndike from Saint Bernard Shaw.'

'How do you ever remember all those lines?' is a question actors often get asked by the public. Beatrice Lillie had a hard time finding the answer, she recalled in 'Every Other Inch a Lady' when she was rehearsing for an American production of Shaw's 'Too True to be Good':

Learning lines was only part of the problem. I hadn't the faintest notion what they meant. In this I was not alone; the rest of the illustrious cast seemed just as much in the dark. I was afraid that I'd end up vaguely like Sarah Bernhardt, who by Alec's account, played Ophelia for one hundred performances, never knowing how 'Hamlet' came out.

I kept the script under my pillow for four weeks, lugging it out when I flopped into bed after the Sutton Club had closed for the night, or shall we say for the morning? I'd study a few pages, then turn out the light to recite the speeches to myself in the dark. Useless. I frantically took up a memory course known as Pelmanism, whose secret is supposedly to concentrate on key words. That only made things worse—now I found I couldn't remember the key words, much less the lines, save only one or two, such as: Sergeant: I'm in a mess. Nurse: Of course, you're in the sergeant's mess. (House in uproar; police called.) The method which finally proved successful, and has been used often since with dialogue, is to work out every one of my lines in longhand. I covered (and still do) miles of odd bits of scrap paper, shirt cardboards, old love notes, bills and hundreds of unanswered gilt-edged invitation cards.

When interviewers asked what was the point of the play, I could only refer them to Mr Shaw. I assumed he might know. When

66. George Bernard Shaw

they speculated that he had written the part for me, I answered, 'God knows. I hope not.' I was always hoping that Noel, who was in New York at the time, would do something in the writing line on my behalf, but he didn't, drat him.

The longest conversation I'd had with G.B.S had consisted of his telling me about a movie short in which he'd just starred, and he rated himself terrific in it. I told him about my movie, 'Why Light Women Float Best', which I thought was just swell. Our meeting didn't exactly amount to a dramatic encounter on the Field of the Cloth of Gold.

Shaw was always irritated by Sir Herbert Beerbohm Tree's methods, especially of rehearsing. And he was furious when he saw that Tree in his highly successful production of 'Pygmalion' had introduced a happy ending by throwing a bunch of flowers to Eliza before the curtain finally came down. The exchange between them afterwards went thus:

TREE. My ending makes money: you ought to be grateful.
SHAW. Your ending is damnable: you ought to be shot.

In 1921 Lawrence Langner, founder and director of the Theatre Guild in New York, went to see Shaw in London and heard about the play cycle he had just completed, 'Back to Methuselah'. He recalled in 'The Magic Curtain':

The play itself was in five separate parts, and since it began with Adam and Eve and stretched over millions of years, it seemed that no member of our Theatre Guild audience was likely to live long enough to be able to disprove any of Shaw's prophetic conclusions. My interest was excited, and I asked for a copy. 'On your way back from the continent, drop in to see me again, and I'll have the plays ready by that time.'

After a while, Mrs Shaw entered. She was a gentle, gracious lady with plain, pleasant features, and of medium height and comfortable build. She was about the same age as Shaw, whom she seemed to regard in much the way a mother would a brilliant young son who needed careful guarding. Perhaps her maternal attitude came from the fact that she married him after nursing him through a rather dangerous illness.

Shaw seemed a little quieter in her presence, as though on his good behaviour, but I sensed a relationship between them which I was to learn afterward was based upon the deepest respect for each other's qualities. Upon the death of Mrs Shaw many years later, the American newspapers printed a ridiculous story that she had left her personal fortune 'to teach the Irish good manners' because of Shaw's lack of them. During the years I was to know them both, I was constantly amazed at Shaw's courtly old-fashioned manners. If Mrs Shaw started to leave the room, Shaw would leap from his chair, dash like a sprinter to the door with his beard waving, so as to arrive ahead of her, and he would hold it open with a deep bow until she had passed into the hall. On the occasion when I first met her, Shaw introduced her in the grand manner, like an impresario displaying a prima donna, a role which did not fit Mrs Shaw in the least. He ostentatiously seated her in a chair, and showed her the photographs of the production, which she admired appreciatively. However, when Shaw pointed out his objection to the doors with the rounded tops, she replied simply, 'What difference does it make?', to which the great man made no reply. I was to learn from many years' friendship with Mrs Shaw that 'the Genius', as she lovingly called him, was guided by her excellent common sense, which often served as an antidote to his tendency to explode fireworks on all occasions. Moreover, she suggested the subjects of some of his best plays, including 'The Doctor's Dilemma' and 'Saint Joan'. Mrs Shaw was most kind to me and invited me to lunch with them when I came back from the continent.

Returning to London a month or so later, I called again on the Shaws. The iron spikes had lost their terror, and seemed even a little friendly as I rang the bell. After being told politely by Shaw that I was not to smoke in the dining room (a wholly unnecessary precaution, since I did not smoke at all then), we had lunch, during which G.B.S. gave me his views on the war and the peace which was in the making. 'I have seen the end of the German Empire,' he said, devouring a goodly helping of cabbage, 'the end of the Russian Empire, and as for the British Empire—' he winked, and ate some more cabbage.

We talked about 'Back to Methuselah', and the best way to present it. Shaw's idea was to have all five plays produced consecutively, so that the audience would have to take the entire dose in one helping. On leaving, he said he would send me the printed proof sheets, and I asked for a contract. 'Don't bother about a contract,' he said, as I stood at the door taking my leave, 'it isn't likely that any other lunatic will want to produce 'Back to Methuselah'!'

From the foreword to 'Cymbeline Refinished':

Plot has always been the curse of serious drama, and indeed of serious literature of any kind. It is so out of place there that Shakespeare never could invent one.

When he was not being impishly insulting about Shakespeare, Shaw wrote about his work with a kind of perceptive affection. This excerpt comes from the preface to 'Back to Methuselah':

Comedy, as a destructive, derisory, critical, negative art, kept the theatre open when sublime tragedy perished. From Molière to Oscar Wilde we had a line of comedic playwrights who, if they had nothing fundamentally positive to say, were at least in revolt against falsehood and imposture, and were not only, as they claimed, 'chastening morals by ridicule', but, in Johnson's phrase, clearing our minds of cant, and thereby shewing an uneasiness in the presence of error which is the surest symptom of intellectual vitality. Meanwhile the name of Tragedy was assumed by plays in which everyone was killed in the last act, just as, in spite of Molière, plays in which everyone was married in the last act called themselves comedies. Now neither tragedies nor comedies can be produced according to a prescription which gives only the last moments of the last act. Shakespear did not make 'Hamlet' out of its final butchery, nor 'Twelfth Night' out of its final matrimony. And he could not become the conscious iconographer of a religion because he had no conscious religion. He had therefore to exercise his extraordinary natural gifts in the very entertaining art of mimicry, giving us the famous 'delineation of character' which makes his plays, like the novels of Scott, Dumas, and Dickens, so delightful. Also, he developed that curious and questionable art of building us a refuge from despair by disguising the cruelties of Nature as jokes. But with all his gifts, the fact remains that he never found the inspiration to write an original play. He furbished up old plays, and adapted popular stories, and chapters of history from Holinshed's 'Chronicle' and Plutarch's biographies, to the stage. All this he did (or did not; for there are minus quantities in the algebra of art) with a recklessness which shewed that his trade lay far from his conscience. It is true that he never takes his characters from the borrowed story, because it was less trouble and more fun to him to create them afresh; but none the less he heaps the murders and villainies of the borrowed story on his own essentially gentle creations without scruple, no matter how incongruous they may be. And all the time his vital need for a philosophy drives him to seek one by the quaint professional method of introducing philosophers as characters into his plays, and even of making his heroes philosophers; but when they come on the stage they have no philosophy to expound: they are only pessimists and railers; and their occasional would-be philosophic speeches, such as The Seven Ages of Man and The Soliloquy on Suicide, shew how deeply in the dark Shakespear was as to what philosophy means. He forced himself in among the greatest of playwrights without having once entered that region in which Michael Angelo, Beethoven, Goethe, and the antique Athenian stage poets are great. He would really not be great at all if it were not that he had religion enough to be aware that his religionless condition was one of despair.

Shaw was once asked by the 'London Evening News' to write his own epitaph. He responded by drawing a tombstone covered in weeds, with the inscription:

HIC JACET

BERNARD SHAW

Who the devil was he?

Richard Brinsley Sheridan

According to Brian Dobbs' 'Drury Lane', Sheridan had great difficulty in getting his plays finished:

'The School for Scandal', Sheridan's masterpiece, was subject to continual delay in the writing. At last complete, Sheridan penned 'Finished, Thank God. RBS' on the title page and handed it to Hopkins the prompter, who added with feeling, 'Amen'. Two years later, he went through the same process with 'The Critic', a lively satire based on Buckingham's 'The Rehearsal'.

The cast and the rest of the theatre's staff got it page by page and began to despair that the play would ever be completed. They got it finished by the adroit device of luring Sheridan into the Green Room where pen and paper, two bottles of port and a plate of anchovy sandwiches awaited him, locking the door and allowing him out only when it was finished. Sheridan was amused, but duly complied.

The delays were even worse for his play 'Pizarro':

The public was lucky to get it at all. Michael Kelly tells us that...at the time the house was overflowing on the first night's performance, all that was written of the play was actually rehearsing and...incredible as it may appear, until the end of the fourth act, neither Mrs Siddons nor Charles Kemble, nor Barrymore had all their speeches for the fifth....
The delays were so long that the after-piece started after midnight to seventeen people in the whole dress circle and twenty-two in the pit.

In Sheridan's 'The Critic, or A Tragedy

Rehearsed', the author, Puff, and his friends watch the duel between Whiskerandos and the Beefeater:

(They fight, and after the usual number of wounds given, WHISKERANDOS falls.)
WHISK. Oh, cursed parry!—that last thrust in tierce
   Was fatal!—Captain, thou hast fencèd well!
   And Whiskerandos quits this bustling scene
   For all eter____
BEEF. ____nity—he would have added, but stern death
   Cut short his being, and the noun at once!
PUFF. O, my dear sir, you are too slow; now mind me. Sir, shall I trouble you to die again?
WHISK. And Whiskerandos quits this bustling scene
   For all eter____
BEEF. ____nity—he would have added....
PUFF. No, sir—that's not it—once more, if you please.
WHISK. I wish, sir, you would practise this without me—I can't stay dying here all night.
PUFF. Very well, we'll go over it by and by—I must humour these gentlemen!
   (Exit WHISKERANDOS.)
BEEF. Farewell, brave Spaniard! and when next....
PUFF. Dear sir, you needn't speak that speech as the body has walked off.
BEEF. That's true, sir—then I'll join the fleet.
PUFF. If you please. (Exit BEEFEATER.) Now, who comes on?

(Enter GOVERNOR, with his hair properly disordered.)

GOV. A hemisphere of evil planets reign!
And every planet sheds contagious frenzy!
My Spanish prisoner is slain! my daughter,
Meeting the dead corse borne along—has gone
Distract! (A loud flourish of trumpets.)
But hark! I am summoned to the fort;
Perhaps the fleets have met! amazing crisis!
O Tilburina! from thy aged father's beard
Thou'st plucked the few brown hairs which time had left!

(Exit GOVERNOR.)

SNEER. Poor gentleman!

PUFF. Yes—and no one to blame but his daughter!

DANGLE. And the planets.

PUFF. True. Now enter Tilburina!

SNEER. Egad, the business comes on quick here.

PUFF. Yes, sir—now she comes in stark mad in white satin.

SNEER. Why in white satin?

PUFF. O Lord, sir—when a heroine goes mad she always goes into white satin—don't she, Dangle?

DANGLE. Always—it's a rule.

PUFF. Yes—here it is. (Looking at the book.)
'Enter Tilburina stark mad in white satin, and her confidant stark mad in white linen.'

(Enter TILBURINA and CONFIDANT mad, according to custom.)

SNEER. But what the deuce, is the confidant to be mad too?

PUFF. To be sure she is: the confidant is always to do whatever her mistress does; weep when she weeps, smile when she smiles, go mad when she goes mad. Now, madam confidant—but keep your madness in the background, if you please.

TILBURINA. The wind whistles—the moon rises—see,
They have killed my squirrel in his cage!
Is this a grasshopper! Ha! no, it is my Whiskerandos—you shall not keep him—
I know you have him in your pocket—
An oyster may be crossed in love! Who says
A whale's a bird? Ha! did you call, my love?
He's here! He's there! He's everywhere!
Ah me! He's nowhere!

(Exit TILBURINA.)

PUFF. There, do you ever desire to see anybody madder than that?

SNEER. Never, while I live!

PUFF. You observe how she mangled the metre?

DANGLE. Yes—egad, it was the first thing made me suspect she was out of her senses.

SNEER. And pray, what becomes of her?

PUFF. She is gone to throw herself into the sea, to be sure—and that brings us at once to the scene of action, and so to my catastrophe—my sea-fight, I mean.

SNEER. What, you bring that in at last?

PUFF. Yes, yes—you know my play is called the Spanish Armada; otherwise, egad, I have no occasion for the battle at all. Now, then, for my magnificence!—my battle!—my noise!—and my procession!

Drinking wine as he watched his Theatre Royal, Drury Lane, burning to the ground, Sheridan remarked: 'Cannot a man take a glass of wine by his own fireside?'

Sarah Siddons

Sarah Siddons earned the dislike of other ladies in the company who thought that Garrick was paying her too much attention —though in this case their attempts to get even involved 'down-staging' rather than 'up-staging', according to 'The Reminiscences of Sarah Kemble Siddons':

He...selected me to present Venus at the revival of 'The Jubilee'. This gained me the malicious appellation of 'Garrick's Venus', and the ladies who so kindly bestowed it on me, so determinedly rushed before me in the last scene, that had he not broken through them all, and brought us forward with his own hand, my little Cupid and myself, whose appointed situations were in the very front of the stage, might as well have been in the Island of Paphos at that moment.

In her 'Reminiscences', Sarah Siddons commented with satisfaction on the effect of her performance in 'Venice Preserv'd' on a party of fashionable people:

They had all wept so much and were so disfigured with red eyes and swollen faces, that they were this morning actually unpresentable, being all confined to their chambers with violent headaches.

Charles Mathews tells, in 'Memoirs', of an incident that threatened Mrs Siddons' poise:

The evening being hot, Mrs Siddons was tempted by a torturing thirst to avail herself of the only relief to be obtained at the moment. Her dresser, therefore, dispatched a boy in great haste to fetch a pint of beer for Mrs Siddons. Meanwhile the play proceeded, and on the boy's return with the frothed pitcher, he looked about for the person who had sent him on his errand, and not seeing her, enquired, 'Where is Mrs Siddons?'

The scene-shifter whom he questioned, pointing his finger to the stage, where she was performing the sleeping-scene of Lady Macbeth, replied, 'There she is.'

To the horror of the performers, the boy promptly walked on to the stage close up to Mrs Siddons, and with a total unconsciousness of any impropriety, presented the porter! Her distress can be imagined; she waved the boy away in her grand manner several times without effect. At last the people behind the scenes, by dint of beckoning, stamping, etc., succeeded in getting him off with the beer, while the audience were in an uproar of laughter, which the dignity of the actress was unable to quell for several minutes.

When Sarah Siddons retired from the public stage, she still gave private readings. R. B. Haydon was at one of them. In 1821, he recalled in his journal:

68. Sarah Siddons by Thomas Lawrence

She acts 'Macbeth', herself, better than either Kemble or Kean. It is extraordinary the awe this wonderful woman inspires. After her first reading the men retired to tea. While we were all eating toast, and tinkling cups and saucers, she began again. It was like the effect of a mass bell at Madrid. All noise ceased; we slunk to our seats like boors, two or three of the most distinguished men of the day, with the very toast in their mouths, afraid to bite. It was curious to see [Sir Thomas] Lawrence in this predicament, to hear him bite by degrees, and then stop for fear of making too much crackle, his eyes full of water from the constraint; and at the same time to hear Mrs Siddons' 'eye of newt and toe of frog!' and then to see Lawrence give a sly bite, and then look awed, and pretend to be listening. I went away highly gratified, and as I stood on the landing-place to get cool, I overheard my own servant in the hall say, 'What! is that the old lady making such a noise?' 'Yes.' 'Why, she makes as much noise as ever!'

Small Ads

Some of the advertisements in the theatrical press can make curious reading:

HAPPY AND JOLLY laughing CLOWN —Vacant Xmas.

DANCE GROUP requires male dancers for tour. Must be keen—lazy-bones won't last two mins.

PERFORMANCE ARTS COMPANY needs a dedicated female performance artist. No money.

SPECIAL ACT required for medieval banquet...e.g. sword-swallowing, walking, fire-eating, knife-throwing etc. Patter acts/illusions not required.

DANCERS, classic and modern, required to help in new book. Also thin, fat and medium ladies for women's book of exercises.

TUMBLER/ACROBAT able to bend double for cabaret act London-based. Work waiting.

CREATIVE AUTHOR is interested in ghosting autobiographies.

COMPERE: experienced modern versatile singer entertainer. Available for odd nights etc.

Eastern Belly/Hawaiian dancer, soubrette, actress.... Clubs, theatres, hotels.

Cream Ponies for panto, also parading, publicity, etc.

Engagements wanted: Brilliant pianist. Play, read anything, double accordion and organ.

LAUGHS GALORE!
    100 ad-libs and heckler stoppers
    100 original saucy limericks
    150 good clean gags
    100 good strong club gags
    100 good stag gags
    Patter routines: 'My Wedding Day',
    'My Army Life'

SEAVIEW GUEST HOUSE: Actors and actresses welcome. Late Breakfasts.

CHIMPANZEES for commercials, publicity tea parties, photography, circus, cabaret, pantomime etc. Chimps also ice skate.

REAL GLAMOUR UNDIES and corsetry, stage, TV and drag specialities. We are famous for cabaret lace-up corsetry. Enormous stocks, ample fitting rooms.

GORILLA COSTUME for sale. Ideal for fancy dress, pantomime, comedy band etc.

INTERNATIONAL BELLY DANCER, with audience participation. Cabarets and Functions.

CLASSICAL SINGER (24), female, with lovely dog, urgently needs accommodation.

WIGS, toppers, beards, sideburns and moustaches. Large stocks, lowest prices, group discounts.

PROFESSIONAL COMEDY WRITERS require names, semi-names, unknowns, who need top-class clean material on one-off or contract basis.

BELLY DANCING and striptease lessons, also femme lessons for drag acts.

FREELANCE ACCOUNTANT available. Based in London, but very mobile.

BODYGUARD-CHAUFFEUR seeks employment. Good references.

Sparks

'Sparks' is the nickname given to electricians and lighting technicians in the theatre and in television. It is a nickname the technicians treat with pride, regarding their profession as an élite. Indeed, when a television film unit was packing up at the end of a day's location shooting, the Sparks looked at the sunset and said happily: 'Well —there goes the Great Sparks in the Sky . . .!'

By 1820 gas lighting had been adopted by the two principal London theatres in place of the oil lamps or candles which theatres previously used. It meant that there could be much greater control of the lighting, and this was further improved by 'limelight'.

Limelight was made by actually burning a stick of lime in a gas-jet. This made it possible to direct a single bright beam on to one performer; coloured glass could be used to vary the colour.

Probably the simplest lighting system ever devised was encountered by a touring company playing in a remote rural hall. The lights were all worked from one socket in the wall. There were two pieces of flex with naked wires instead of plugs at the end. These were simply stuck into the socket and held with match sticks. One flex was linked to the main lights in the hall: the 'house' lights. When it was time for the show to start, someone simply took the flex out and stuck in the other one, which was connected to the stage lights. At the end of the show, the process was reversed.

Alistair Wilson was a member of Perth

Repertory Company in Scotland during the 1950s when David Stuart was artistic director. In that role he did a great deal to build up the theatre's reputation, but his tendency to be somewhat vague had its drawbacks, especially when he occasionally acted in one of the plays:

In a superb production of 'Midsummer Night's Dream', he was an impressive Oberon, in black cloak, green eye make-up, but was not always there on cue and when he was, was thinking of other things. The stage management were always nervous when he was performing and on the Thursday night of the week's run, David was busy talking to a young actress in the wings about the part she was to play the next week. He was giving kindly advice when the ASM raced round to hiss: 'Mr Stuart, you're on!' David blinked and nodded and strode on to the stage, followed by his train, to see Titania haughtily waiting. The line was the famous: 'Ill met by moonlight, proud Titania!' David stopped short, peered at her, broke out in a big smile and advanced, saying, 'He-llo!' Titania sagged in horror and the ASM screamed the line at him. David looked round. 'Moonlight? Moonlight?' He blinked up and around at the superb forest setting. 'Ah, yes,' he said, nodding with satisfaction, 'so it is. Very nice too. Er—Titania— moonlight—' He drew her attention to the realistic lighting effect, with a wave of his hand. 'Yes—and ill-met by it, too, indeed!'

David Stuart sometimes played major roles. But it could be a problem trying to cope with the technical side of the production as well as performing in it, as Alistair Wilson recalls:

Playing Othello, he had trouble with the lights. He told Sandy the electrician that

69. A limelight man

there was too much light on the murder of Desdemona scene. On the Tuesday, Sandy checked the dimmers down a notch. David, about to smother Desdemona, stopped dead, looked around, edged over to the prompt corner (on the stage right, at Perth) where Sandy was up in his gantry, and whispered in a clear, carrying aside: 'Too much light, Sandy.' He then carried on to asphyxiate Desdemona. On the Wednesday, he stopped again, left Desdemona high and dry, to edge right and whisper the same instruction. He did the same on the Thursday and Sandy, annoyed, checked the dimmers down to one. On the Friday, setting the dimmers at one, Sandy scowled down at the almost totally dark stage. David proceeded so far, stopped, muttered a polite 'excuse me', to Desdemona, shuffled sideways to DR, and whispered, 'Not enough light, Sandy.' Sandy, furious, slammed every dimmer up to full. David blinked around in the glare, chewed his lip thoughtfully for a moment, then said, 'Ah! That's too much, Sandy!'

Speaking Up

This is the first part of Hamlet's instructions to the Players (Act III, Scene 2):

HAMLET. Speak the speech, I pray you, as I pronounced it to you, trippingly on the tongue: but if you mouth it, as many of your Players do, I had as lief the town-crier had spoke my lines. Nor do not saw the air too much with your hand, thus, but use all gently; for in the very torrent, tempest, and—as I may say—whirlwind of passion, you must acquire and beget a temperance that may give it smoothness. Oh, it offends me to the soul to hear a robustious periwig-pated fellow tear a passion to tatters, to very rags, to split the ears of the groundlings, who for the most part are capable of nothing, but inexplicable dumb-shows and noise: I would have such a fellow whipped for o'erdoing Termagant: it out-Herods Herod. Pray you avoid it.

PLAYER. I warrant your honour.

HAMLET. Be not too tame neither, but let your own discretion be your tutor. Suit the action to the word, the word to the action, with this special observance: that you o'erstep not the modesty of Nature; for anything so o'erdone, is from the purpose of playing, whose end both at the first and now, was and is, to hold as 'twere, the mirror up to Nature; to show Virtue her own feature, Scorn her own image, and the very age and body of the Time, his form and pressure.

Charles Lamb, 'On the Tragedies of Shakespeare':

How far the very custom of hearing anything spouted, withers and blows upon a fine passage, may be seen in those speeches from 'Henry the Fifth', etc., which are current in the mouths of schoolboys, from their being to be found in Enfield's Speaker, and such kind of books! I confess myself utterly unable to appreciate that celebrated soliloquy in 'Hamlet', beginning 'To be or not to be', or to tell whether it be good, bad or indifferent, it has been so handled and pawed about by declamatory boys and men, and torn so inhumanly from its living place and principle of continuity in the play, till it is become to me a perfect dead member.

It may seem a paradox, but I cannot help being of opinion that the plays of Shakespeare are less calculated for performance on a stage, than those of almost any other dramatist whatever. Their distinguishing excellence is a reason that they should be so. There is so much in them, which comes not under the province of acting, with which eye, and tone, and gesture, have nothing to do.

Peter Hall, from David Addenbrooke's 'The Royal Shakespeare Company, the Peter Hall Years':

I think that my greatest achievement in the theatre (if I may be immodest) is to have started a Shakespeare company which conscientiously began to understand what Shakespeare's verse was about and how to speak it. But because we made a different 'noise', everybody said: 'They're not speaking the verse!' In fact to my mind no one had been speaking the verse before —except great stars, idiosyncratic actors who had their own way of making the verse work. That's all now gone and forgotten. We caused a revolution in the speaking of Shakespeare's verse. And, at the gate of heaven, if I was asked to justify myself, I would say that is the best thing I've done in my life.

Stage Fright

Almost everything nowadays has been the subject of scientific experiment, at some time or other: and stage fright is no exception. Actors have been wired up and monitored, to discover what state they are in before they go on stage. And some have been found to be in a state of nervous anxiety so great that their heart beat is the same as that of someone who has just had a bad car accident. (Yes—there must have been a scientist there to monitor *that*, too.)

If an actor can gauge his performance right in rehearsal, the first night will be the time when he hits his peak. But it can happen that nerves cause his performance to go down suddenly into a kind of listlessness. At the other end of the scale some actors are notorious for keeping their acting deliberately low key until the first night, when their performance suddenly 'takes off like a rocket' as one actor put it sourly. He was remembering how such sudden bravura acting astonished the rest of the cast and put them completely off balance.

It is not by any means uncommon for actors to be physically sick before first nights: and there are even some who vomit regularly before every performance.

Actors getting up from their dressing-room chairs to go on stage have suddenly found that one leg is shaking so violently that they are hardly able to stand. And on stage, one of the trickiest things to cope with is having to stretch out your hand to accept a cup of tea: there's grave danger that the hand and arm will be shaking so much that the cup will rattle in the saucer. One actor solved this problem by asking the assistant stage manager to put a piece of plasticine on the saucer so the cup would stick to it just enough as he drew the saucer towards him.

Some actors say that stage fright doesn't get any less with experience: you just learn how to cope with it, using ruses like the stuck-together cup and saucer. Age and eminence don't seem to do any good either. Robert Stephens recalled on a recent radio programme how he was standing in the wings with Laurence Olivier, waiting to *go on, when he suddenly noticed the great man was visibly nervous. Sir Laurence remarked dolefully: 'This is no profession for an adult person. . . .'*

Sarah Bernhardt remembered the stage fright from which she suffered before her first appearance in London in 'Phèdre'. It was a familiar sensation, she recalled in 'Memoirs':

I wanted to return home at once, for I was acting that night for the first time, and I felt rather wretched and despairing. There were several persons awaiting me at my house in Chester Square, but I did not want to see anyone. I took a cup of tea and went to the Gaiety Theatre, where we were to face the English public for the first time. I knew already that I had been elected the favourite, and the idea of this chilled me with terror, for I am what is known as a 'traqueuse'. I am subject to the 'trac' or stage-fright, and I have it terribly. When I first appeared on the stage I was timid, but I never had this 'trac'. I used to turn as red as a poppy when I happened to meet the eye of a spectator. I was ashamed of talking so loud before so many silent people. That was the effect of my cloistered life, but I had no feeling of fear. The first time I ever had the real sensation of stage-fright was in the month of January 1869, at the seventh or perhaps the eighth performance of 'Le Passant'. The success of this little masterpiece had been enormous, and my interpretation of the part of Zanetto had delighted the public, and particularly the students. When I went on the stage that day I was suddenly applauded by the whole house. I turned towards the Imperial box, thinking that the Emperor had just entered. But no, the box was empty, and I realized then that all the bravos were for me. I was seized with a fit of nervous trembling, and my eyes smarted with tears which I had to keep back. Agar and I were called back five times, and on leaving the theatre the students, ranged on each side, gave me three cheers.

70. Sarah Bernhardt and M. Coquelin

Stage~struck

Thomas Snagge, 'Recollections of Occurrences':

It frequently came to my lot to assist and attend at the theatre (at Their Majesties' Command of a Play) for the fixing and regulating the canopy they sit under, where I have indolently and insolently lolled in the same chairs of State to be graced after with the King and Queen.

This with other vocations in the line of my profession soon gave me ingress and regress to the fascinating scenes from whence Thespian passions are engendered.

Not the delightful fields of Elysium can more captivate a first beholder when newly ferried over the Styx, than the Scenes, Flies, Traps, and all the Pantomimical apparatus behind the curtain of a theatre can a stage struck hero of the Buskin. Every circumstance creates pride, pomp and admiration—not a bowl or dagger, Harlequin's mask or sword, trick, lamp or warning bell, but raises wonder. Every call boy, lamplighter, carpenter, sweeper and attendant grows into consequence to the emulating enlisting Knight of this mimic, honour-be-sotting state.

Arthur Murphy, 'The Apprentice':

GARGLE. And then, Sir, I've found out that he went three times a week to a Spouting Club.

WINGATE. A Spouting Club, friend Gargle? What's a Spouting Club?

GARGLE. A meeting of prentices and clerks, and giddy young men, intoxicated with plays; and so they meet in public houses to act speeches; there they all neglect business, despise the advice of their friends, and think of nothing but to become actors.

WINGATE. You don't say so! A Spouting Club! Wounds, I believe they are all mad.

Noel Coward's great creation, Mrs Worthington's daughter, had her exact equivalents, two hundred years earlier:

A cousin too she has, with squinting eyes,
With waddling gait, and voice like London
    Cries,
Who, for the stage too short by half a
    storey,
Acts Lady Townly—thus—in all her glory.
And, while she's traversing her scanty
    room,
Cries: 'Lord, my lord, what can I do at
    home!'
In short, there's girls enough for all the
    fellows,
The ranting, whining, starting, and the
    jealous,

The Hotspurs, Romeos, Hamlets, and
       Othellos.
Oh! Little do those silly people know,
What dreadful trials actors undergo.

**The story of many a successful stage career
has begun with the Mrs Worthington-style
advice: 'Don't!' This was the advice of Vivian
Van Damm, general manager of the Windmill
Theatre, to Kenneth More, after he had given
him a job as a stage-hand. He recalled the
occasion, in his book 'More or Less':**

'There is just one thing I would like to
warn you about,' said Van Damm seriously.
'Not drink. And not girls. Acting. You must
never, ever become a bloody actor. Acting
is the end. It is death and destruction to
become an actor, and I know what I'm
talking about. You stick to me, Kenny, and
I'll teach you how to run a theatre. But
whatever you do, forget acting. Put that
right out of your mind.'

71. Candidates for a Christmas pantomime at Drury Lane Theatre

Constantin Stanislavski

Constantin Stanislavski, in 'Building a Character', wrote that actors who achieve the greatest pinnacle of their art have a special quality, which he defined like this:

That quality of the unexpected which startles, overwhelms, stuns me. Something that lifts the spectator off the ground, sets him in a land where he has never walked, but which he recognizes easily through a sense of foreboding or conjecture. He does, however, see this unexpected thing face to face, and for the first time. It shakes, enthrals, and engulfs him.

And in 'An Actor Prepares', translated by Elizabeth Reynolds Hapgood:

Technique alone cannot create an image that you can believe in and to which both you and your spectators can give yourselves up completely. So now you realize that creativeness is not a technical trick. It is not an external portrayal of images and passions as you used to think.

Our type of creativeness is the conception and birth of a new being—the person in the part. It is a natural act similar to the birth of a human being.

If you follow each thing that happens in an actor's soul during the period in which he is living into his part, you will admit that my comparison is right. Each dramatic and artistic image, created on the stage, is unique and cannot be repeated, just as in nature.

As with human beings, there is an analogous, embryonic stage.

In the creative process there is the father, the author of the play; the mother, the actor pregnant with the part; and the child, the role to be born.

There is the early period when the actor first gets to know his part. Then they become more intimate, quarrel, are reconciled, marry and conceive.

In all this the director helps the process along as a sort of matchmaker.

Actors, in this period, are influenced by their parts, which affect their daily lives. Incidentally the period of gestation for a part is at least as long as that of a human being, and often considerably longer. If you analyse this process you will be convinced that laws regulate organic nature, whether she is creating a new phenomenon biologically or imaginatively.

You can go astray only if you do not understand that truth: if you do not have confidence in nature; if you try to think out 'new principles', 'new bases', 'new art'. Nature's laws are binding on all, without exception, and woe to those who break them.

Getting Started

imitate you. By taking the initiative, you allow the parrot no alternative but to be itself, which proves once again that attack is often the best defence. At the age of two, I apparently did a passable imitation of Lloyd George, and later on I added Hitler, Mussolini and Aristide Briand to my gallery as these gentlemen became available in the public domain. I also did a complete voyage round Europe by radio while hidden behind a curtain, which was remarkable by virtue of the fact that we possessed no radio in the house until 1936.

Joyce Grenfell, in 'Joyce Grenfell Requests the Pleasure':

I had played my first part on any stage as a tinsel fairy in an improvised version of 'Hansel and Gretel', in Aunt Nancy's drawing-room at Cliveden in the First World War, before an audience of wounded soldiers. I was five. The role of the fairy was demanding. I had to hold a wand with a star on it in one hand and a single leaf in the other. The part called for me to trip on lightly, spot the unfortunate children sleeping on the ground and drop my leaf as a means of disguising their presence from the wicked villains who were out to get them. Not only was this a first time on any stage, it was also a first time of wearing proper, long, grown-up white stockings—joy,

Peter Ustinov, in 'Dear Me':

...I had been used by my father as a cabaret, which was my first introduction to show business. My ability to imitate had manifested itself very early on, as well as my instinctively unconventional way of going about it. After all, I had started this tendency by imitating a parrot, which is unusual, in that a parrot is supposed to

oh joy, the feel of them, buttoned on to what was inaccurately known as a Liberty bodice by tapes sewn to their tops. Tape doesn't yield, so after I had knelt to deliver my leaf and risen jerkily to a standing position there were sagging knees to the white stockings and quite a lot of wrinkling at the ankles. It seems I was in no hurry to get off the stage and stood there smiling in my tinselly sparkle and wobbly wings while my stockings crept down my legs.

Danny Kaye:

I don't think anybody breaks out on the scene overnight. The audience may see them break out overnight, but I think most of it is preparation. I think one of the reasons we're not developing as many new young people as we used to in the past, is because there's no place to train any more. With television you know, creating the demand for so many new things all the time, people do not have the place to go and practise and develop: to put it strangely, there's no place to be lousy any more.

Roy Hudd, on the old type of concert party as a training ground:

You never get this sort of training anywhere now; now the small shows are dropping out, I don't know where the nursery's going to be next. People say it's moved into the working men's clubs now, but it hasn't really, because this is just basically a solo act you're doing, going out there; whereas in concert party you had to do production, you had to learn how to dance, you had to learn how to play sketches, sing, as well as doing your own act, you know. In other words, you learned everything which you should really need to know for the business. I mean the perfect example really is that they say Bruce Forsyth was an overnight success, a sensational success, when he compered the London Palladium Show. He'd been about seventeen years in concert party before then: as a dancer, a light comedian, everything. So when the big break came, he had all the talent and everything there, absolutely at his finger-tips, he knew just what to do when the occasion arose. But where are people going to learn these sorts of things now?

Ed Berman describes in the introduction to 'Ten of the Best British Short Plays' some of the early manifestations of his Ambiance theatre group and the resourcefulness needed to keep it going:

At the time of the first bankruptcy of the Ambiance Restaurant we took to the streets with James Saunders' 'Dog Accident', previously a radio play, set in a busy street at lunch-time. I had wanted to do it in its appropriate venue in any case. The restaurateur didn't have to go bankrupt to reinforce my environmental tendencies. We were going to use a real dog for this play, but couldn't find a dead one that looked real enough. Finally, we used a wired-up stuffed dog, radio controlled, that twitched and screamed when I twiddled a dial some twenty yards away—a very special effect by the man who had created the special effects for the Battle of Britain film.

Having lost the original Ambiance Restaurant, our next temporary home was the Green Banana Restaurant. Before it went the way of all good green bananas, we produced the premiere of Tom Stoppard's 'After Magritte'. Tom was attracted to us, I think, by the whole idea of Inter-Action—both the theatre and community sides. Letting us do his play was a gift beyond the call of curiosity, however.

The Green Banana was a basement restaurant measuring 14ft x 25ft with a pillar in the middle (for a world premiere, no less). Every morning at 5.00 a.m. during the run of 'After Magritte' a removal lorry would pull up outside the restaurant in the empty Frith Street of Soho. By that time of night everyone else seemed to have finally found a stage on which to rehearse their own branch of the entertainment industry.

The pieces of the box set of 'After Magritte' would emerge from the lorry. Stacked on the pavement, the pieces waited. Then the entire contents of the Green Banana, basement night club extraordinaire, were carried up to the street and loaded into the lorry. Next the pieces of the set were carried down the narrow winding stair by two dedicated stage managers. These tortuous acrobatics completed, the set was ensconced for lunch by 11.00 a.m.

Television

Frances Donaldson, on actors 'being themselves' in television interviews ('The Actor-Managers'):

Actors often appear to be playing a part and, when one enters a room and hears a voice on television replying to the questions of an interviewer, one can normally tell when it belongs to a member of the acting profession. The timing is invariably too good, the modesty—so desirable on television, yet so difficult to achieve—too easily handled, the lines thrown away in a manner impossible to the ordinary man. Spending all his professional life in impersonation, the actor finally loses his own identity and becomes naturalistic rather than natural—a tendency which becomes more obvious as fashion and mannerisms are no longer in the style of the day.

American television and theatre dramatist Corinne Jacker contrasts the attitudes of West Coast TV producers with people putting on theatre plays:

In California they eat writers—grind them up and spit them out. And that means they need more writers than they have. Writers are a valuable commodity right now, so when you are 'out there' you are worth something: they've got to have words, and they're running out of writers. If you add up the number of television hours every night and multiply that by three networks and public television and the syndicated shows—well, they are obviously desperate for writers. So they treat you with a different kind of interest from the theatre. In the theatre, we're not meeting an economic demand, so you feel as though they're doing you a favour putting on your play.

A producer who brought some of the liveliest directors into television in the pioneer days of TV drama was once having a slanging

match in the studio gallery with one of these directors:

PRODUCER. You can't talk to me like that! I brought you up from the gutter!
DIRECTOR. From the gutter, to you, is UP?!

A television director is chatting to a friend who works in the less ruthless world of radio:

FRIEND. How are things over at the television centre these days?
DIRECTOR. Worse than ever. It's getting so bad now, that people are even stabbing each other in the chest!

When TV drama was transmitted live, one ambitious BBC production was an old Easter Play, performed in a Bristol church, using Outside Broadcast cameras. The medieval crowd was recruited from local drama groups, and controlled by the director's assistant, who was dressed as a monk. When the actor playing Christ was ready to walk up the nave with his cross, the jostling crowd, all anxious to be in shot, blocked the route. The monk moved with reverence among them, apparently muttering a prayer. What he was really saying was: 'Get the hell out of it, you bloody idiots! Clear the nave! Sod off, blast you!' and other words to that effect. The nave was clear in time for the big moment — and luckily, no live microphones were anywhere near the cowled figure.

When television started up again in Britain after the Second World War, one actor remarked glumly to another that he could see a whole new field of unemployment opening up.

Ellen Terry

Ellen Terry made her first stage appearance in 1856 at the age of nine, playing Mamillius in 'The Winter's Tale'. At ten, she was playing Puck in 'A Midsummer Night's Dream'. At the end of one performance she caught her foot in one of the stage traps. Someone said later that she had been very brave to think of the audience and not cry. She answered: 'I wasn't thinking of the audience. I was thinking of Mr Shakespeare's play.'

Ellen Terry played Portia in 'The Merchant of Venice' in London in 1875. It was a memorable first night, as Alice Comyns Carr recalls:

As the curtain rose upon Nell's tall and slender figure in a china-blue and white brocade dress, with one crimson rose at her breast, the whole house burst forth in rapturous applause. But her greatest effect was when she walked into the court in her black robes of justice, and I remember my young husband, who had rushed out between the acts to buy the last bouquet in Covent Garden, throwing his floral tribute to her feet amidst the enthusiasm of the audience.

Alan Haydock's radio feature 'Darling Nell' included several personal reminiscences. First, Dame Sybil Thorndike remembered the remarkable voice of Ellen Terry:

. . . that lovely rather husky voice, with infinite, infinite, gradation of tone she had, and there was a slight blur over it, a slight faint husk which was charming. And she could do anything with her voice. A low one for low sounds, and wonderful high sounds, and she never could laugh out loud —isn't that funny? She'd go into paroxysms of laughter but it was all silent. I heard that and thought—I noticed in Beatrice, she never laughed aloud, she never laughed aloud at all as Portia but Portia didn't laugh aloud much—silly old girl.

During the First World War, when Ellen Terry was nearing seventy, her grandson Edward Craig stayed with her at a farmhouse in Kent:

73. Ellen Terry as Portia in 'The Merchant of Venice', 1880

like a tailor. She always—at any moment—just sat on the floor like a tailor, cross-legged, and she used to get on the bed, sit cross-legged, put this candle beside her and start off, you know. And first of all she'd tell me about the scene, how it was laid, and probably a little bit about Irving and his make-up or something like that. And then she'd start off. And we'd go through the whole of 'Hamlet'. So I've even seen her as the First Grave-Digger—which is more than anybody else has seen...and Horatio and all the rest of them.

About three o'clock in the morning I was nodding off a bit, specially as it was getting to the end of Shakespeare which is always a bit noddable, and then Grannie'd say: 'Well, we'd better go to bed.' Off she'd toddle, because she was sleepy by then. She went through 'Hamlet', she went through 'The Merchant of Venice', 'Romeo and Juliet', 'The Tempest', and 'Macbeth', which of course was my favourite. And I was willing to hear that over again any time she liked.

Of course, when I was a small boy, because I heard her always talking about Henry and about Shakespeare I took it for granted that she and Henry were brother and sister and that Shakespeare was their father. It was quite some years before I realized that this wasn't true.

Hilda Barnes, Ellen Terry's companion in the last years of her life, remembered:

Her skin was beautiful. But she never used make-up, but three pennyworth of prepared chalk from Mr Boots in which she rubbed her powder-puff which was in a bag. And that was all she used. Her skin was beautiful. Beautiful. She cleaned it with cream that an old man in Chicago used to send her. And he sent her six bottles for her birthday and six again for Christmas. She'd no make-up. She'd sometimes take a pencil and rub it on to her eyebrows and look at me and grin. She had a lovely chuckle and a lovely grin.

Ellen Terry once gave this advice to Gladys Cooper on the playing of a tear-jerking scene: 'Now dear, don't be sorry for yourself. Let the audience cry—don't you cry.'

I used to have a bed in her bedroom and I used to wake up in the middle of the night and hear her quoting from 'The Brook' by Tennyson—she loved Tennyson. You know, there's a refrain in it 'Men may come and men may go, but I go on forever'. This voice was booming away in this four-poster bed. And I'd be very excited about this and start chatting to her, which she loved. And then time passed and she looked on me as a sort of another night-bird, which of course I was. And she used to come and give me a good old prod and say 'Are you awake, Teddy?' And I'd say 'Yes, yes, Gran.' 'Oh, I thought you were. Shall we read 'Hamlet' together?'

There she was with a candle, probably dripping it on me, and she'd sit cross-legged

Theories
and Theatre

Peter Brook, 'The Empty Space':

I can take any empty space and call it a bare stage. A man walks across this empty space whilst someone else is watching him, and this is all that is needed for an act of theatre to be engaged.

Peter Hall:

I believe that theatre begins with the word. In the beginning there is the word. Absolutely! Because, without the word there is little possibility for all the other things of the theatre. If the theatre is only word then it's literary and boring and thin and academic. But I know that a silence on the stage means nothing—unless it's surrounded with the most marvellous words. The more marvellous the words are, the better the silence.

The director and playwright Roger Planchon, who runs the Théâtre National Populaire at Villeurbanne in France (the TNP), said:

Like everybody else, I can't use the word popular except in inverted commas. To say that workers never go to the theatre except to build them is all the more heartbreaking in that, in a very autobiographical way, I know that there is a cultural divide and that it is strong, real and brutal. I don't believe that theatre can make much impact on a state of affairs that only a change in civilization could modify. I hope to live to see the dawn of this change, but in the meantime what a theatre like the one I run can do is to go on making people aware that there is a violent cultural divide.

Our job is to keep the wound open. And in our work in the provinces, we're trying to make it so that it's the trade unions, the workers and teachers, the youth organizations, that form the body of our support. This support is important because the theatre always runs a serious risk of becoming marginal.

Peter Brook, 'The Empty Space':

It is always the popular theatre that saves the day. Through the ages it has taken many forms, and there is only one factor that they all have in common—a roughness. Salt, sweat, noise, smell: the theatre that's not in a theatre, the theatre on carts, on wagons, on trestles, audiences standing, drinking, sitting round tables, audiences joining in, answering back; theatre in back rooms, upstairs rooms, barns; the one-night stands, the torn sheet pinned up across the hall, the battered screen to conceal the quick changes—that one generic term, theatre, covers all this and the sparkling chandeliers too. I have had many abortive discussions with architects building new theatres—trying vainly to find words with which to communicate my own conviction that it is not a question of good buildings and bad: a beautiful place may never bring about explosion of life, while a haphazard hall may be a tremendous meeting place; this is the mystery of the theatre, but in the understanding of this mystery lies the only possibility of ordering it into a science.

Arthur Miller commented in 'On Social Plays' on the sense of identity which the ancient Greeks had with others in their *polis* or city-state and foresaw a return to drama which would ask the ultimate philosophical questions:

The world, I think, is moving toward a unity, a unity won not alone by the necessities of the physical developments themselves, but by the painful and confused re-assertion of man's inherited will to survive. When the peace is made, and it will be made, the question Greece asked will once again be a question not reserved for philosophers and dramatists; it will be asked by the man who can live out his life without fear of hunger, joblessness, disease, the man working a few hours a day with a life-span probability of eighty, ninety, or perhaps a hundred years. Hard as it is for most people, the sheer struggle to exist and to prosper affords a haven from thought. Complain as they may that they have no time to think, to cultivate themselves, to ask the big questions, most men are terrified at the thought of not having to spend most of their days fighting for existence. In every sphere, and for a hundred hard reasons, the ultimate questions are once again becoming moot, some because without the right answers we will destroy the earth, others because the peace we win may leave us without the fruits of civilized life. The new social drama will be Greek in that it will face man as a social animal and yet without the petty partisanship of so much of past drama. It will be Greek in that the 'men' dealt with in its scenes—the psychology and characterizations—will be more than ends in themselves and once again parts of a whole, a whole that is social, a whole that is Man. The world, in a word, is moving into the same boat. For a time, their greatest time, the Greek people were in the same boat—their polis. Our drama, like theirs, will, as it must, ask the same questions, the largest ones. Where are we going now that we are together? For, like every act man commits, the drama is a struggle against his mortality, and meaning is the ultimate reward for having lived.

Ed Berman, introduction to 'Ten of the Best British Short Plays':

It is in its difference from TV and films that theatre must find its role. The impossible competition of the media in the areas of theatre's traditional roles of storytelling and holding a mirror up to reality forces such a change. The mirror of theatre has been eclipsed by the silver screen and the non-reflecting tube.

Live theatre will now look to its assets to find its survival:
- that it can use and change its environment at the point of playing
- that it can respond to the audience
- that it can allow the audience to respond and, in turn, change itself accordingly
- that it can physically and verbally involve the audience
- that it involves the risk of accident by being live

Perhaps most important of all is that theatre, because of its live confrontation potential, can create a sense of event or can be an event—a celebration of, or an attack on reality.

Lunch-hour theatre is hardly the epitome of this crystal-ball gazing. It is one of the modest ways in which dozens of theatre companies in the last few years in Britain have sought to find new directions—socially, politically, financially, structurally and even aesthetically.

By the nature of the relatively small size of theatre audiences, theatre becomes exclusive. Theatre is for this reason the wrong place to claim political influence. In the modern state, where theatre is subsidized by the taxpayer, modesty should prevail in our medieval guild of craftsmen.

The extraordinary privilege of being paid to express ourselves to limited numbers of our paymasters is an enviable position in our world. We should remember that it fills neither sufficient bodies nor souls to claim a shattering social or political role.

'Rough theatre' is the name coined by John Miles and Tony Allen to describe the street-theatre plays they perform in west London. They must be among the very few playwrights who can claim that some of their lines have become so popular, they even reappear scrawled up as graffiti.

That's what happened to Tony Allen's line: 'I always thought Home was an ex-prime minister until I discovered squatting.'

They coin some splendidly bitter titles for their plays too. One, about a council worker who smashes up his own home because that is what the official form says, is called 'Dwelling Unit Sweet Dwelling Unit'.

Antonin Artaud, 'The Theatre of Cruelty—Second Manifesto':

Admittedly or not, conscious or unconscious, the poetic state, a transcendent experience of life, is what the public is fundamentally seeking through love, crime, drugs, war, or insurrection.

The Theatre of Cruelty has been created in order to restore to the theatre a passionate and convulsive conception of life, and it is in this sense of violent rigour and extreme condensation of scenic elements that the cruelty on which it is based must be understood.

This cruelty, which will be bloody when necessary but not systematically so, can thus be identified with a kind of severe moral purity which is not afraid to pay life the price it must be paid.

Jean Genet, 'Reflections on the Theatre':

If I am so insistent about the bright lights, both the stage and house lights, it is because I should in some way like both actors and audience to be caught up in the same illumination, and for there to be no place for them to hide, or even half-hide.

The actor must act quickly, even in his slowness, but his speed, lightning-like, will amaze. That and his acting will make him so beautiful that, when he is snatched up by the emptiness of the wings, the audience will experience a feeling of sadness, a kind of regret: they will have seen a meteor loom into view and pass by. This kind of acting will give life to the actor and to the play. Therefore: appear, shine, and, as it were, die.

H. L. Mencken:

The acting that one sees upon the stage does not show how human beings actually comport themselves in crises, but simply how actors think they ought to. It is thus, like poetry and religion, a device for gladdening the heart with what is palpably not true.

The designer Edward Gordon Craig, who had a great influence on twentieth-century design, costume and production, believed that the mask should once again take an important place in theatrical presentation and made these arguments for it in a radio broadcast:

The mask was used by the ancients in their ceremonies, when faces were held to be too weak, too slight an element; used by those artists of the theatre, Aeschylus, Sophocles and Euripides; found essential to their highest drama by the Japanese masters of the ninth and fourteenth centuries. Rejected later on in the eighteenth century by the European actors and relegated by them to the toy shop and the fancy-dress ball, the mask has sunk now to the level of the dance, of pantomime and of the marionette. From being a work of art, carved in wood or ivory, and sometimes ornamented with precious metals or precious stones, and later made in leather, it has frittered itself away to a piece of paper, badly painted, or covered with black satin or with pink....

It is as important now as it was of old and is in no way to be included among the things which we put aside as old fashioned. It must in no way be looked upon merely as a curiosity, for its existence is vital to the art of the theatre....

Masks carry conviction when he who creates them is an artist, for the artist limits the statements which he places upon these masks. The face of the actor carries no such conviction: it is over-full of fleeting expressions, frail, restless, disturbed, and disturbing to us.... The mask will return to the theatre, of that I grow ever more and more assured...the spirited reticence and passionate desire which led men to use the mask in past ages should be the same now as it ever was, and it should never die. It is such an inspiration as this that we should turn to, and in which we should trust entirely.

Sybil Thorndike

Sybil Thorndike described her very first audition:

I went up with Mother. Oh, I looked such a sight! I put on a veil, God knows why! We climbed up the stairs—it was in Bedford Street in an awful room high up on about the fourth floor. And there was that little man, Fred Topham, a wonderful principal and a brilliant old actor. 'Well, would the girl like to do something for me?' he said, and then he gazed at me and added, 'No, I don't think I'll bother her to do anything—she looks as if she can act.' And I said, 'Of course I can act. I've acted since I was four. Anybody can act, it's the easiest thing in the world.'

Ralph Richardson first acted with Sybil Thorndike in 1932 in 'The Knight of the Burning Pestle' at the Old Vic. He soon got to know how good Dame Sybil was with other actors—and how kind:

Sybil sees sermons in stones and good in everything. She even saw good in my Othello, which was an incredible piece of observation.

She can make an actor act. Any actor. I've seen her do it. She could act with a tailor's dummy and bring it to life. Anything she touches comes to life—just as it does with Chaplin.

Dame Sybil was ninety-three when she died in 1976, but she had never settled down to passive old age: she remained alert, courageous and twinkling with humour, as Richard Baker recalls:

Not long before she died I went to interview Dame Sybil for BBC Radio's 'Start the Week'. When I arrived at the block of flats in Chelsea where she lived, the hall porter said: 'Good morning Mr Baker. I'm sorry to tell you Dame Sybil has had a fall.'

'Oh, then I won't bother her now,' I said.

'Oh, but you must go up,' said the porter, 'Dame Sybil's companion wants you to help get her up.'

I went up to the flat and was told Dame Sybil had fallen out of bed.

We went into the bedroom where the great lady was indeed on the floor beside her bed, but ebulliently cheerful as always.

'Oh, I'm so glad you've come,' she said. 'What a pickle I'm in! You didn't know I was a fallen woman, did you?'

We raised her to the bed, and I suggested we should cancel the interview, or she could do it in bed. Not at all. She insisted on doing it as arranged in the sitting-room. Her companion brought in some brandy.

'I don't need it,' she said, 'but Richard probably does!'

Beerbohm Tree

Her Majesty's Theatre in London, where Sir Herbert Beerbohm Tree staged many of his lavish productions, was sometimes a strange scene during their preparation, as Frances Donaldson wrote in 'The Actor-Managers':

Rehearsals under Tree's management were well known for their chaotic character. An unmotivated anarchy reigned, people came in and out of the theatre, sat and talked to Tree, who every now and then produced a witticism at which he and all his henchmen laughed, the stage staff rushed about in all directions, people bellowed at each other and stood distractedly about. At one rehearsal, overcome by the attempts of his stage manager to impose some order on the scene, Tree knelt and prayed: 'Dear Lord, do look at Bertie Shelton now.' There is no explanation of what magic ultimately restored order in time for the curtain to go up on the vastly complicated and magnificent scenes for which this theatre was famous.

Sir Herbert Beerbohm Tree was so delighted with his own skill at coining epigrams that he would sometimes ask his secretary to write down something he had just said. One such convivial quip was: 'It is better to drink a little too much than much too little.'

Upstage

Ronald Hayman, 'Gielgud':

John Gielgud asked Fred Terry for advice when he was constantly being upstaged in a scene by a crafty old actor. Terry replied: 'Walk in front of him while he's speaking, old boy. He'll have to come down level with you then, otherwise the audience won't be able to see him.'

The advice worked.

A young actor in his first job with a small town repertory company used to drink occasionally in an out-of-the-way pub where the barman was friendly and sympathetic. And his sympathy was needed: the young actor always had doleful tales of how he had been totally upstaged by a scene-stealing veteran in the company, who seemed prepared to go to any lengths to make sure the audience's attention stayed on him. But one day the barman was surprised to see the young man in high spirits when he came in.

'This time I've got him!' said the actor gleefully.

'What do you mean?'

'Next week's play has a big courtroom scene. I play the prosecuting counsel, and I have a big dramatic speech. He plays the judge, and doesn't have a single line during the whole scene. Not one! There's no way he can upstage me this time.'

During the rehearsal period the actor continued in a great state of elation. But the day after the play opened, the barman was surprised to see him come into the pub looking suicidally gloomy. He leaned heavily on the bar and ordered a treble. The barman asked him what was wrong, and the actor said with cold fury: 'The bastard drank the ink!'

A young actress had to make her big speech, kneeling at the feet of a Great Lady of the Theatre. Each time she knelt, the Lady moved right upstage, so that the actress had to turn away from the audience. One night, the young actress made sure she knelt on one knee, planting the other foot firmly on the edge of the long flowing gown of the older woman. When the Lady turned to move upstage, she found herself anchored to the spot. She smiled sweetly at the young actress, and said out of the corner of her mouth: 'You're learning!'

A leading impresario and theatre manager was walking down Shaftesbury Avenue with a man who had directed several plays for him. It was a warm, sunny afternoon, and the director remarked: 'Lovely day!' The impresario magnanimously smiled and said: 'Thank you very much.'

Wartime Theatre

In 1944 and early 1945 Joyce Grenfell and Viola Tunnard did two tours doing shows for the troops, visiting North Africa, the Middle East, the Persian Gulf and India. They went to fourteen countries altogether and had to perform in some difficult conditions, as 'Joyce Grenfell Requests the Pleasure' recounts:

Singing or speaking out-of-doors is always hard work. Nature and other hazards intruded in our concerts, indoors and out, particularly in hot weather. I often had to compete with birds, usually sparrows. The more I sang the more they sang too, piercingly and without stopping. They were always the winners. In India we had to play in a yard between two three-storey hospital buildings where the patients watched us from balconies above. It was a crick-in-the-neck occasion for me, not made any easier by crows and green parrots, both vocal and both raucous. That day every low-flying plane in the area came just over my head; ox-carts rumbled by, creaking, and an Indian carrying a letter scrabbled his big black boots on the asphalt path. Out of sight, just behind the trellis against which I stood, someone watered the flowers from a trickling hose. An uphill concert but good training for concentration.

One day during a sandstorm, when stones on the roof of the Nissen hut made so much noise that we had to pause between gusts to be heard at all, Viola opened the piano and out fell a scorpion. The same night I was battling through a song at full voice when a mouse ran over my foot, but so diligent was my effort that I didn't notice it; Viola did and for the rest of the concert played without pedals, keeping her feet up on the rungs of her chair. Cockroaches of a kind I'd never seen before, enormous and

bright brown, became a commonplace; I did not get fond of them, or of ants. We were warned to shake our shoes before we put them on in case of snakes. Thank Heaven I never saw one.

The English audience was never more phlegmatic than during the Second World War; Grace Webb was in Ivor Novello's company in the early part of the war, when London was being constantly attacked by air raids:

A bomb used to usually come down in the middle of one of Ivor's quietest scenes, you know. But we never saw anybody get up and go out—they just sat there. The sirens used to go, and there was a terrifying feeling that there was nothing between you and that, except the roof of the theatre—but nobody ever went out.

76. A play put on by Australian POWs at Oflag VIIB Eichstatt

Tennessee Williams

Tennessee Williams, 'Memoirs':

Most of you belong to something that offers a stabilizing influence: a family unit, a defined social position, employment in an organization, a more secure habit of existence. I live like a gypsy, I am a fugitive. No place seems tenable to me for long any more, not even my own skin.

I have made a covenant with myself to continue to write, since I have no choice, it is so deeply rooted as a way of existence and a form of flight....

77. Tennessee Williams

Donald Wolfit

Ken Tynan, when he became a drama critic, often reviewed performances by Donald Wolfit, but much earlier it happened that Wolfit reviewed one by Tynan. 'The Gloucestershire Echo' had asked Wolfit to comment on the Oxford University Players' production of the First Quarto 'Hamlet'

produced by Tynan.... Wolfit wrote—in the course of his review:

The producer himself gave us an effective ghost, which would be even better if he'd discarded the modern craze for crediting Hamlet's father with sepulchral asthma.

78. Donald Wolfit and Patricia Jessel in 'The Solitary Lover'

W.B. Yeats

Denis Johnston:

When Yeats reached the Olympian heights of trying to light a play, I remember on one particular occasion a dawn effect was required, and he tried it this way and he tried it that way, and still nothing was to his liking. Indeed, it didn't look like a dawn to me. But finally, at the back of the stage a strange kind of red, roseate glow started coming up. And Yeats suddenly leapt in his seat and said: 'Yes, that's it! That's what I want, that's what I want!'...to be interrupted by the electrician, who stuck his head out from the side and said: 'Well, you can't have it—the place is on fire!'

Joseph Holloway wrote in his journal on 8 October 1903:

Mr W. B. Yeats was called after both his plays, and held forth at the end of 'Cathleen ni Houlihan' in his usual thumpty-thigh, monotonous, affected, preachy style, and ended by making a fool of himself in 'going' for an article that appeared in this morning's 'Independent'. He generally makes a mess of it when he orates. Kind friends ought to advise him to hold his tongue.

79. W. B. Yeats

Credits

The publishers and compiler have made every effort to contact copyright holders in all sources quoted and apologise to any whom they have not been able to trace. They are grateful to the following for permission to quote copyright matter:

QUOTATIONS

ACTAC (Theatrical & Cinematic) Ltd for an extract from a speech by Harold Pinter;

W. H. Allen & Co. Ltd for an extract from 'All Above Board' by Wilfred Brambell;

W. H. Allen & Co. Ltd for extracts from 'Dames of the Theatre' by Eric Johns;

W. H. Allen & Co. Ltd for extracts from 'Every Other Inch a Lady' by Beatrice Lillie;

W. H. Allen & Co. Ltd for extracts from 'Memoirs' by Tennessee Williams;

George Allen & Unwin Ltd for an extract from 'Henry Irving and the Victorian Theatre' by Madeleine Bingham;

Angus & Robertson (UK) Ltd for extracts from 'George S. Kaufman — An Intimate Portrait' by Howard Teichmann;

Atheneum Publishers for extracts from 'What is Theatre?' by Eric Bentley;

Mrs Beatrice Behan for an extract from a broadcast by Brendan Behan;

Victor Borge for an extract from a broadcast interview;

Peggy Branford and the BBC for an extract from her radio biography of Maria Malibran;

British I. T. I. Publications for extracts from articles and statements by Corinne Jacker, Roger Planchon, Alan Plater, Sam Shepard and Tom Stoppard, published in 'Theatre Quarterly';

Jonathan Cape Ltd for extracts from 'The History of the National Theatre' by John Elsom and Nicholas Tomalin;

Jonathan Cape Ltd for an extract from 'The Sound of Two Hands Clapping' by Kenneth Tynan;

Cassell Ltd for extracts from 'Drury Lane' by Brian Dobbs;

John Casson for an extract from a broadcast by Dame Sybil Thorndike;

Chatto and Windus Ltd for an extract from the introduction by Alan Ayckbourn to his plays, 'Joking Apart', 'Ten Times Table' and 'Just Between Ourselves';

Chatto and Windus Ltd and David Garnett

for an extract from 'The Cherry Orchard and Other Plays' by Anton Chekhov, translated by Constance Garnett;

Collins Publishers for an extract from 'King Charles II' by Sir Arthur Bryant;

Collins Publishers for an extract from 'Mink Coats and Barbed Wire' by Ruth Kaminska;

Collins Publishers for an extract from 'The Mousetrap Man' by Peter Saunders;

Edward Craig for an extract from a broadcast;

The Edward Gordon Craig Estate for an extract from a broadcast by Edward Gordon Craig;

The Cultural Relations Committee, Department of Foreign Affairs, Dublin, for an extract from 'Theatre in Ireland' by Mícheál MacLiammóir;

Curtis Brown Ltd for an extract from 'All for Hecuba' by Mícheál MacLiammóir, published by Methuen & Co. Ltd;

The 'Daily Mail' for an extract from a news report;

James Dale for an extract from his autobiography, 'Pulling Faces for a Living', published by Victor Gollancz;

Peter Davies Ltd for extracts from 'Life is a Cucumber' by Peter Bull;

J. M. Dent and Sons Ltd, Everyman's University Library, for extracts from 'Victorian Melodramas' by James L. Smith;

Gerald Duckworth & Co. Ltd for an extract from 'The Cult of Shakespeare' by F. E. Halliday;

E. P. Publishing for an extract from 'The Story of Pantomime' by A. E. Wilson;

John East for an extract from a broadcast;

Eyre Methuen Ltd for extracts from 'Mediations' by Martin Esslin;

Eyre Methuen Ltd for extracts from 'Brecht on Theatre' by John Willett — original title 'Schriften zum Theater', published by Suhrkamp Verlag, Frankfurt am Main, all rights reserved. Copyright © 1957 by Suhrkamp Verlag, Frankfurt am Main;

Eyre and Spottiswoode (Publishers) Ltd for an extract by Michael Booth from the introduction to 'Hiss the Villain', edited by Michael Booth;

Faber and Faber Ltd for an extract from 'Stage and Bar' by George Pleydell Bancroft;

Faber and Faber Ltd for an extract from 'Comedians' by Trevor Griffiths;

ILLUSTRATIONS

Index